D1587853

THOMAS REID AND THE STORY OF EPISTEMOLOGY

The two great philosophical figures at the culminating point of the Enlightenment are Thomas Reid in Scotland and Immanuel Kant in Germany. Reid was by far the more influential across Europe and the United States well into the nineteenth century. Since that time his fame and influence have been eclipsed by his German contemporary.

This important book by one of today's leading philosophers of knowledge and religion will do much to reestablish the significance of Reid for philosophy today. Nicholas Wolterstorff has produced the first systematic account of Reid's epistemology. Relating Reid's philosophy to present-day epistemological discussions, the author demonstrates how they are at once remarkably timely, relevant, and provocative.

No other book both uncovers the deep pattern of Reid's thought and relates it to contemporary philosophical debate. This book should be read by historians of philosophy as well as all philosophers concerned with epistemology and the philosophy of mind.

Nicholas Wolterstorff is Noah Porter Professor of Philosophical Theology at Yale University. His previous Cambridge University Press books are *Divine Discourse* (1995) and *John Locke and the Ethics of Belief* (1996).

MODERN EUROPEAN PHILOSOPHY

General Editor
Robert B. Pippin, *University of Chicago*

Advisory Board
Gary Gutting, *University of Notre Dame*
Rolf-Peter Horstmann, *Humboldt University, Berlin*
Mark Sacks, *University of Essex*

Some Recent Titles:

THOMAS REID AND THE STORY OF EPISTEMOLOGY

NICHOLAS WOLTERSTORFF

Yale University

CAMBRIDGE
UNIVERSITY PRESS

PUBLISHED BY THE PRESS SYNDICATE OF THE UNIVERSITY OF CAMBRIDGE
The Pitt Building, Trumpington Street, Cambridge, United Kingdom

CAMBRIDGE UNIVERSITY PRESS
The Edinburgh Building, Cambridge CB2 2RU, UK
40 West 20th Street, New York, NY 10011-4211, USA
10 Stamford Road, Oakleigh, VIC 3166, Australia
Ruiz de Alarcón 13, 28014 Madrid, Spain
Dock House, The Waterfront, Cape Town 8001, South Africa

http://www.cambridge.org

First published 2001

Printed in the United States of America

Typeface Baskerville 11/12 $\frac{1}{2}$ pt.   *System* QuarkXPress [BTS]

A catalog record for this book is available from the British Library.

Library of Congress Cataloging in Publication Data
Wolterstorff, Nicholas.
Thomas Reid and the story of epistemology / Nicholas Wolterstorff.
p.   cm. – (Modern European philosophy)
Includes index.
ISBN 0-521-79013-1
1. Reid, Thomas, 1710–1796.   2. Knowledge, Theory of.   I. Title.   II. Series.
B1537.W65 2000
121′.092 – dc21   00-028943

ISBN   0 521 79013 1   hardback

Contents

Preface

There are signs today of a renaissance of interest in the philosophy of Thomas Reid; whether those signs are a portent remains to be seen. If so, it will indeed be a *renaissance*. Reid has almost disappeared from the canon used for teaching modern philosophy in the universities of the West. Yet from the last decade or two of the eighteenth century, on through most of the nineteenth, he was probably the most popular of all philosophers in Great Britain and North America and enjoyed considerable popularity on the continent of Europe as well. I myself judge him to have been one of the two great philosophers of the latter part of the eighteenth century, the other being of course Immanuel Kant.

Why has Reid almost disappeared from the canon? No doubt for a number of reasons; let me mention just three. For one thing, the reception of Reid's philosophy both trivialized and misunderstood him. It trivialized him by giving looming importance to his doctrine of Common Sense; it misunderstood him by failing to see the radicality of his rejection of the prior tradition of modern philosophy and treating him as if he justified us in forgetting about Hume and returning to Locke.

Second, scholarship in the history of philosophy lives and thrives on challenges to the interpretive skills of the scholar and on the controversies that ensue from different ways of meeting such challenges: Is there or is there not a vicious "Cartesian circle," and so forth. Reid provides relatively little by way of such challenges. Certainly he's been misunderstood. Nonetheless, he is one of the most lucid writers in the history of philosophy; and never does he suggest that he is revealing to us astonishing, hitherto undreamt of, realms of truth. In short, he's not a very rewarding subject for the historian of philosophy. A great many people, upon reading Reid, have become "Reidian" in one or another aspect of their thinking; but they haven't dwelt on him. They've gone on to think for themselves along Reidian lines. That's been Reid's role in the history of philosophy.

I speculate that a third reason is the following. The history of modern philosophy was first written by Hegel and his followers. A Hegelian history of anything whatsoever structures the cultural material into triads of thesis, antithesis, and synthesis. All those who have ever encountered modern philosophy have been inducted into the Hegelian structure for this material: continental rationalists, British empiricists, and synthesis in Kant and Hegel. Reid is not plausibly regarded as an empiricist; he does not believe, for example, that all concepts are "derived from experience." But neither is he a rationalist. As we will see, one of the deepest themes in his thought is opposition to what he regarded as the exaggerated claims made for reason by the modern philosophers – empiricists included!

Reid thus had the great misfortune not to fit what became the canonical schematization of the history of modern philosophy! So much the worse for the scheme, one wants to say. What happened was the opposite. Since the bed was too small for Procrustes, Procrustes' legs were cut off. I call this a "speculation" on my part. To make it more than speculation, with this point in mind one would have to study, among other things, the early Hegelian histories. I have not done that, nor am I aware that anyone else has done so.

It was about twenty years ago that I first read Reid, for reasons that I now cannot recall. I had the sense of discovering a philosophical soul mate: a metaphysical realist who was also, in his own way, an antifoundationalist. I suppose I also had the vague sense of having discovered a religious soul mate, less I think because Reid was a Christian philosopher, though he was, and more because of the fundamental role in his thought of ungrounded trust. I resonated with his antirationalism.

For these reasons, and many others, I found him fascinating but in equal measure baffling. What *was* he getting at? Why *did* he say *that*? I now know that some of my bafflement – by no means all – had its source in looking for Reid's answers to the questions of contemporary epistemology; I had to learn that some of those questions were not Reid's questions but only ours. What kept me going was that, as with all the great philosophers, one had the sense of so much intelligence at work that one hesitated a long time before settling on the conclusion that the source of bafflement was not obtuseness on one's own part but confusion and mistake on the part of the philosopher.

The blend of fascination and bafflement lasted many years. The fascination remains; the bafflement has now considerably diminished. Hence, this book.

A word about the book's genre. This is an *interpretation* of Reid's epistemology. By no means is it a full treatment of his epistemology; that would have to be much longer. Instead it offers a line of interpretation, a way of reading. That's one thing I mean. I also mean to suggest that it's not an exegetical study. When discussing a given topic, I don't assemble all the relevant passages so as to find out what Reid actually said, with all its ambiguities, obscurities, inconsistencies, and so on. I will in fact attend to ambiguities, obscurities, and all of that; but my aim throughout is not so much to present what Reid said as to discover what he *was trying to say*. Not, be it noted, to discover what he was trying *to get at*, understanding that in the way in which it is understood by Gadamer; that is to say, I do not interpret Reid with the aim of trying to make what he says come out true. Sensible, intelligent, but not necessarily true. My goal is to discover the line of thought that he was trying to clarify and articulate.

I have one more thing in mind. This is not an engagement with the scholarly literature on Reid – of which there isn't very much in any case. I do not carry on debates with those with whom I disagree; and I do not very often mention the points at which my interpretation accords with that of others. That too would have required a longer book. More relevantly, it would repeatedly have diverted the reader's attention from the way of reading Reid's epistemology that I offer. Rightly or wrongly, I judge the need of the day to be a guide to reading Reid, so that his genius can come to light. What I *will* do, every now and then, is bring into the discussion some contemporary alternative to Reid's position; by having a contrast before her, the reader can better see what it is that Reid was trying to say and the significance thereof.

There is much in Reid's thought that is highly provocative. Now and then I have responded to the provocation and gone beyond presenting Reid's views to discussing them. For the most part, though, I have restrained myself and simply presented my interpretation of what Reid was trying to say.

During the twenty years that I have been reading and reflecting on Reid I have talked about him with many people, mainly philosophers and historians, given lectures on him at many places, most extensively at St. Andrews University, and taught courses on him at Calvin College, the Free University of Amsterdam, Notre Dame University, and Yale University. I have learned much from many. To single out some from those without mentioning all is to do injustice to those not singled out. But my memory isn't up to mentioning all. It might seem best then to be just and mention no one. But that would be taken as ingratitude. So let me mention those who, for one or another reason, sensible or quirky, happen right now to be in the forefront of my mind as ones from whom I have either learned about Reid, or been aided in thinking about what he said: William P. Alston, Alexander Broady, Andrew Chignell, Keith de Rose, Andrew Dole, Richard Foley, John Haldane, Lee Hardy, Gordon Graham, Joseph Huston, Alvin Plantinga, Del Ratzsch, Huston Smit, James van Cleve, Edwin van Driel, René van Woudenberg, Allen W. Wood, Crispin Wright, Steve Wykstra.

I have used two editions of Reid's works. First, the standard edition by William Hamilton of Reid's complete published works, along with certain of his letters; I have employed the fifth edition, published in Edinburgh in 1858 by Maclachlan and Stewart. Secondly, the critical edition of the *Inquiry* prepared recently by Derek R. Brookes and published in Edinburgh in 1997 by Edinburgh University Press. This is the first volume in what will be The Edinburgh Edition of Thomas Reid.

I will employ the following system of references: References to Reid's *An Inquiry into the Human Mind* (1764) will be cited by the abbreviation IHM, followed by chapter and section number, followed by page and column in the Hamilton edition, and page in the Brookes edition, thus: IHM V, ii [121a; B 58]. *Essays on the Intellectual Powers of Man* (1785) will be cited by the abbreviation EIP, followed by essay and chapter, followed by page and column in the Hamilton edition, thus: EIP IV, iii [375b]. *Essays on the Active Powers of the Human Mind* (1788) will be cited by the abbreviation EAP, followed by essay and chapter, followed by page and column in the Hamilton edition. References to passages in Reid's letters will be identified by recipient and date, and by page and column in the Hamilton edition.

I should add that I myself fail to see any significant change in Reid's views from his early *Inquiry into the Human Mind* to his late *Essays on the Intellectual Powers* and *Essays on the Active Powers*; elaboration, yes, significant change, no. Thus it's not the views of early Reid nor the views of late Reid but just the views of Reid that I will be articulating. It's for that reason that, in the references I offer, I will move freely back and forth between the early *Inquiry* and the late essays.

CHAPTER I

Reid's Questions

ENTERING REID'S THOUGHT

Reid's thought is not easy to enter. He was the greatest stylist of all who have written philosophy in the English language. No one can match him for wit, irony, metaphor, humor, and elegance. Yet his thought is elusive. Why that is so, I do not entirely understand. Partly it's because central elements of the pattern of thought against which he tirelessly polemicized – the *Way of Ideas*, he called it – have been so deeply etched into our minds that we find it difficult even to grasp alternatives, let along find them plausible. Partly it's because Reid's understanding of the philosophical enterprise makes it seem to many that he's not practicing philosophy but opting out. Yet these factors, though certainly relevant, seem to me only partly to explain the elusiveness.

Be that as it may, the question before us is how to enter. The one thing everyone knows about Reid is that his philosophy became known as *Common Sense Philosophy*. It acquired that name because the phenomenon Reid called "common sense" played a prominent role in his thought. But it's not what is deepest. And one lesson to be drawn from the fate of Reid's thought is that if one tries to enter through the doorway of his views on Common Sense, one will never get far. The profundity of his thought will be blocked from view by that peculiar mindlessness that talk about common sense induces in readers. It's common sense not to try fishing in a lake immediately after a hard rain. That's an example of what we customarily understand by common sense. If we approach Reid's thought with that understanding in mind, his genius will elude us.

Common Sense comes into prominence in Reid's discussion when he engages in methodological reflections on how philosophizing should be conducted after certain of the ideological underpinnings of the *Way of Ideas* have been rejected. But Reid's methodological reflections presuppose the conclusions arrived at in his substantive reflections. It is with those substantive reflections that we must begin. A consideration of what Reid has to say about Common Sense will come at the end.

What were the fundamental questions that shaped Reid's substantive reflections? Before I say, let me mention a set of questions that many of us are tempted to take to be Reid's questions, though they were not.[1] Beliefs come with a variety of distinct truth-relevant merits and demerits. They are warranted, reliably formed, entitled, justified, rational, cases of knowledge, fit for inclusion within science, and so forth. Contemporary epistemology in the analytic tradition has been preoccupied, in recent years, with the attempt to offer analyses of such merits as these, and criteria for their application. A person trained in this tradition will naturally assume that Reid is engaged in the same enterprise. She will be inclined to try to extract from Reid a theory of warrant, a theory of entitlement, a theory of justification, or whatever. That inclination will be reinforced by the fact that John Locke, against whom Reid never tires of polemicizing, clearly did develop a theory of knowledge and a theory of entitlement. Given the polemic, one naturally supposes that Reid was doing the same and disagreeing with Locke's theories. But nowhere in Reid does one find a general theory of any doxastic merit (*doxa* = belief, in Greek). Naturally one can extract *assumptions* that Reid is making about such merits. He remarks, for example, that "it is the universal judgment of mankind that the evidence of sense is a kind of evidence which we may securely rest upon in the most momentous concerns of mankind" (EIP II, v [259a]). If one wishes, one can even oneself develop a "Reidian" theory concerning one and another doxastic merit.[2] But it was not Reid's project to develop

---

[1] I myself, at an earlier stage in my attempt to understand Reid, succumbed to this temptation. See my "Thomas Reid on Rationality" in Hart, van der Hoeven, and Nicholas Wolterstorff, eds., *Rationality in the Calvinian Tradition* (Lanham, Md.: University Press of America, 1983), pp. 43–69. And my "Hume and Reid," *The Monist* 70 (1987): 398–417.

[2] Alvin Plantinga's theory of *warrant* is a good example of such a "Reidian" theory; see his *Warrant and Proper Function* (Oxford: Oxford University Press, 1993). The reason Plantinga's theory is a "Reidian" theory, but not Reid's theory, is that Plantinga did not develop his theory, and could not have developed his theory, by simply exegeting and elaborating Reid.

any such theory. Contemporary analytic epistemology is closer to Locke than to Reid on this point; that makes Locke more accessible to those who work in this tradition than Reid is.

The reason one finds in Reid no general theory for any truth-relevant doxastic merit is not that Reid had no interest in such a project. He clearly indicates an interest in developing a general theory of "good evidence," of "just ground[s] of belief" (EIP II, xx [328b]). But he found his interest stymied. Here's what he says in the decisive passage:

> The common occasions of life lead us to distinguish evidence into different kinds, to which we give names that are well understood; such as the evidence of sense, the evidence of memory, the evidence of consciousness, the evidence of testimony, the evidence of axioms, the evidence of reasoning. All men of common understanding agree, that each of these kinds of evidence may afford just grounds of belief, and they agree very generally in the circumstances that strengthen or weaken them.
>
> Philosophers have endeavoured, by analyzing the different sorts of evidence, to find out some common nature wherein they all agree, and thereby to reduce them all to one. . . .
>
> I confess that, although I have, as I think, a distinct notion of the different kinds of evidence above mentioned, and perhaps of some others, which it is unnecessary here to enumerate, yet I am not able to find any common nature to which they may all be reduced. They seem to me to agree only in this, that they are all fitted by nature to produce belief in the human mind; some of them in the highest degree, which we call certainty, others in various degrees according to circumstances. (EIP II, xx [328a–b])[3]

Let it not be thought, Reid adds, that because he lacks a general theory of evidence, he is incapable of making good judgments about evidence. "A man who knows nothing of the theory of vision, may have a good eye; and a man who never speculated about evidence in the abstract, may have a good judgment" (EIP II, xx [328a]). Theory comes *after* practice, not before.

---

[3] That last clause, "they are all fitted by nature to produce belief in the human mind; some of them in the highest degree, which we call certainty, others in various degrees according to circumstances," won't do badly as an epigrammatic summary of Plantinga's theory of warrant. Hence, its "Reidian" character. Consider also, in the following passage, Reid's striking anticipation of Plantinga's account of probability: "I think, in most cases, we measure the degrees of evidence by the effect they have upon a sound understanding, when comprehended clearly and without prejudice. Every degree of evidence perceived by the mind, produces a proportioned degree of assent or belief" (EIP VII, iii [482b]).

I submit that all of Reid's substantive (as opposed to method-ological) thought in his early book, *An Inquiry into the Human Mind*, and in his late *Essays on the Intellectual Powers*, revolves around a pair of extraordinarily deep, yet easily formulated, questions. They are these: What accounts for the fact that we get enti-ties in mind in such a manner as to be able to form beliefs and other modes of thought about them, and to speak about them? In particular, what accounts for the fact that we get *nonmental* enti-ties in mind in such a manner, and experienced events from the past? And secondly, what accounts for the fact that often we do not merely *entertain thoughts* about the entities we have in mind but *form beliefs* about them?

Formulating the questions, as I say, is easy; explicating their sig-nificance will take some work. Let's begin that work by distin-guishing between two distinct ways of describing what a person believes. One way is to state, in a that clause, the proposition which she believes: She believes that the days are getting longer, she believes that the crocuses are about to bloom, and so forth. The other way of describing what a person believes is to pick out that entity about which she believes something and then to state what it is that she believes about that entity. For example: She believes, about the tree in the far corner of the garden, that it is rotten and has to go. Let's follow the now customary practice of calling these styles, respectively, the *de dicto* style and the *de re* style – or to keep before us the structure of the latter style, let us often call it the *de re*/predicative style.

The reason for distinguishing these two styles of belief descrip-tion is that we need both styles if we are to describe fully the sim-ilarities and differences in the contents of our beliefs; the styles are not just rhetorical variants on each other. Here is an example of the point. Suppose I express a belief of mine by saying, "Felix sounded ill," referring to our cat Felix with the proper name "Felix." Using the *de dicto* style, we can describe the belief I expressed thus: I believed that Felix sounded ill. And using the *de re*/predicative style we can describe it this way: I believed, about Felix, that he sounded ill. That is to say: There is a cat, Felix, about which I believed that he sounded ill. Given the former style of description, truth attaches to my belief if and only if the propo-sition *that Felix sounded ill* is true. Given the latter style, truth attaches to my belief if and only if Felix satisfies my predicative thought *that he sounded ill*. Whether other things also satisfy that same predicative thought makes no difference; Felix has to satisfy it.

By contrast, suppose I have a belief that I express thus: "The cat making all that noise under the window last night sounded ill." And suppose that that cat, unbeknownst to me, was our cat Felix. Then, using the *de re*/predicative style of description, we can correctly describe my belief in the same way that my preceding belief was described; namely, I believed, about Felix, that he sounded ill. But if we use the *de dicto* style, we could not correctly describe this belief in the same way. I did not express the belief that Felix sounded ill – in spite of the fact that Felix was in fact the cat making all that noise under the window. An additional difference is this: Using the *de re*/predicative style of description, what we said about the preceding case is that truth attaches to my belief if and only if Felix satisfies my predicative thought *that he sounded ill.* By contrast, what has to be said about the present case is that truth attaches to my belief if and only if the cat which was in fact making all that noise under the window, *be it Felix or some other cat*, sounded ill. What accounts for this difference is that, in the second case, the fact that my belief was about Felix was a matter of (extramental) happenstance, whereas in the former case, it was by no means a matter of happenstance.

For these reasons, then, we need both styles of description if we are to say all that we want to say about the similarities and differences among the contents of our beliefs. It's not that there are two kinds of beliefs, propositional and *de re*/predicative. It's rather that these two styles of description enable us to get at different dimensions of the content of beliefs.[4]

There is a vast philosophical literature on the matters that I have just now been discussing; very much more could be said on the topic than what I have just now said. For our purposes here, however, it will be satisfactory to brush past all the elaborations, refinements, and controversies to say that if we are to grasp the significance of Reid's questions, we must work with the *de re*/predicative style of description. Judgment, says Reid, "is an act of the mind, whereby one thing is affirmed or denied of another"

---

[4] In my *Divine Discourse* (Cambridge: Cambridge University Press, 1997), p. 138 ff., I distinguished what I called the *noematic* content of beliefs from what I called the *designative* content. The connection between that distinction, and the one above, is this: the *de dicto* style of description gets at the *noematic* content, the *de re*/predicative style gets at the *designative* content.

(EIP VI, i [413b]). No doubt Reid would not have repudiated the *de dicto* style if the issue had been put to him; but it's not the style he works with.

To move on, let me again work with an example. Among my *de re*/predicative beliefs is my belief, about the car I presently own, that it is red. My having that, or any other *de re*/predicative belief, presupposes my having the general ability to believe something about something. So fundamental in our human constitution is this ability, so pervasive in our lives, its exercise, that we rarely take note of it. But there it is: the ability to believe something *about* something. And that, in turn, is just a special case of *thinking* something about something. For a while, let me speak of thinking something about something, coming back later to *believing* something about something.

If my possession of that highly general ability, to think something about something, is to be actualized by my thinking, about the car I presently own, that it is red, I must, for one thing, get that car in mind – gain a mental grip on it. In Reid's words, "It is true of judgment, as well as of knowledge, that it can only be conversant about objects of the mind, or about things which the mind can contemplate. Judgment, as well as knowledge, supposes the conception of the object about which we judge; and to judge of objects that never were nor can be objects of the mind, is evidently impossible" (EIP VI, iii [427b–428a]).[5] What I am calling "having in mind" is what some philosophers have called "mental reference." I shall avoid that terminology – mainly because to speak of "reference" to something is to invite the quest for some entity that the person *uses* to refer to the referent. But when one has something in mind, there isn't – or needn't be – anything that one uses to refer to the thing one has in mind. One can just have it in mind by virtue of its being present to the mind and one's being aware of that.[6]

---

[5] Cf. EIP I, vii [243a], p. 66: "without apprehension of the objects concerning which we judge, there can be no judgment. . . ."

[6] Now and then Reid takes note of the fact that making a judgment requires not just having in mind the thing about which one is making the judgment but also requires having in mind *the judgment itself*: "even the weakest belief cannot be without conception. He that believes, must have some conception of what he believes" (EIP IV, i [360b]; cf. EIP IV, iii [315a]). Immediately after taking note of this connection between judgment and conception, Reid goes on to take note of the connection which is of more concern to him – namely, the one mentioned in the text above.

Second, if that general ability of mine, to think something about something, is to be actualized by my thinking, about the car I presently own, that it is red, I must think about it the predicative thought *that it is red*. This itself is the exercise of an ability, a capacity, on my part. Before I ever thought, about my car, that it is red I had the *capacity* to think the predicative thought, about it, that it is red; now I actualize the capacity. To have this capacity is to possess the *concept* of *being red*. That capacity was, as it were, stored in my mind awaiting actualization; in thinking the predicative thought I did, I brought the capacity out of storage for actual use. How we acquire those capacities that constitute possession of a concept has, of course, been a topic of much philosophical discussion; Reid will have a few things to say.

The way I just described possessing the concept of *being red*, though not inaccurate, is misleading. I described it as the capacity to think, about my car, that it is red. That capacity, though implied by possessing the concept, is not identical with it. The capacity that constitutes possessing the concept is the capacity to think, *about anything at all*, that it is red. All concept-possession is general in that way. Hence it is that, for anything I have in mind, I can think about it any of the predicative thoughts (concepts) I'm capable of thinking. Of course many of those thoughts couldn't be true of it.

I described my thinking that it is red, about the car I presently own, as the actualization of a capacity I had already acquired – namely, the capacity to think about anything at all that it is red. There are many capacities of this sort which I have not acquired; natural scientists, for example, possess a huge repertoire of capacities for predicative thoughts (i.e., concepts) which I have not acquired. The concept of being red is one I have already acquired. It should not be assumed, however, that every case of thinking some predicative thought about something consists of actualizing some capacity one already possesses; sometimes experience brings it about that one thinks some predicative thought without that thought being the actualization of a preexisting capacity. When this happens, does thinking the predicate thought always then in turn evoke the capacity to think the thought henceforth. Does it evoke the concept? Good question!

It may be noted that whereas I described thinking a predicative thought about something as (typically) an actualization of the stored capacity to do so, I did not similarly describe having some thing in mind as an actualization of a stored capacity to have it in mind. That's because very often it's not that. If I'm capable of remembering the thing, that will be the case; I then have the capacity to *bring it to mind*; likewise if I possess the conceptual material for getting it in mind by means of a singular concept. But if I perceive something for the first time without previously having had any thought of its existence, my thereby getting it in mind is not the actualization of a stored capacity to *bring* it to mind. Obviously I have to possess the perceptual capacities that make it possible for me to see it; but that's like the general capacity to *acquire* concepts, it's not like those capacities which *are* concepts. These belong to the furniture of the mind.

With these explanations in hand, let us once again have before us Reid's two fundamental questions. The first is this: What brings it about that we have things in mind? Apart from some polemical comments about the theories of his predecessors, Reid doesn't have much to say about that highly general ability of ours to think something about something; he pretty much just takes for granted that we have this ability to form *de re*/predicative thoughts. The question that grabs his attention is, once again: What brings it about that we have things in mind – have a thing in mind in such a manner as to be able to form some predicative thought about *that thing* rather than about some other thing? What brings it about that I have the car I presently own in mind in such a way that, from among all the things there are, I can attach *to it* my predicative thought that it is red?

Reid also has things to say on the topic of what brings it about that we possess concepts – what brings it about that I, for example, possess the concept of being red, and thus am capable of thinking, of something, that it is red. He assumes, though, that possessing some concept consists of possessing the capacity to think some particular property as possessed by something – having the concept of being red consists of having the capacity to think redness as possessed by something. And this presupposes having a mental grip on redness. Accordingly, he treats the question, what accounts for our possession of concepts, as a special case of the general question on his docket: What accounts for our having entities in mind? What accounts for my having the property of redness in mind?

That was the first of Reid's two fundamental questions. The other is this: What in general accounts for the fact that often we don't just *think* predicative thoughts about things that we have in mind but *believe* those things about those things? Few questions in philosophy go deeper than these two.

WHAT REID MEANS BY "CONCEPTION"

Though most if not all of Reid's present-day commentators have discerned that vast stretches of his thought are devoted to giving an account of belief formation, relatively few have discerned the centrality in his thought of the prior question of how it comes about that we have things in mind. There are a number of reasons for this oblivion on the part of Reid's readers. It's important for my exposition that I single out what seems to me the most important of them.

I have been using the locution, "having something in mind." Though Reid sometimes uses that locution, and closely similar locutions, for the phenomenon in question, his official terminology is "having a conception of something." I submit that therein lies one of the principal obstacles to our grasping Reid's thought. For we take it for granted that Reid's locution, "having a conception of," is synonymous with our locution, "possessing a concept of"; and we automatically understand this latter in the sense in which I used it some paragraphs back. I said that to think, about my car, that it is red, I must possess the concept of being red. Between us and Reid looms Kant, who powerfully shaped our understanding of what we call *conception*. We automatically connect conception with concepts. But much of what Reid says makes no sense if that is how we understand his locution, "having a conception of." And since his thoughts about conception are more fundamental than anything else in his thought, misunderstanding at this point blocks from view the whole pattern of his thinking.

In his account of perception, Reid over and over says that in perception the perceived object evokes in the percipient a conception of the object and an immediate belief about it that it presently exists as something external. Here is just one passage from among hundreds that might be cited: "by an original principle of our constitution, a certain sensation of touch both suggests to the mind the conception of hardness, and creates the belief of it" (IHM V, ii [121a; B 58]). In his account of memory he likewise speaks of memory as incorporating a conception of the event remembered and the immediate belief about it that it did once exist. And in his account of consciousness he speaks of consciousness as incorporating a conception of the mental act or state of which one is conscious and the immediate belief about it that it presently exists as something subjective. Over and over, the pairing: conception of some entity and the immediate belief about it that it does or did exist.

On our quasi-Kantian construal of such language this yields either a puzzling interpretation or too narrow an interpretation. Suppose one takes Reid to be saying that in perception the perceived object evokes *a general concept* of itself. That's puzzling. Which concept of itself does the perceived object evoke – for example, which concept of itself does my perception of a table evoke? Reid never tells us. Does he mean, perhaps, *any* concept? If so, how does the claim that an object evokes some concept or other of itself contribute to our understanding of what goes on in perception?

Alternatively, suppose one takes Reid to be saying that in perception the perceived object evokes *a singular concept* of itself. Reid does in fact think that usually this is what happens. The perceived object evokes a belief, about itself, that it presently exists as something external. In order to have such a belief we must have the perceived entity in mind. And usually we have the perceived entity in mind by means of some singular concept which that entity satisfies – for example, the concept of *the hardness of the object which I am touching*. But though getting things in mind by means of some singular concept is one way of getting them in mind, for Reid's purposes it's indispensable that we recognize that this is not the only way.

The thing to do is set aside our Kantian lens and give full weight to Reid's own official explanation of what he has in mind by "conception." It goes like this:

Conceiving, imagining, apprehending, understanding, having a notion of a thing, are common words, used to express that operation of the understanding, which the logicians call *simple apprehension.* . . . Logicians define simple apprehension to be the bare conception of a thing, without any judgment or belief about it. (EIP IV, i [360a])

Conception is *apprehension*. The clue to what Reid means, in turn, by "apprehension" is its etymology. Apprehension is *having a grip* on something. A *mental* grip, of course. Reid suggests that sometimes we have a mental grip on something without having any belief about that on which we have the grip; what he means is not believing that it does or did exist. In Chapter III we'll see what he has in mind by that claim. The point here is that whether or not one's mental grip on something comes as part of a package that includes a belief about its past or present existence, the conception is just the grip. Conception is apprehension.[7]

Reid's explanation of how he will use "conception" is thus eminently clear.[8] But I judge that it will prove next to impossible for us to put out of mind our quasi-Kantian understanding of "conception" and "conceive." Accordingly, in expounding Reid I will rather often avoid the word "conception" and use instead Reid's own alternative locution, "apprehension." Along, now and then, with the locutions "having a mental grip on" and "having in mind." For that is exactly what Reid officially means by "conception": *having in mind.*

And now for a passage in which Reid emphasizes how fundamental in the life of the mind is this phenomenon of *apprehension* – in part, though not entirely, because of the pervasiveness of

---

[7] In his essay, "Reid on Perception and Conception" (in M. Dalgarno and E. Matthews, eds., *The Philosophy of Thomas Reid* [Dordrecht: Kluwer Academic Publishers, 1989]), William. P. Alston shows that he is aware of the fact that "Reid by no means confines conception to the use of 'general concepts', to the exercise of capacities for classification, or predication, to thinking of something as being of a certain *sort.*" In particular, Alston briefly considers the possibility that, for Reid, "the conception of an external object that is involved in perception can be understood as a direct awareness of that object, rather than as the application to it of some general concept" (pp. 43, 44). But this is the closest he gets to the interpretation of Reid on conception which I am proposing.

[8] Nonetheless, it must be noted that Reid does not always use "conception" in accord with his official explanation; for he speaks of conceiving something *to be* so-and-so, and of conceiving *that* something is so and so. In such cases, Reid is using "conceive" to mean *believe* or *understand.* Here is an example of the former usage: "no man can conceive any sensation to resemble any known quality of bodies" (IHM V, ii [121b; B 57]). Here is an example of the latter: "May not a blind man be made to conceive, that a body moving directly from the eye, or directly toward it, may appear to be at rest" (IHM VI, ii [133b; B 79])? About these uses of "conceive" on Reid's part, it should be noted that he himself observes that it is "hardly possible" to avoid this use of the word "conception." It was Reid's view that in addition to using "conceive" in the way that he officially explains, we also, in ordinary speech, use it to "signify our opinions, when we wish to express them with modesty and diffidence" (EIP IV, i [361a]; cf. EIP I, i [223a]).

belief in the life of the mind.[9] Most of what Reid says in this
passage turns out plausible, or at least intelligible, if we interpret
his word "conception" in our familiar post-Kantian way as synonymous with "having a concept of," rather than in his own way,
as synonymous with "apprehension" – which goes to show how
easy it is for us to miss the pattern of Reid's thought. Read in that
way, his point would be the rather bland observation that one
cannot have beliefs without possessing the concepts that are constituents of the proposition believed. The passage occurs just a
page after Reid's official explanation, which I cited above, of what
he means by "conception," and it ends with a repetition of that
explanation. It's most unlikely, then, that Reid means anything
other by "conception" than what he has just said he means by it
and says again – namely, one cannot have a belief *about* some
entity without having a mental grip on that entity.

although conception may be without any degree of belief, even the
weakest belief cannot be without conception. He that believes, must
have some conception of what he believes. . . .
　[C]onception enters as an ingredient in every operation of the mind.
Our senses cannot give us the belief of any object, without giving some
conception of it at the same time. No man can either remember or
reason about things of which he has no conception. When we will to
exert any of our active powers, there must be some conception of what
we will to do. There can be no desire nor aversion, love nor hatred,
without some conception of the object. We cannot feel pain without
conceiving it, though we can conceive it without feeling it. These things
are self evident.
　In every operation of the mind, therefore, in every thing we call
thought, there must be conception. When we analyze the various operations either of the understanding or of the will, we shall always find this
at the bottom, like the *caput mortuum* of the chymists, or the *materia prima*
of the Peripatetics; but though there is no operation of the mind without
conception, yet it may be found naked, detached from all others, and
then it is called simple apprehension, or the bare conception of a thing.
(EIP IV, i [360b–361a])[10]

---

[9] After running through some of the many ways in which belief is involved in mental
activity, Reid observes that "as faith in things divine is represented as the main spring
in the life of a Christian, so belief in general is the main spring in the life of a man"
(EIP II, xx [328a]).

[10] Cf. EIP VI, iii [431b]: "nothing can be more evident than this, that all knowledge, and
all judgment and opinion, must be about things which are, or may be immediate objects
of our thought. What cannot be the object of thought, or the object of the mind in
thinking, cannot be the object of knowledge or of opinion."

CONCEPTUAL APPREHENSION

Let's move on to begin looking at what Reid has to say on the first of the two questions fundamental in his thought – namely, the question of how it comes about that we can have entities in mind. Let's work with an example. Suppose I now judge, about that person who was the fifth president of the United States, that he held office before the Civil War. That implies that right now I have an apprehension of him – a mental grip on him – firm enough to make it the case that my judgment is a judgment about *him* rather than about any of the other things that judgments can be about. How did I acquire this apprehension? How did I get this person in mind? And what is the character of this particular apprehension?

I don't know the name of that president. If I once knew it, I've forgotten it and haven't now bothered to look it up. To make things simpler, let's suppose I never knew it. And let's also suppose that I have never seen either a portrait, or a photographic reproduction of some portrait, of him that was identified for me as such. I do, however, possess the singular concept of *the fifth president of the United States*; and as a matter of fact, this concept is satisfied. The combination of the fact that I possess that singular concept with the fact that it is satisfied puts me in a position to have this person in mind, if I wish, and to go on and form a predicative thought about him. I can have him in mind with the concept of *that person who was in fact the fifth president of the United States.*[11]

Someone might reply that by itself that's not enough; that in addition I have to *know* that this singular concept is satisfied. Of course in this particular case I do know that; but it seems to me that such knowledge is in fact not necessary, indeed, not even the *belief* that the concept is satisfied is necessary. Though I know that Bill Clinton is something more than the fortieth president of the United States and something less than the fiftieth, my knowledge on this matter doesn't go beyond that; I don't know how many presidents the United States has had. So I don't know whether

---

[11] If an individual is "unknown, it may, when an object of sense and within reach, be pointed out to the senses; when beyond the reach of the senses, it may be ascertained by a description, which, though very imperfect, may be true and sufficient to distinguish it from every other individual" (EIP IV, i [364b]).

anything satisfies, say, the singular concept of *being the forty-seventh president of the United States*. I don't even have a belief on the matter. But, assuming that the United States has in fact had (at least) forty-seven presidents, that ignorance on my part does not prevent me from having someone in mind with the concept of that person who is or was the forty-seventh president of the United States, and then forming the predicative thought, about him, that he was or is a Republican. The thought would be true just in case that person, whoever he might be, was or is a Republican.

Not only do I apprehend him; it's obvious, from what has been said, that it's possible to distinguish the *mode* of my apprehension from its object – that is, from the entity apprehended. I apprehend him by what I shall call the "apprehensive use" of a singular concept – in distinction from the "predicative" use. If I had available to me some other mode of apprehending that person – if I could apprehend him by perception, say – then I could form about him not only the predicative thought that *he was or is a Republican*, but also the predicative thought *that he is the forty-seventh president of the United States*.

To explain that last point a bit: Apprehending him by the apprehensive use of the singular concept, *that person who was the forty-seventh president of the United States*, is different from forming the predicative thought *about* him, *that* he is the forty-seventh president of the United States. One and the same singular concept can function both apprehensively and predicatively – both as that by means of which I have something in mind and as that which I predicate of something. We can both use a singular concept to get something in mind (viz., that which satisfies the concept); and we can think, about something that we already have in mind, that it satisfies the singular concept.

Kent Bach, in his discussion of these matters in his book *Thought and Reference*,[12] denies that definite descriptions (singular concepts) enable us to have things in mind. "If *all* your thoughts about things could only be descriptive," he says, "your total conception of the world would be merely qualitative. You would never be related in thought to anything in particular. Thinking of something would never be a case of having it 'in mind'. . . ." He offers the following reason for this claim: Whatever be the nature of that

---

[12] Oxford: Clarendon Press, 1987.

special relation which holds between an entity and a person when the person has that entity in mind,

it is different from that involved in thinking of something under a description. If we can even speak of a relation in the latter case, it is surely not a real (or natural) relation. Since the object of a descriptive thought is determined SATISFACTIONALLY, the fact that the thought is of that object does not require any connection between thought and object. However, the object of a *de re* thought is determined RELATION-ALLY. For something to be the object of a *de re* thought, it must stand in a certain kind of relation to that very thought. The relation that makes something the object of a *de re* thought is a causal relation, of a special kind to be explained in due course." (p. 12)

Bach does not distinguish, as I have been distinguishing, between having something in mind and forming some *de re*/predicative thought about something. But given this distinction, it's clear what he wishes to argue. Definite descriptions (singular concepts) do not enable us to get things in mind in a manner and degree adequate for having thoughts that can be described, in *de re*/predicative style, as being *about* particular things. Earlier I claimed that if I believe that the cat making all that noise under the window last night sounded ill, and Felix is that cat, then it would be correct to say that I believed, about Felix, that he sounded ill. So Bach's claim is a direct challenge to the line of thought that I have been laying out.

What is Bach's argument? Singular concepts, he says, do not constitute or provide a "real" or "natural" relationship between object and thought – by which he means, do not constitute or provide a *causal* relation. The relation is purely satisfactional. The person forms the singular concept, *the cat making all that noise under the window last night*; and if the world happens to be such that there was exactly one cat making all that noise under the window last night, then that thing stands to the concept in the relation of satisfying it.

All true. But why isn't *satisfaction* a "real" relation? What's "unreal" about the relation in which Felix stands to the concept of *the cat making all that noise under the window last night* when he satisfies that concept? It's not, indeed, the causal relation; but why is it on that account "unreal"? And how, in any case, does the conclusion follow? Bach grants that a descriptive thought does, in his words, "determine" an object. Why isn't determination – be it a "real" relation or not – sufficient for having the object in mind in a manner and degree adequate for forming thoughts which can be correctly described, in *de re*/predicative fashion, as *about* the determined object?

Bach doesn't say why "determination" isn't sufficient. It's true that if Fluffy rather than Felix had been the cat making all that noise, then, for my belief to be true, my predicative thought *that he sounded ill* would have to be satisfied by Fluffy, rather than by Felix. But that seems entirely compatible with the fact that, as things stand in the world, it was about Felix that I believed *that he sounded ill* rather than about Fluffy. Which entity it is that I have in mind is not determined merely by my thoughts but by the world and how the world is related to my thoughts. I submit that one of the relationships between world and mind that brings about having something in mind is the satisfaction relationship.

In summary: one way of arriving at an apprehension of an entity that is sufficient for having a thought that can be correctly described, in *de re*/predicative fashion, as *about* that entity, is by apprehensive use of a singular concept that that entity satisfies.[13] I have been working with my own examples in developing the point. An example Reid offers, of apprehending an entity by means of a singular concept, is the following:

---

[13] A word should be said about that final clause, "that that entity satisfies." Suppose – to use an example now current in the philosophical literature, that I say, "The man over there drinking a martini is . . ."; might I not both have him in mind with that description and communicate to someone else who I have in mind, even though it's not a martini he's drinking but, say, Dutch gin? Yes, definitely. And that's because, though there's some thought I have, or some aspect of a thought I have, which is doing the designative work – serving to get the person in mind – the words I use prove, unbeknownst to me, to be a defective expression of that thought. The words "drinking a martini" prove not to be doing any designative work in this case. Furthermore, there may be persons in the situation who know that my words are a defective expression of that aspect of my thought which is actually doing the designative work because they are able to surmise who I have in mind and they know it's not a martini he's drinking. A related point is that, by virtue of the role played by contextual factors, both I and my auditor may get some thing in mind by my use of a singular concept of the form 'the K that is f' – for example, "the book on the table last night" – even though there are many things which satisfy the concept. In such cases, it's not the singular concept by itself which is doing the designative work but the singular concept in conjunction with one and another contextual factor. One more complication: I might pick something out with an expression of the form 'the K that is f' even though I myself do not possess the concept of *the* K. I myself might not know what, say, a trilobite is; nonetheless, I might use the word to pick out a trilobite. I would be using it with the intent that it express the concept that those who are in the know about trilobites use the concept to express.

Westminster bridge is an individual object; though I had never seen or heard of it before, if I am only made to conceive that it is a bridge from Westminster over the Thames, this conception, however imperfect, . . . is sufficient to make me distinguish it, when it is mentioned, from every other object that exists. (EIP IV, i [364b])

NOMINATIVE APPREHENSION

Let's move on to what I shall call the *nominative* mode of apprehension of entities. I hold various beliefs about Aristotle. And I am furthermore capable of actively entertaining those beliefs about Aristotle – which presupposes my having the capacity of *actively apprehending* Aristotle. How did I acquire this capacity of actively having Aristotle in mind?

Almost certainly I acquired it by being confronted, several decades ago now, by someone's referring to Aristotle with the name "Aristotle." Thereupon I had Aristotle in mind – mentally apprehended him. My mode of apprehension was by means of a name; I apprehended him by means of the name "Aristotle." Not only was I thereby placed in the position of *being able to think* one thing and another about Aristotle; I'm sure that as a matter of fact I did at once begin thinking things about him – indeed, forming *beliefs* about him.

Though I'm quite sure that my original apprehension of Aristotle was in the nominative mode, that would not have prevented my later apprehending him in the conceptual mode – by means of the concept, say, of *that person who was Plato's most gifted student.* So too, by looking up his name I can bring it about that I apprehend in the nominative mode that person whom I previously apprehended in the conceptual mode with the concept, *the fifth president of the United States.* The general point is this: From the fact that one originally apprehended X by means of some singular concept it doesn't follow that one's present apprehension of X is by means of that concept – nor even by some concept or other. And conversely, from the fact that one originally apprehended X in some nominative mode it doesn't follow that one's present apprehension of X is in that nominative mode – nor indeed, in some nominative mode or other. Indeed, one may have lost one's ability to think of him in that mode; one may have forgotten his name.

I must clarify one aspect of what I mean when I speak of having something in mind *in the nominative mode*. My guess is that I first acquired a notion of Aristotle by being confronted, several decades ago, with some philosophical discourse in which the writer or speaker used the name "Aristotle" to refer to Aristotle. But I have completely forgotten the episode; so it cannot be the case that when I now have Aristotle in mind, I have him in mind as the person who was denoted by that particular token of the name "Aristotle." But I also can't have him in mind as the person who bears the name "Aristotle," since so many people do.

Let us suppose that Saul Kripke is right, in essentials, about the workings of proper names.[14] Schematically it goes like this: Someone, call him A, takes the proper name "Aristotle" and in some way or another attaches it to some person as that person's name. Thereafter A uses that name in the presence of persons B and C with the (successful) intent of thereby referring to the person he named "Aristotle." Thereafter B uses the name in the presence of another person D with the (successful) intent of thereby referring to the person whom A referred to when A used the name in the presence of B; and C uses the name in the presence of yet another person E with the (successful) intent of thereby referring to the person whom A referred to when A used the name in the presence of C. And so forth. Call the use of a particular proper name in this branching, chainlike fashion, going back to the naming of a particular entity with the name, a *reference-specific usage* of the name.

Long before I was first confronted with the name "Aristotle" being used to refer to Aristotle, I had gotten the hang of how proper names work. So I think it likely that, even on that original occasion, I regarded myself as confronted with a token of a reference-specific usage of "Aristotle," and thought of Aristotle as the person denoted by that particular reference-specific usage, rather than as the person referred to by *that particular token*. Upon hearing the name "Aristotle" used to refer to Aristotle, I acquired an apprehension and concept of that particular reference-specific usage of the name which goes back to an original naming of Aristotle and which, by a chain of referrings, eventuated in the production of that particular token of the name which I first heard

[14] Saul A. Kripke, *Naming and Necessity* (Oxford: Basil Blackwell, 1980).

or read in philosophical discourse several decades ago. In any case, when I now apprehend Aristotle in the nominative mode, that's surely how I apprehend him. I have him in mind as the person to whom that particular usage of the proper name "Aristotle" is attached.

APPREHENSION BY ACQUAINTANCE

Apprehension in the conceptual and nominative modes is not, and cannot possibly be, the totality of our apprehensions; it is not the case, and cannot possibly be the case, that we get things in mind exclusively by means of names of those things and singular concepts that they satisfy. The point can be argued in many ways. In his theory of perception and of memory, Reid will provide us with the materials for one way of arguing the point. Since those theories still await us, let me argue it in a different way.

I apprehend the fifth president of the United States by apprehensive use of the singular concept, *that person who was the fifth president of the United States.* But what then about my apprehension of that singular concept itself? In principle that too can be by apprehensive use of a singular concept. And so forth. But somewhere this sequence has to end with an apprehension of some singular concept that is not an apprehension of it by use of some other singular concept, or there will never be my apprehension of the fifth president of the United States. And as for names, the crucial point is that someone has to do something that gives the person or thing that name. Consider that reference-specific usage of the name "Aristotle" that is attached to the Greek philosopher Aristotle: Someone must name Aristotle "Aristotle" if there is even to be that particular usage of the name. For this to happen, the namer must have a mental grip on Aristotle – have him in mind, apprehend him. How could he achieve that? Well, in principle his apprehension of Aristotle could be in the conceptual mode: While apprehending Aristotle by apprehensive use of some singular concept, he could do whatever is necessary to name the person he thereby has in mind, "Aristotle." But if he is to apprehend Aristotle by such use of a singular concept, he has to have an apprehension of that singular concept. And though that singular concept could in turn be apprehended by apprehensive use of another singular concept, the chain, as we just saw, must end somewhere with an apprehension of a concept that is not in the conceptual mode. And then there is the matter of the working of the name itself. If I am to apprehend something in the nominative mode, I must have an apprehension of the name – strictly, of a reference-specific usage of the name and of tokens of that usage. Those apprehensions could in turn be in the conceptual, and indeed in the nominative, mode; but once again, the chain must end somewhere with apprehensions that are not in those modes.

Singular concepts and names do indeed enable us to get a mental grip on things. The grip is real, no doubt of that, and it is strong enough to enable us to form thoughts about the things thus gripped. There can be chains of such grips on things. But the chains must somewhere end with mental grips on things which aren't purely conceptual or nominative. Examples of the requisite apprehensions are legion. I *grasp* the property of *being the fifth president of the United States*; I am *aware* of my present state of feeling dizzy. Though I can get a mental grip on *your* feeling of dizziness by apprehensive use of the singular concept, the *dizziness that you are presently experiencing*, my mental grip on my own present feeling of dizziness is very different: I *feel* it, and am fully aware of doing so. It's *present* to me, and I'm aware that it is.

What word shall we use to pick out this third mode of apprehension? I propose using the word that Bertrand Russell used for exactly the same purpose: "acquaintance."[15] When I am aware of feeling uncomfortably warm, I am *acquainted with* that feeling of mine. And speaking of the converse relation, my uncomfortably warm feeling is *present* to me. Though I can mentally apprehend *your* state of feeling uncomfortably warm, I do not and cannot have acquaintance with it; it is not and cannot be present to me. So too, in grasping the property of being a prime number I am acquainted with that property; that property is present to me. Intellection *presents* to me in the intellective mode the property of *being a prime number*; consciousness *presents* to me in the mode of consciousness my uncomfortably warm feeling. Apprehension of some entity in the acquaintance mode is what

---

[15] See Russell's "On the Nature of Acquaintance" in B. Russell's *Logic and Knowledge: Essays 1901–1950*, ed. R. C. Marsh (London: Allen & Unwin, 1956).

the grand philosophical tradition up to and including Locke called "knowledge."

Objects of acquaintance constitute a subset of what I shall sometimes call the *intuitional* contents of the mind, meaning by this, the contents of consciousness. I borrow the word "intuition" from English translations of Kant, where it is standardly used to translate *Anschauung*. Fundamental to the life of the mind is intuitional content; were a mind devoid of all intuitional content, it would be no mind at all. It's because your feeling of dizziness is not part of the intuitional content of my mind that I can get a mental grip on it only by the apprehensive use of some singular concept, not by acquaintance. Since it does not belong to the intuitional content of my mind, it cannot be present to me.

It's mainly because we fail to attend to all that belongs to the intuitional content of the mind – fail to be aware of it, fail to take note of it – that the intuitional content extends beyond what we have acquaintance with. Our attention is focused on other things. Most of the time, in the discussion that follows, this lack of coincidence between what one is conscious of (the intuitional content of the mind) and what one attends to, and hence is acquainted with, won't make any difference. When it does, I will call attention to it.[16]

I am well aware of the fact that in speaking of "presence" and "presentational content" I am waving a red flag in the face of deconstructionists. Deconstructionists profess to deny all forms of *presence*. We are all prisoners in the house of interpretation. But of course it is assumed that *the interpreted* is present to us – and that, conversely, we have acquaintance with it. So in spite of all their bluster, deconstructionists, along with the rest of us, assume presence; their point is that what is present to us is always already shaped by concepts. The issue is not *whether* there's presence but

---

[16] The distinction between being conscious of something, and *being acquainted with it* was of indispensable importance for Reid's purposes. Likewise, the distinction between being awarely conscious of it, and *reflecting* on it, was important for his purposes. (Reid's "reflection" is a synonym of our "introspection.") "In order ... to our having a distinct notion of any of the operations of our own minds, it is not enough that we be conscious of them, for all men have this consciousness: it is further necessary that we attend to them while they are exerted, and reflect upon them with care, while they are recent and fresh in our memory" (EIP II, v [258a]). "Reflection upon any thing, whether external or internal, makes it an object of our intellectual powers, by which we survey it on all sides, and form such judgments about it as appear to be just and true" (EIP VI, i [420b]).

what is present; and more generally, not *whether* there's intuitional content but *what* that content is.

Perception, recollection, introspection, and intellection are of course different in important ways. Just as important for our subsequent purposes is their similarities. All of them yield apprehensions of entities. More precisely: they don't *yield* apprehensions; they *are* or *incorporate* apprehensions. My perception of my car incorporates an apprehension of my car sufficient for me to form a *de re*/predicative thought about it. There's nothing else I have to do to have it in mind than perceive it. And my awareness of my dizziness just is an apprehension of it – of the acquaintance sort.

What is furthermore distinctive of these modes of apprehension is that each of them yields (or makes available) information about the world or oneself. To perceive my car is thereby to gain information, or to be in a position to gain information, about my environment; to be aware of my dizziness is thereby to gain, or to be in a position to gain, information about my mental state; to recollect learning that "walk" is spelled with an "l" is thereby to recover information about my past. By contrast, I do not gain information about my environment when apprehending someone with the singular concept, *that person who was in fact the fifth president of the United States*; nor do I gain information about my environment when apprehending a person by a particular usage of the name "Aristotle." Again, in grasping a concept I thereby gain information, or am in a position to gain information, about that concept; I am, for example, in a position to judge whether proposed analyses of the concept are correct or incorrect. By contrast, I do not gain information about that concept if my apprehension of it is purely conceptual – for example, if I apprehend it as *that concept which Wittgenstein worked so hard to understand in <u>On Certainty</u>*.

CHAPTER II

The Way of Ideas: Structure and Motivation

Reid believed that the Way of Ideas held his philosophical predecessors so firmly in its grip that without an accompanying
polemic against that alternative his own view would be rejected
out of hand. I judge that at many points the connection between
affirmation and polemic goes even deeper than that. It's not just
that we won't take Reid's arguments *for* his position seriously
unless we are also given arguments *against* the opposition. Often
it's difficult even to grasp what Reid is affirming without being
aware of the position he is rejecting and of his reasons for doing
so. Thus in my exposition I will, in good measure, follow Reid's
own practice of allowing the presentation of his own view to
emerge out of his polemic against the Way of Ideas.

THE WAY OF IDEAS

In its main outlines the Way of Ideas is as familiar as anything in
modern philosophy. I will not exegete the various statements Reid
offers of what he wants his expression, "the Way of Ideas," to cover
– that is, of the theses that he wants included. Those statements
are not entirely consistent with each other, and I see no point in
dwelling on the inconsistencies here.[1] What I will rather do is
outline the system of thought which Reid attributes to his forebears and whose totality he sometimes, at least, has in mind by
"the Way of Ideas."

I will also not pursue the historical query of whether Reid does
full justice to his predecessors in attributing to them this system
of thought. Though it's my view that Reid did in fact capture the

---

[1] For an exegetical approach to what Reid had in mind by "the Way of Ideas," see John
Greco, "Reid's Critique of Berkeley and Hume: What's the Big Idea?" *Philosophy and
Phenomenological Research* 55 (1995): 279–96.

23

fundamental drift of their line of thought, I concede that he tended to ignore the disagreements among those who espoused the theory. When compared to the fine texture of particular expositions, Reid's formulation is often idealized and stereotypical; the hesitations expressed and the qualifications introduced by particular proponents of the Way of Ideas tend to go unremarked. Locke seems usually to have functioned for him as the paradigmatic figure, while Hume takes the brunt of his polemical ire. Seldom, however, does this make any difference to Reid's purposes. Reid was not so much offering an exegesis as composing a rational reconstruction of a line of thought that gripped his predecessors – gripped them so firmly that, whatever their hesitations and qualifications, they never took the step of discarding the fundamentals of the theory as fatally flawed. Rather than developing a new theory they tinkered around the edges of the Way of Ideas, drew out its implications, and so forth. Reid was the first to have had the philosophical imagination to liberate himself sufficiently to develop a significant alternative.

In contrast to those present-day theorists who profess to deny all presence, the seventeenth and eighteenth century proponents of the Way of Ideas unambiguously held that items of reality are presented to each of us for our acquaintance. However, from within the totality of reality, only items of a few, very limited, sorts can ever be present to any of us. Assuming the tenability of the ontological distinction between mental entities and all others, the Way of Ideas held that, at any moment, that with which one has acquaintance consists at most of oneself, of one's present mental acts and objects, and of those of one's present mental states that one is then actively aware of – along with various facts, contingent and necessary, consisting of the interrelationships of these. Thus, mental acts such as judging and regretting; mental objects such as visual and auditory images; mental states such as emotions, feelings, and those concepts and beliefs that one is actively aware of at the time; and facts consisting of the interrelationships among these. Acquaintance with one's self occupies an unsteady position in the theory. There are strong impulses in the Way of Ideas to deny such acquaintance; yet usually, in the working out of the theory, it is assumed.

One explanatory qualification, not to my knowledge made by any of the theorists themselves, is crucial for understanding the theory. Many of those acts and states of one's self that would presumably be classified as mental are relational acts of a kind such that one's performing the act consists of acting on some entity of a sort other than those mentioned above, and relational states of a kind such that one's being in the state consists of standing in a relation to some entity of a sort other than those mentioned. My perceiving our cat would be an example of such a relational act; my believing, about Paul, that he will be late, would be an example of such a relational state. The Way of Ideas theorists held that such 'mixed' acts and states are not candidates for acquaintance. Though my perceiving our cat definitely bears some relation to our cat, nonetheless, since it's impossible to have acquaintance with our cat, my perception of our cat does not have acquaintance with our cat as an ingredient. It follows that I cannot be acquainted with the act of my perceiving our cat. Likewise, since I cannot have acquaintance with Paul, I cannot have acquaintance with my believing something about Paul. It's typical of theorists of the Way of Ideas to postulate a purely mental correlate, of one sort and another, for each of such 'mixed' states and acts. With these correlates we have acquaintance.

This specifies the candidates for objects of acquaintance – not very precisely, admittedly, but well enough for our purposes. It does not, so far, say anything about what actually brings about an episode of acquaintance. Reid regards the thesis on this matter which was offered by theorists of the Way of Ideas as constituting the fundamental motivation for the theory as a whole; accordingly, rather than discussing the issue here, let me set it aside, get the rest of the theory in hand, and then return.

Suppose I have acquaintance with a certain mental state – a certain *dizziness*, say – and with various mental facts of which that dizziness is a constituent. That acquaintance will evoke various *de re*/predicative judgments (and beliefs) about that mental state: that it exists, that it is a case of dizziness, that it's mine, that it is an unusually serious case of dizziness, and so forth. Specifically, my awareful acquaintance with some mental fact evokes in me a judgment or belief whose propositional content corresponds to the fact with which I am acquainted. My acquaintance with the fact that this present state of mine is a case of dizziness evokes in me the belief that this present state of mine is a case of dizziness. In addition, one's acquaintance *justifies* the corresponding belief which it evokes. Such judgments and beliefs are singled out by theorists of the Way of Ideas as *certain*. When what one judges and believes to be true is simply the propositional counterpart to some fact with which one is acquainted, how could error intrude itself?

It's worth adding that Locke eventually conceded that the causal power, possessed by acquaintance with mental facts, to cause corresponding *de re* judgments and beliefs, may be inhibited, in particular instances, by strongly held beliefs one already has to the effect that one is *not* acquainted with that fact. For example, if I believe some trusted mathematician who tells me that a certain mathematical proposition has just been proved false, I may no longer believe the proposition even though the mathematician is mistaken and I am, in fact, acquainted with the corresponding mathematical fact.[2]

The typical Way of Ideas theorist did not deny that there's more to reality than his own mind and its acts, states, and objects; he was not typically a solipsist. With the exception of Berkeley, and possibly Hume, he was a realist concerning the existence of external, spatially located, objects. He furthermore held that we form *de re*/predicative judgments and beliefs about those – which presupposes that we somehow get them in mind; what he denies is that we have, or can have, acquaintance with them. The great challenge facing such Way of Ideas theorists was then how to explain the nature and acquisition of our apprehensions of nonmental entities, and the formation and justification of *de re*/predicative judgments and beliefs about them.

In particular, then, how did such Way of Ideas theorists analyze perception? And let it be recalled that everyone assumed that perception incorporates presentational content of *some* sort. His analysis was guided by the use of reflective images as a model. Suppose one is gazing at a reflection that a mountain produces of itself in a lake. Now ask oneself the question: "Do I see the mountain?" The immediate reply of most of us would be, "No, I see its reflection." Probably some of us would not feel entirely happy with leaving the matter there. We would want to add some such comment as this: "I certainly don't see the mountain directly, or immediately. Maybe I see it indirectly, by way of seeing its reflection; but I don't see it directly."

---

[2] See John Locke, *Essay concerning Human Understanding*, IV, 20. For a discussion of the significance of this passage in the *Essay*, see my *John Locke and the Ethics of Belief* (Cambridge: Cambridge University Press, 1996), pp. 94–8.

Whatever be the truth on that matter, what surely is true is that one's direct and immediate perception of the reflective image of the mountain gives one the basis for inferential knowledge, of a special kind, about the mountain. I get a mental grip on the mountain by the apprehensive use of the singular concept, *that entity that is producing this reflection of itself*; and then, by inference from beliefs that get formed in me by gazing at the reflection and noticing its properties, I arrive at judgments and beliefs about the mountain and its properties. In particular, with respect to some properties of the reflection I infer that the mountain has those properties. Or if one prefers to think nominalistically: with respect to some qualities of the reflection, I infer that the mountain has qualities similar to those.[3] For example, from the reflection's whiteness I infer the existence of the mountain's whiteness; and from the reflection's contour I infer a similar contour of the mountain. In making the inference I assume that the reflection is, in these respects, an image of the mountain, a simulacrum. Others of my inferences will not assume that the mountain has a property identical with, or a quality similar to, the property or quality of its reflection; for example, from certain properties or qualities of the reflection I will infer no more than that the mountain has whatever properties or qualities are required for causing properties (or qualities) in its reflection.

Our cognitive grip on the mountain, in such a case, is of course a conceptual apprehension. The singular concept used is of a sort worth singling out for special attention, however. Sometimes the singular concept by means of which we apprehend something has purely universal constituents. Not so in this case. I apprehend the mountain with the concept, *that entity which is causing this reflec-*

[3] It was the practice of the medieval philosophers to use the Latin word '*quale*' (plural, '*qualia*') for those abstract particulars which are cases of properties, and of predicables generally. Examples of such entities are this paper's whiteness and this table's hardness. I will follow in the footsteps of the medievals by using the English word 'qualities' for what they called '*qualia*'; by and large, Reid did the same. It's tempting to follow even more closely in the footsteps of the medievals by simply using their word '*qualia*.' However, in recent years the word '*qualia*' has been regularly used in philosophy of mind discussions to refer to what Reid calls "sensations"; to use it in our discussion to refer to abstract particulars rather than sensations would be to court confusion. (So far as I can tell, the current usage in philosophy of mind was adopted in complete oblivion to the medieval usage.) As we shall see, Reid thought that the fundamental objects of perception were qualities. For a discussion of some of the ontological issues involved, see Chapter 6 of my *On Universals* (Chicago: University of Chicago Press, 1970). For Reid on qualities, see, in particular, EIP V, iii [394a ff.].

tion. To grasp this concept – that is, to be actively acquainted with it – I must be actively perceiving that spatially located particular which is *this reflection* of the mountain. For that particular is a constituent of the concept, and my access to that particular is by perception. Concepts of this sort – call them *causal particular* concepts – play an indispensable role in the account of perception offered by the Way of Ideas, as do inferences based on the assumption of similarity between image and imaged.

Theorists of the Way of Ideas regularly used reflective images, and our cognitive interaction with such, as their model for analyzing the nature of perception. Nowadays, photographic images would do as well. To get going on using images of this sort as a model for analyzing perception we have to find something mental that bears a relation to external objects like that which the reflection of the mountain bears to the mountain; specifically, we have to find something that *represents* external objects to us in the way that a reflective image represents to us the thing reflected.

What might these entities be? Whatever they might be, the seventeenth- and eighteenth-century theorists proposed calling them "ideas"; twentieth-century theorists have preferred calling them "sense data." Let's suppose, says the Way of Ideas theorist, that in every case of what we ordinarily call "perception" there's some idea or sense datum in the mind which images some external object in the same way that an ordinary reflective image images the object reflected; and let's furthermore suppose that our only access to the external object is by way of our access to its image. There's nothing like looking up at the mountain itself. The Way of Ideas theorists drew the conclusion that, strictly speaking, it's only one's ideas, one's sense data, that one perceives. Locke says of the mind that "it perceives nothing but its own ideas" (quoted by Reid at EIP II, ix [275b]), and Hume says that "the existences which we consider, when we say, *this house*, and *that tree*, are nothing but perceptions in the mind" (quoted by Reid at EIP II, xiv [302b]).

When discussing the mountain and its reflective image I noted that though all of us would say that we don't really see the mountain when looking at its reflection, probably some of us would wish to add that perhaps we see the mountain *indirectly*. Reid takes note of a similar ambivalence and tendency in the Way of Ideas theorists. In one passage he asks "whether, according to the opinion of philosophers, we perceive the images or ideas only, and infer the existence and qualities of the external object from what we perceive in the image? or, whether we really perceive the external object as well as its image? (EIP II, vii [263b]). And he then observes that "The answer to this question is not quite obvious." After excepting Berkeley and Hume, he says that philosophers "believe the existence of external objects of sense, and call them objects of perception, though not immediate objects." But what they mean by that, he does "not find clearly explained." Possibly they mean that, speaking literally, "we perceive both the external object and its idea in the mind. If [this] be their meaning, it would follow that, in every instance of perception, there is a double object perceived: that I perceive, for instance, one sun in the heavens, and another in my own mind." Reid finds it doubtful that this is what they do in fact mean. More likely "their opinion is, that we do not really perceive the external object, but the internal only; and that when they speak of perceiving external objects, they mean it only in a popular or in a figurative sense." He offers three reasons for thinking this is what they mean. One is that "if we do really perceive the external object itself, there seems to be no necessity, no use, for an image of it." A second is that "since the time of Descartes, philosophers have very generally thought that the existence of external objects of sense requires proof, and can only be proved from the existence of their ideas" (EIP II, vii [263b]).

The upshot is that sometimes Reid will take the Way of Ideas theorists as holding that always, in perception, there are two objects perceived: the external object and its internal image.[4] He will say, for example, that according to the Way of Ideas theorists

---

[4] He regards Hume as the first to have seen, with full clarity, the absurdity of this view: "Mr. Hume saw further into the consequences of the common system concerning ideas than any other author had done before him. He saw the absurdity of making every object of thought double, and splitting it into a remote object, which has a separate and permanent existence, and an immediate object, called an idea or impression, which is an image of the former, and has no existence, but when we are conscious of it. According to this system, we have no intercourse with the external world, but by means of the internal world of ideas, which represents the other to the mind.

"He saw it was necessary to reject one of these worlds as a fiction, and the question was, which should be rejected? Whether all mankind, learned and unlearned, had feigned the existence of the external world without good reason? or whether philosophers had feigned the internal world of ideas, in order to account for the intercourse of the mind with the external? Mr. Hume adopted the first of these opinions, and employed his reason and eloquence in support of it.

"Bishop Berkeley had gone so far in the same track as to reject the material world as fictitious; but it was left to Mr. Hume to complete the system" (EIP III, vii [356b]).

"things which do not now exist in the mind itself, can only be perceived, remembered, or imagined, by means of ideas or images
of them in the mind, which are the immediate objects of perception, remembrance, and imagination" (IHM VII [210b;
B216]). More often he will interpret their view in accord with the
conclusion drawn in the passage above: In perception, the only
thing really perceived is 'ideas.'

The detailed analysis of perception offered by the Way of Ideas
theorists went, then, like this: The occurrence of sense data
evokes acquaintance with those sense data and with various of the
mental facts pertaining thereto. These factual acquaintances in
turn cause judgments and beliefs whose propositional content
corresponds to those facts. Such judgments and beliefs are
formed in the person immediately. That is to say, the person does
not arrive at them by inferring them from other beliefs; the
person's acquaintance with the mental facts causes the corresponding judgments and beliefs without further ado. Furthermore, her acquaintance with those mental facts constitutes her
evidence for those judgments and beliefs; a person's evidence
for her belief that she presently has a red-sphere sense datum
is not some other belief she has but just the presence to her
of that red-sphere sense datum. Her acquaintance with the
mental facts pertaining to that sense datum is both the *immediate
cause* of judgments and beliefs whose propositional content
corresponds to those facts, and her *evidence* for those judgments
and beliefs.

Then, as the output of inference from those beliefs, the new
judgment (and belief) is formed in her that this sense datum of
hers has been caused by some external, spatially located, object
of which the sense datum is an image. This belief might be mistaken; she might be having an hallucination, or an illusion. But
suppose it is correct. She is then in a position to apprehend some
external object with the singular concept, *that entity which is
causing* this sense datum *which is an image of itself.* This apprehension is of course a conceptual apprehension; it's not a case of
acquaintance. More specifically, it is a causal particular concept.
With this conceptual apprehension in hand she then forms judgments and beliefs about that external entity by making inferences
from beliefs about the phenomenal properties or qualities of the
sense datum. At this point the celebrated distinction between

primary and secondary properties or qualities enters into the philosopher's description of the situation. She infers that the object has a spatial shape resembling the spherical shape of the sense datum; whereas, with respect to the redness of the sense datum, she infers only that the object has the disposition (under standard conditions, etc.) to cause sense data with that particular property or quality. Of course these inferences from the phenomenal features of the image to the features of the object usually take place swiftly and unreflectively.

I have been presenting Reid's understanding of the account of perception offered by theorists of the Way of Ideas. Let me give Reid the chance to state the core of the view in his own voice:

philosophers maintain, that, besides [real things], there are immediate objects of perception in the mind itself: that, for instance, we do not see the sun immediately, but an idea; or, as Mr. Hume calls it, an impression in our own minds. This idea is said to be the image, the resemblance, the representative of the sun, if there be a sun. It is from the existence of the idea that we must infer the existence of the sun. But the idea being immediately perceived, there can be no doubt, as philosophers think, of its existence. . . .

Mr. Locke, and those that were before him . . . [held that] there are substantial and permanent beings called the sun and moon; but they never appear to us in their own person, but by their representatives, the ideas in our own minds, and we know nothing of them but what we can gather from those ideas. (EIP II, xiv [298b–299a])

Are inferences of the sort indicated, to the existence and character of external objects, reliable? That is the great 'problem of the external world' which loomed before these Way of Ideas theorists. What generates the problem is not the conviction that in some cases the inferences yield false conclusions. What generates it is the query whether we can know, or have good reason to believe, of *any* such inference that it has yielded a true conclusion. Can we know, or have good reason to believe, concerning *any* sense datum that some external object is causing it? If so, can we *know* anything about its properties or qualities; or more weakly, are there any *beliefs* that we can have good reason to hold about its properties or qualities? All parties concede that a sensory experience need not be caused by something external — certainly not by something external of which the experience is an image. Might it be that none is so caused?

What resources does the Way of Ideas theorist have for dealing with this particular form of skepticism? Not many. He's confined to using as evidence the deliverances of that faculty which, on his view, does yield acquaintance; namely, consciousness (reason being understood as that special use of consciousness which yields acquaintance with logical relations among concepts and thoughts). His strategy is to try to assemble a satisfactory body of evidence on which it is highly probable that sense data are caused, in normal cases at least, by external objects of which those sense data are the imagistic representations. The fact that that proposition is probable on that evidence must, of course, be something with which he has acquaintance; it must be a deliverance of reason. And as to the character of the evidence itself, it too must consist of facts with which he has acquaintance; thus it must be confined to the deliverances of consciousness, including reason. And in its totality it must be sufficiently ample in scope, and representative – that is, not skewed. Descartes was the first, but only the first, of the great modern philosophers to attempt to construct an argument that satisfied these peculiar and stringent demands.

It was typical in Reid's time, and it remains typical to this day, for theorists of the Way of Ideas to say far less about memory than about perception. It's clear, though, that the analysis they had in mind proceeded along lines parallel to that which they developed for perception. They claimed or assumed that when we recollect, we have memory images before the mind with which we have acquaintance, as we do with various facts pertaining to these images. These factual acquaintances cause judgments and beliefs about the images, the content of these judgments and beliefs corresponding to the facts with which one has acquaintance. The judgments and beliefs are formed *immediately*, that is, noninferentially, and they are justified by one's acquaintance with the facts; they are *certain*. But it's also characteristic of us to infer from such beliefs that our memorial images are caused by prior mental events of which they are the imagistic representations. On the supposition, in a given case, that this inference is correct, one is in a position to form a conceptual apprehension of a prior mental event by means of the causal particular concept, *that event which did in fact cause <u>this present memorial image</u> of itself.* And then, by drawing further inferences from the judgments and beliefs formed in one immediately by one's acquaintance with facts pertaining to the memorial image, and justified by that acquaintance, one arrives at *mediately formed* judgments and beliefs about that prior mental event. The theorist of the Way of Ideas attempts to answer the skeptic's question concerning the reliability of these inferences in the same way that he does the parallel question concerning perceptual beliefs.

Reid states the core of the analysis like this:

> when I remember, or when I imagine any thing, all men acknowledge that there must be something that is remembered, or that is imagined; that is, some object of these operations. The object remembered must be something that did exist in time past. The object imagined may be something that never existed. But, say the philosophers, besides these objects which all men acknowledge, there is a more immediate object which really exists in the mind at the same time we remember or imagine. This object is an idea, or image of the thing remembered or imagined. (EIP II, xiv [298b])

In this passage Reid not only refers to the analysis of memory offered by the Way of Ideas theorists but also alludes to their analysis of imagination: We sometimes just imagine things, form plans for doing or making things, grasp abstract entities of one sort or another – for example, imagine a certain sort of person for the novel we are writing, plan an item of furniture to build, grasp a proposition or think of a tune. "Bare conception" and "simple apprehension" are Reid's terms for the activity in question – the significance of the modifiers "bare" and "simple" being that we have no impulse whatsoever to believe that what we are imagining or planning or grasping actually exists (as a substance or spatiotemporal particular).[5] Nonetheless, acquaintance is involved – as can be seen when we contrast imagining a character, composing a plan, or grasping an argument, with getting any of those in mind with a singular concept. As with perception and recollection, the theorist of the Way of Ideas holds that the

---

[5] Reid avoids the word "imagination," as a synonym for his "conception," for the following reason: "I take imagination, in its most proper sense, to signify a lively conception of objects of sight. This is a talent of importance to poets and orators, and deserves a proper name, on account of its connection with those acts. According to this strict meaning of the word, imagination is distinguished from conception as a part from the whole. We conceive the objects of the other senses, but it is not so proper to say that we imagine them. We conceive judgment, reasoning, propositions, and arguments; but it is rather improper to say that we imagine these things" (EIP IV, iii [375b]).

acquaintance involved in intellection (i.e., Reid's "bare conception") is acquaintance with some mental image, or some other sort of mental entity, existing at the time of the conceiving. In this case, however, there is no suggestion that these mental entities function representationally. The situation is not that in reasoning and intellection we are dealing with various abstract entities – propositions, universals, etc. – which are represented by certain mental states and objects. We are dealing just with certain objects, specifically with concepts and the logical relations among them.

One last point of exposition remains. The Way of Ideas theorists embraced an account of concept formation that was intimately connected with their claim that ingredient in perception are images of external objects. This account claimed that all concepts are either evoked by acquaintance with mental entities to which the concepts apply or derived from such by the processes of abstraction, generalization, distinction, and combination. Concepts thus derived constitute the totality of our conceptual repertoire – including, then, the repertoire of concepts available to us for our conceptual apprehension of entities in the external world and for our predications about those entities. From this it follows, of course, that those Way of Ideas theorists who hold that there is an external world and that we can form correct beliefs about it are assuming deep-seated resemblances between the external world and our sense data.[6] It's because there are such deep-seated resemblances that concepts derived from sense data provide us with the conceptual repertoire necessary for apprehending entities in the external world and for making true predications concerning them. And it's because this present sense datum of mine

---

[6] Berkeley and (probably) Hume run the argument in the other direction: if there were an external world, there would have to be such resemblances; but there aren't, so there isn't. Speaking about the debate between Berkeley and Hume, on the one side, and their realist-concerning-the-external-world opponents, on the other, Reid says this: "in all this debate about the existence of a material world, it hath been taken for granted on both sides, that this same material world, if any such there be, must be the express image of our sensations: that we can have no conception of any material thing which is not like some sensation in our minds; ... Every argument brought against the existence of a material world either by the bishop of Cloyne or by the author of the Treatise of Human Nature, supposeth this" (IHM V, vii [127b; B 69]; cf. IHM V, viii [131bff.; B 74 ff.], for Reid's spelling out of Berkeley's argument). Given the assumption, Reid thinks that Berkeley and Hume easily win the argument. In the *Inquiry*, II, vi [109 a–b; B 33–6], there is a hilarious passage in which Reid develops the thought that "Ideas seem to have something in their nature unfriendly to other existences."

is an image of the external object that caused it that I can, using that repertoire, gain considerable knowledge of that object.

Let's allow Reid to make these points in his own words. "The natural furniture of the human understanding is of two kinds," he says. First, the

> *notions* or simple apprehensions which we have of things: and, secondly, the *judgments* or the belief which we have concerning them. As to our notions, the new system [i.e., the Way of Ideas] reduces them to two classes; *ideas of sensation* and *ideas of reflection*: the first are conceived to be copies of our sensations, retained in the memory or imagination; the second, to be copies of the operations of our minds whereof we are conscious, in like manner retained in the memory or imagination: and we are taught, that these two comprehend all the materials about which the human understanding is, or can be, employed. As to our judgment of things, or the belief which we have concerning them, the new system . . . holds it to be the acquisition of reason, and to be got by comparing our ideas, and perceiving their agreements and disagreements

and then, from the beliefs thus acquired, making inferences to the external world on the assumption that our sensory ideas are caused by external objects and are images of the objects that cause them (IHM VII [208a; B 213–14]).

REID'S DIAGNOSIS OF WHAT LED TO THE WAY OF IDEAS

If we are to understand Reid's attack on the Way of Ideas and his alternative thereto, we must not only understand the structure of the theory – we now have that before us – but also his diagnosis of its motivation. By the seventeenth century the central elements of what may be called "our causal picture of perception" had emerged. The picture, as it applies to vision, goes like this: light reflected from physical objects travels in straight lines to the eye, where it produces images on the retina; this excites the optic nerve, which then transmits a 'message' from the retina to the brain. The outcome of this, in turn, is the occurrence of a visual experience.

Philosophers, says Reid, have not been content to combine a description of the workings of the mind in perception with what this causal picture tells us about the physical conditions under which these workings occur. They have wanted to take the further step of *explaining* perception – of giving a *causal account* of it. The Way of Ideas is the product of this attempt to explain perception.[7] The Way of Ideas theorists have not made any new and striking observations. They have not observed that external objects are not immediately perceived, they have not observed that sense data caused by external objects are the only things really perceived (in the act that we ordinarily call "perception"), they have not observed that these sense data resemble the external objects that cause them, they have not observed that perceptual beliefs are inferred from beliefs about these sense data. These are not facts they have discovered, to be added to those discovered by natural scientists. But neither are they logical implications of the facts discovered by scientists. The causal picture of perception informs us about the physical conditions under which perception occurs; that's all it does. The Way of Ideas, assuming this picture, is offered as an explanation of what we ordinarily call "perception" and of the formation of perceptual beliefs. It's arrived at by inference to what is supposedly the best – or only possible – explanation.[8]

The thesis that in perception there are mental images of external objects, that strictly speaking it's only these that we perceive, and that from beliefs about these we make inferences to external objects, was not an inductive generalization from facts observed but belonged, instead, to the theoretical superstructure of the account. Mental images functioning thus were not noticed but

[7] I doubt that Reid is entirely right about this. No doubt the attempt to explain perception was one of the factors that gave rise to the Way of Ideas. But it appears to me that this factor had little role in Descartes' thought. In fact, though Reid definitely regards Descartes as representative of the Way of Ideas, he never discusses Descartes' theory of perception; Locke, Berkeley, and Hume are his principal targets. My guess as to the reason for this is that Reid realized that much of his attack on the account of perception offered by what he calls the Way of Ideas doesn't apply to Descartes. The motivations behind Descartes' account of perception are complex; but if I had to boil it down, I would say that it was motivated more by Descartes' quest for certainty and by his views about God than by any attempt at explanation.

[8] "There is no phenomenon in nature more unaccountable, than the intercourse that is carried on between the mind and the external world: there is no phenomenon which philosophical spirits have shown greater avidity to pry into and to resolve. . . . Philosophers must have some system, some hypothesis, that shews the manner in which our senses make us acquainted with external things. All the fertility of human invention seems to have produced only one hypothesis for this purpose . . . : and that is, that the mind, like a mirror, receives the images of things from without . . ." (IHM VI, vi [140a–b; B 91]).

postulated.[9] In the Dedication to his *Inquiry* Reid explicitly speaks of the Way of Ideas as a "hypothesis."

This feature of the explanation was sufficient by itself to make it unacceptable to Reid. For Reid sternly opposed hypotheses in science, insisting that natural science confine itself to induction. More precisely: Reid insisted that scientific *belief* be confined to that for which we have inductive evidence. "Let hypotheses . . . suggest experiments, or direct our inquiries; but let just induction alone govern our belief" (EIP II, iii [251a]).[10] If all that is to be said in favor of hypothesizing certain entities is that, if there were those entities, some phenomenon would be explained, then that is not sufficient reason for believing that there are those entities. In the absence of evidence for their existence, "to apply them to

[9] Reid cites (EIP II, xiv [299b]) the following passage from Hume as one illustration of his general point that it is philosophy rather than 'common sense' that gives rise to the belief in mental representations: "It seems evident that men are carried by a natural instinct, or prepossession, to repose faith in their senses; and that without any reasoning, or even almost before the use of reason, we always suppose an external universe, which depends not on our perception, but would exist though we and every sensible creature were absent or annihilated. . . . It seems also evident, that when men follow this blind and powerful instinct of nature, they always suppose the very images presented by the senses to be the external objects, and never entertain any suspicion, that the one are nothing but representations of the other. . . . But this universal and primary notion of all men is soon destroyed by the slightest philosophy, which teaches us, that nothing can ever be present to the mind, but in image or perception; and that the senses are only the inlets through which these images are received, without being ever able to produce any immediate intercourse between the mind and the object."

[10] Reid offers his fullest account of the role of hypotheses in science in his letter of Dec. 16, 1780, to Lord Kames: "I would discourage no man from conjecturing, only I wish him not to take his conjectures for knowledge, or to expect that others should do so. Conjecturing may be a useful step even in natural philosophy. Thus, attending to such a phenomenon, I conjecture that it may be owing to such a cause. This may lead me to make the experiments or observations proper for discovering whether that is really the cause or not; and if I can discover, either that it is or is not, my knowledge is improved; and my conjecture was a step to that improvement. But, while I rest in my conjecture, my judgment remains in suspense, and all I can say is, it may be so, and it may be otherwise.

"A cause that is conjectured ought to be such that, if it really does exist, it will produce the effect. If it have not this quality, it hardly deserves the name of a conjecture. Supposing it to have this quality, the question remains – Whether does it exist or not. And this, being a question of fact, is to be tried by positive evidence. . . . All that we know of the material world, must be grounded on the testimony of our senses. Our senses testify particular facts only: from these we collect, by induction, general facts, which we call laws of nature, or natural causes. . . . This is the analytical part of natural philosophy. The synthetical part takes for granted, as principles, the causes discovered by induction, and from these explains or accounts for the phenomena which result from them. This analysis and synthesis make up the whole theory of natural philosophy" (56b–57a).

the solution of phenomena, and to build a system upon them, is . . . building a castle in the air" (EIP II, iii [250a].[11]

> The most uninstructed peasant has as distinct a conception, and as firm a belief of the immediate objects of his senses, as the greatest philosopher; and with this he rests satisfied, giving himself no concern how he came by this conception and belief. But the philosopher is impatient to know how his conception of external objects, and his belief of their existence, is produced. This, I am afraid, is hid in impenetrable darkness. But where there is no knowledge, there is the more room for conjecture: and of this philosophers have always been very liberal.
>
> The dark cave and shadows of Plato, the species of Aristotle, the films of Epicurus, and the ideas and impressions of modern philosophers, are the production of human fancy, successively invented to satisfy the eager desire of knowing how we perceive external objects; but they are all deficient in the two essential characters of a true and philosophical account of the phenomenon: for we neither have any evidence of their existence; nor, if they did exist, can it be shown how they would produce perception. (EIP II, xx [326b])[12]

Reid's argument will be that we neither have evidence for the existence of images of external objects, as an ingredient in perception, nor, if there were such entities, "can it be shown how they would produce perception."

The explanation offered by the Way of Ideas theorists of perception, recollection, inner awareness, and the phenomenon analyzed by Reid as acquaintance with abstract entities (I have been calling it "intellection"), was framed in the context of certain general principles that they assumed any tenable explanation of these phenomena must satisfy. It was Reid's conviction that it was those general principles that were the principal culprit in the

---

[11] "We laugh at the Indian philosopher, who to account for the support of the earth, contrived the hypothesis of a huge elephant, and to support the elephant, a huge tortoise. . . . His elephant was a hypothesis, and our hypotheses are elephants. Every theory in philosophy, which is built on pure conjecture, is an elephant . . ." (IHM VI, xix [180a; B 163]). Cf. the vivid passage making the same point at EIP II, xv [309a–b].

[12] Part of Reid's argumentation for his position on hypotheses is theological: "Although some conjectures may have a considerable degree of probability, yet it is evidently in the nature of conjecture to be uncertain. In every case, the assent ought to be proportioned to the evidence; for to believe firmly, what has but a small degree of probability, is a manifest abuse of our understanding. Now, though we may, in many cases, form very probable conjectures concerning the works of men, every conjecture we can form with regard to the works of God, has as little probability as the conjectures of a child with regard to the works of a man. The wisdom of God exceeds that of the wisest man, more than that of the wisest man exceeds the wisdom of a child" (EIP I, iii [235a]). Reid elaborates the point over several following pages.

affair; the principles drove the invention of the hypotheses. One sees him struggling, over and over, to identify the principles in question; they were never, in their totality, explicitly affirmed by his opponents. Here is perhaps his best formulation of the results of his reflections:

There are two prejudices which seem to me to have given rise to the theory of ideas in all the various forms in which it has appeared in the course of above two thousand years. . . . The *first* is, that in all the operations of the understanding there must be some immediate inter-course between the mind and its object, so that the one may act upon the other. The *second*, that in all the operations of understanding there must be an object of thought, which really exists while we think of it; or, as some philosophers have expressed it, that which is not, cannot be intelligible. . . .

It is by these principles that philosophers have been led to think, that in every act of memory and of conception [i.e., intellection], as well as of perception, there are two objects. The one, the immediate object, the idea, the species, the form; the other, the mediate or external object. . . . These principles have not only led philosophers to split objects into two, where others can find but one; but likewise have led them to reduce the three operations now mentioned to one, making memory and conception [intellection], as well as perception, to be the perception of ideas. (EIP IV, ii [368b–369b])

The formulation is extremely compact and calls for some exe-gesis. Take any mental phenomenon that has a self/act/object structure. Reid's diagnosis was that in constructing their account, adherents of the Way of Ideas were, in the first place, guided by the general principle that any such phenomenon will fit into the causal texture of nature in one or the other of two ways: Either it will consist of the object acting immediately upon the self or it will consist of the self acting immediately upon the object.

Our concern here is with cases of apprehension (Reid's *con-ception*). Reid's diagnosis is that the Way of Ideas theorists oper-ated with this fundamental thesis: *The immediate object of any act of apprehension is identical with the immediate cause thereof.* By an *imme-diate* object of an act of apprehension Reid means an object of an act of apprehension which is not mediated by an imagistic repre-sentation of that entity. (More about this in the opening pages of Chapter VI.) By telling us how apprehension fits into the causal order, the thesis tells us what can and what cannot be the imme-diate object of an act of apprehension: only if it is the immediate cause of the act of apprehension is an entity the immediate object of the act. On Reid's diagnosis, this thesis was the most fundamental and fateful assumption of the Way of Ideas.

A word about "immediate cause": A can *indirectly* bring about a change in C by acting on B in such a way as to bring about the effect of B's acting on C in such a way as to bring about that change in C. But the fundamental reality in such a case is A's acting directly on B, and B on C – that is, acting on them with no causal mediation, *immediately*. We express an important truth when we say that A acted indirectly on C; but that truth consists entirely in those causally unmediated actings occurring in that chainlike relationship.

The application of the point to the matter at hand goes like this: An act of apprehension will be an effect of a vast number of events whose effectuation of that act is causally mediated. But always there will be something that produces the effect *immediately*. And that, on the assumption of the Way of Ideas theorists, is the immediate object of the act of apprehension. (It was also assumed that every act of apprehension has an immediate object.) Given this identification of the immediate object of apprehension with the immediate cause thereof, we can now employ certain general principles about causal activity, as well as the emergent causal picture of perception, to specify the region in which we must look for the immediate objects of apprehension that are ingredient in perception. Science can, in this way, tell us what we are and are not acquainted with.

We have learned from physics, physiology, and neurology that when I perceive a tree there's a whole chain of causal mediation between the tree and my mental act: light rays transmitted from the tree to my eye, followed by the transmission of neural impulses from my eye to my brain, followed by alterations in my brain. Reid's eighteenth-century cohorts were guided in their eliciting of such causal chains by a highly general principle concerning immediate causal action; namely, there is no immediate causal action at a distance. A can *indirectly* (mediately) bring about a change in C without being contiguous to C. But if A indirectly has an effect on C by acting on B in such a way as to bring about the effect of B's acting on C in such a way as to bring about that change in C, A must be contiguous with B, and B with C. Reid cites Samuel Clarke, along with Porterfield, as two of the Way of

Ideas theorists who explicitly embraced this causal principle of contiguity with the elegant formulation: *Nothing can act, or be acted upon, where it is not.* Reid agrees: "That nothing can act immediately [directly] where it is not, I think, must be admitted; for I agree with sir Isaac Newton, that power without substance is inconceivable. It is a consequence of this, that nothing can be acted upon immediately where the agent is not present" (EIP II, xiv [301a]).[13]

When the principle identifying the immediate objects of acts of apprehension with the immediate causes of those acts is supplemented with this ancillary causal principle of contiguity, what follows is the principle of *no immediate apprehension at a distance*, and in particular, *no acquaintance at a distance.* And when this principle is coupled with the emerging causal picture of perception, it obviously follows that external objects – chairs, cats, ducks, etc. – cannot be immediate objects of apprehension. They're always too far away for that. They cannot act immediately upon the mind to produce immediate apprehensions of themselves. Thus it is that the Way of Ideas theorists were forced into proposing entities of some other category as the immediate objects of those acts of apprehension that are ingredients in perception; namely, images that represent the objects. "Philosophers, ancient and modern, have maintained, that the operations of the mind, like the tools of an artificer, can only be employed upon objects that are present in the mind, or in the brain, where the mind is supposed to reside. Therefore, objects that are distant, in time or place, must have a representative in the mind, or in the brain; some image or picture of them, which is the object that the mind contemplates" (EIP II, ix [277b]).

A second principle of causation to which, on Reid's diagnosis, his predecessors appealed, was stated by him in these words: "In all the operations of understanding there must be an object of thought, which really exists while we think of it; or, as some philosophers have expressed it, that which is not, cannot be intelligible." Again, it's a dark saying. I think Reid is best understood here as drawing out an implication of the principle, no immediate causal action at a distance, and formulating it with an eye on

---

[13] Once we learn that Reid was an occasionalist, this principle, on which Reid says he agrees with his predecessors, wears a quite different mien from what it wears at first!

how the implication was used by the Way of Ideas theorists in their attempt to give a causal explanation of recollection, and with an eye on how it was used to reject the suggestion that we have acquaintance with abstract entities.[14] The principle is that whereas an indirect (mediate) cause of some effect may be long over when the effect occurs, the *immediate* cause has to exist at the time of its bringing about the effect. There is no immediate action at a spatial distance and no immediate action at a temporal distance. It follows that the event which I remember as having occurred in my first-grade classroom cannot be the immediate cause of that episode of responsiveness which is my recollection, and hence cannot be the immediate object of the apprehension which is ingredient in my recollection.

How, given these principles, do the Way of Ideas theorists propose to explain perception? We know the answer: the immediate cause of perception, and hence its immediate object, is an internal image of some sort that represents the object and evokes acquaintance with itself. Reid notes that some believed the images in question were physical images located in the brain,[15] and that when we perceive, we are acquainted with these images. Others held that they were mental images. On the latter view, the penultimate link in the causal chain is something in the brain causing mental images; these mental images then, as the final link in the chain, cause that episode of receptivity that is acquaintance with the image. Either way, "as the external objects of sense are too remote to act upon the mind immediately, there must be some image or shadow of them that is present to the mind, and is the immediate object of perception" (EIP IV, ii [368b]). Along the same lines, the explanation of recollection proposed by the Way of Ideas theorists is that the immediate object of apprehension, in episodes of recollection, is presently existing imagistic representations of the prior events.

Some of this sounds very strange to us today, even a bit wacky – so much so that one is suspicious of the accuracy of Reid's diag-

---

[14] On this last, see especially EIP IV, ii [369a ff.].

[15] Reid wryly observes: "We have not the least evidence, that the image of any external object is formed in the brain. The brain has been dissected times innumerable by the nicest anatomists; every part of it examined by the naked eye, and with the help of microscopes; but no vestige of an image of any external object was ever found. The brain seems to be the most improper substance that can be imagined for receiving or retaining images, being a soft moist medullary substance" (EIP II, iv [257b]).

nosis. Did his predecessors really propose, some of them anyway, that one is acquainted with images in one's brain? Did they really assume that the mind has a spatial location, or that mental acts have spatial locations, so that entities can be contiguous to it or to them? Did they really propose that mental images cause acquaintance with themselves? And so forth.

Strange though it sounds, I judge the main points of Reid's diagnosis to be undeniably correct. His Way of Ideas predecessors endeavored to explain perception – that primarily, and secondarily, recollection and what Reid identified as intellection.[16] To do so, they made a general assumption about how acquaintance in particular, and apprehension more generally, fits into the causal order; specifically, they assumed that the immediate object of an act of apprehension is identical with its immediate cause. That done, they were then in a position to determine the immediate objects of apprehension by applying the causal picture of perception plus certain current assumptions concerning causal possibilities and impossibilities. Had they not identified the immediate object of apprehension with its immediate cause, the principles about no immediate causation at a spatial or temporal distance could not have been used to get the conclusion of no immediate apprehension at a distance.

When one adds to these speculations about *how they must have been thinking* the amplitude of quotations that Reid gives from his contemporaries, Reid's diagnosis becomes compelling. Here, for example, is what Samuel Clarke said: "The soul cannot perceive what it is not present to, because nothing can act, or be acted upon, where it is not" (EIP II, xiv [301a]). Thus "the soul, without being present to the images of the things perceived, could not possibly perceive them. A living substance can only there perceive,

---

[16] To recollection, inner awareness, and perception, Reid added what I call "intellection" as a distinct mode of apprehension – namely, acquaintance with abstract entities such as universals. With the possible exception of Descartes, the Way of Ideas proponents denied that there are any abstract entities, hence none for us to apprehend; they were all conceptualists on the issue of universals. Reason, which they took to be a mode of acquaintance, was viewed by them as a species of consciousness. Thus on the matter of intellection, Reid's polemic with his predecessors took a different form from that which it took for perception and recollection. None of them denied that there is perception and recollection (though Berkeley denied that the objects of perception were extra-mental entities); nor did they deny that these both have intuitional content. Reid's dispute with them on those matters was over the nature of that intuitional content and how it functioned.

where it is present, either to the things themselves, as the omnipresent God is to the whole universe, or to the images of things, as the soul is in its proper *sensorium*" (EIP II, xiv [300b–301a]). And here is an even more explicit passage from Porterfield:

> How body acts upon mind, or mind upon body, I know not; but this I am very certain of, that nothing can act, or be acted upon, where it is not; and therefore, our mind can never perceive any thing but its own proper modifications, and the various states of the sensorium, to which it is present: so that it is not the external sun and moon which are in the heavens, which our mind perceives, but only their image or representation impressed upon the sensorium. How the soul of a seeing man sees these images, or how it receives those ideas, from such agitations in the sensorium, I know not; but I am sure it can never perceive the external bodies themselves, to which it is not present. (EIP II, xiv [301a])[17]

I doubt that anyone today would be willing to affirm what Porterfield says in this passage. Yet there lives on in our intellectual culture the belief that physical objects are too distant for us to have immediate apprehension of them; our knowledge of them has to be mediated by mental representations. The thought, though influential among us, is vague and unarticulated. It is to the credit of the seventeenth- and eighteenth-century theorists of the Way of Ideas that they were not content with vagueness and inarticulateness at this point; they tried to articulate the belief and its implications, and to defend it. Thereby they increased their vulnerability to Reid's attack. Reid could attack not only their theory itself but the argumentation advanced for the theory. We will begin our consideration of Reid's attack by looking at his attack on the argumentation for the theory.

---

[17] Add the following passage from Malebranche that Reid quotes: "every one will grant that we perceive not the objects that are without us immediately, and of themselves. We see the sun, the stars, and an infinity of objects without us; and it is not at all likely that the soul sallies out of the body, and, as it were, takes a walk through the heavens to contemplate all those objects. She sees them not, therefore, by themselves; and the immediate object of the mind, when it sees the sun, for example, is not the sun, but something which is intimately united to the soul; and it is that which I call an idea: so that by the word *idea*, I understand nothing else here but that which is the immediate object, or nearest to the mind, when we perceive any object. It ought to be carefully observed, that, in order to the mind's perceiving any object, it is absolutely necessary that the idea of that object be actually present to it. Of this it is not possible to doubt" (EIP II, vii [265a]).

CHAPTER III

Reid's Opening Attack: Nothing Is Explained

The "avidity to know the causes of things," that is, to explain them, "is the parent of all philosophy true and false," says Reid (EIP II, vi [260b]). In particular, this "avidity" is the parent of that false philosophy which is the Way of Ideas. "An object placed at a proper distance, and in a good light, while the eyes are shut, is not perceived at all; but no sooner do we open our eyes upon it, than we have, as it were by inspiration, a certain knowledge of its existence, of its colour, figure, and distance" (ibid.). "This is a fact which every one knows." "The vulgar are satisfied with knowing the fact," and don't bother trying to explain it. The philosopher wants "to know how this event is produced, to account for it, or assign its cause" (ibid.).

It was this "avidity" to explain that gave rise to the Way of Ideas. Not all by itself, of course. As with anyone who attempts to explain something, the Way of Ideas theorists operated with convictions as to the principles that an explanation of perception and memory, to be satisfactory, would have to satisfy. It was their attempt to explain, coupled with their commitment to these principles, that drove the Way of Ideas theorists to postulate "ideas" as an essential ingredient in perception and memory.

As we have seen, the account offered for (what is ordinarily called) perception ran, in its essentials, as follows: the conditions for a satisfactory explanation carry the implication that perception cannot incorporate immediate apprehension of some external object; the external object is always too far away for that. Such apprehension as we may acquire of the external object must be mediated by an imagistic representation of the object. What happens in perception thus is this: That brain state which is the final link in the chain of physical and neurological events constituting the causal conditions of perception of some object is either itself an imagistic representation of the object or the cause of an imagistic representation of the object in the mind; this representation, be it in brain or mind, causes acquaintance with itself. Beliefs about these imagistic representations are formed immediately in us; from these beliefs about the image which represents the object we then make inferences to the existence and character of the external object. In the case of our perception of primary qualities, these inferences presuppose that the representation resembles the primary quality. Lastly – a matter of usage rather than argument – strictly speaking, we do not perceive external objects. To perceive something requires having immediate apprehension of it – that is, apprehension not mediated by a representation of the object in the way that a mirror or photographic image of an object represents it. In what the vulgar call "perception" we have immediate apprehension only of the reflective, imagistic representations of those objects in mind or brain, not of the external objects themselves.

One of Reid's fundamental arguments against this theory is that it simply doesn't do what it set out to do, namely, explain perception and memory. And since the postulation of "ideas" was defended on the ground that the only way to explain perception and memory is to suppose that there are such entities, the postulation proves groundless.

NOTHING EXPLAINED

Reid has two main points that he wants to make concerning the Way of Ideas attempt to explain. The first goes as follows. The Way of Ideas theorist wants to explain how it is that brain states cause that very different thing which is perception. He regards his cohorts working in physics and physiology as on the way to explaining how the external object causes the brain state; he intends to make his contribution at the final point, where the transition from brain states to perception occurs. The criteria with which he works, for the construction of a satisfactory explanation, lead him to deny that the apprehension which is ingredient in perception is ever immediate apprehension of an external object; that would be truly inexplicable. The explanation he offers, to state it yet one more time, is that the final brain state either is itself a reflective image that causes acquaintance with itself or it causes a reflective image in the mind which then causes acquaintance with itself.

What, asks Reid, does this hypothesis explain? The project was to explain how it is that a series of physical and physiological events brings about the mental act of perception. The Way of Ideas theorist tells us that the final brain state either is or causes an image of the external object, this image in turn causing acquaintance with itself.[1] But we already knew that the brain event causes a mental act; that was what was to be explained. The Way of Ideas theorists can debate with each other as to whether the core of perception consists of direct acquaintance with an image in the brain or of direct acquaintance with an image in the mind. But whichever analysis they adopt, they have not explained how it is that physical and physiological events cause the mental act of perception; analysis is not explanation. Of course if images always caused acquaintance (or some other mode of apprehension) of themselves, that would count for something. But obviously they don't.

There's just no explanation here at all. None. The point is not that the explanation offered is false, or ungrounded. What's offered is simply not an explanation. To recognize this we don't need some *theory* of explanation. Quite to the contrary: Any theory of explanation that has as its consequence that this is an explanation is for that reason an unacceptable theory of explanation.

Suppose, says Reid, that we go along with the theory and postulate "an image in the mind, or contiguous to it; we know as little how perception may be produced by this image as by the most distant object" (EIP II, xiv [302a]). Even if one accepts the two principles, that the immediate object of an act of apprehension must be identical with its immediate cause and that the immediate cause of any occurrence must be spatially contiguous to it, declaring that it is reflective images in brain or mind that are the immediate objects of those acts of apprehension ingredient in perception does nothing to explain how physical and physiological events cause that mental event of apprehension. "This power of perceiving ideas is as inexplicable as any of the powers

---

[1] The Way of Ideas theorists disagreed with each other as to what this causal relation came to; Descartes, for example, denied that material bodies have causal *power* over minds.

[supposedly] explained by it: and the contiguity of the object con-
tributes nothing at all to make it better understood; because there
appears no connection between contiguity and perception . . ."
(EIP II, xiv [306a]).

Perhaps that last point needs just a bit of elaboration. Physical
causes don't in general have immediate apprehension of themselves among their immediate effects – not even if they are images;
if they did, the Way of Ideas theorist who argues that perception
is not immediate apprehension of external objects but of certain
brain events would at least have taken note of an interesting law
– though he would not, of course, have *explained* this law. But
the truth of the matter is obviously that "two things may be in
contact without any feeling or perception; there must therefore
be in the percipient a power to feel or to perceive," and that
power must be activated if perception is to occur (EIP II, xiv
[305b]). But the Way of Ideas offers no explanation whatsoever
either of that power or of its activation and no explanation of
why certain brain states should cause mental acts of immediate
apprehension.

In short,

We are at a loss to know how we perceive distant objects; how we
remember things past; how we imagine things that have no existence.
Ideas in the mind seem [to the Way of Ideas theorist] to account for all
these operations. They are all by the means of ideas reduced to one
operation; to a kind of feeling, or immediate perception of things
present, and in contact with the percipient; and feeling is an operation
so familiar, that we think it needs no explication, but may serve to
explain other operations. But this feeling, of immediate perception, is
as difficult to be comprehended, as the things which we pretend to
explain by it. (EIP II, xiv [305b])

Speaking in his own voice in his recent (1994) Dewey Lectures,
Hilary Putnam states Reid's point exactly: "Notice how peculiar
the suggested 'explanation' is. . . . It is not, after all, as if the
'Cartesian' epistemologist had any mechanism to offer to explain
just *how* events in the brain produce 'sense data,' or how the mind
'immediately observes' the postulated objects. . . . The explanation starts with a familiar fact . . . and offers an 'explanation' in
terms of utterly mysterious entities and processes – one that lacks
all detail at just the crucial points, and possesses no testability

whatsoever. Such an 'explanation' would not even be regarded as *intelligible* in serious natural science."[2] This Reidian point seems to me indubitably correct.

Both Reid and Putnam sometimes phrase their point in a way that might give one pause in accepting the point made. Reid, in the passage last quoted, said that the immediate perception of ideas "is as difficult to be comprehended, as the things which we pretend to explain by it." And Putnam says that the Way of Ideas theorists offer "an 'explanation' in terms of utterly mysterious entities and processes." To this, it might be replied that we all regard Newton's appeal to gravity as explaining a great deal even though, to this day, it remains itself unexplained and "mysterious."

In the course of his attack on the Way of Ideas in the second Essay of the *Essays on the Intellectual Powers*, Reid inserted a brief chapter on "What It is to Account for a Phenomenon in Nature"; in this chapter he cites Galileo's gravitational and inertial account of the motion of falling bodies as a good example of an explanation. It will help to understand how Reid is thinking, in his attack on the Way of Ideas, if we look briefly at what he says in this chapter.

Consider the following phenomenon, says Reid: "that a stone, or any heavy body, falling from a height, continually increases its velocity as it descends; so that if it acquire a certain velocity in one second of time, it will have twice that velocity at the end of two seconds, thrice at the end of three seconds, and so on in proportion to the time" (EIP II, vi [261a]). This "accelerated velocity in a stone falling must have been observed from the beginning of the world," says Reid. But Galileo was the first to explain it. His explanation assigns two causes to the phenomenon, inertia and gravity. "1st, That bodies once put in motion, retain their velocity and their direction, until it is changed by some force impressed upon them. 2ndly, That the weight or gravitation of a body is always the same." These, says Reid, are "laws of nature." They are "confirmed by universal experience"; and "they are precisely adequate to the effect ascribed to them; they must necessarily

---

[2] Hilary Putnam, "Sense, Nonsense, and the Senses: An Inquiry into the Powers of the Human Mind," *Journal of Philosophy*, XCI, No. 9 (Sept. 1994).

produce that very motion in descending bodies which we find to take place; and neither more nor less" (EIP II, vi [261b]). This, then, is a "just and philosophical" explanation of the phenomenon in question.

Reid goes on to observe that "the causes assigned of this phenomenon are things of which we can assign no cause. Why bodies once put in motion continue to move; why bodies constantly gravitate toward the earth with the same force, no man has been able to explain." What he means is that we have no *scientific* explanation to offer. Inertia and gravity "must no doubt have a cause; but their cause is unknown, and we call them laws of nature, because we know no cause of them but the will of the Supreme Being" (ibid.). Reid concedes that scientists may eventually discover a scientific explanation of inertia and gravity. But the fact that Galileo had no explanation of inertia and gravity does not imply that he did not offer an explanation of the motion of falling bodies.

So the point Reid wishes to make against the "explanation" of perception offered by the Way of Ideas theorists is not that their explanation leaves certain things unexplained; that's true of every explanation. His point is rather that the postulated phenomena – images in mind or brain – simply do not explain what was to be explained; what is offered as an explanation does not satisfy the fundamental conditions for an explanation. The phenomenon to be explained was how physical and physiological events cause the mental act of perception – in particular, how they cause the mental event of apprehension which is ingredient in perception, whatever be the object of that apprehension. The Way of Ideas theorist tells us that, contrary to what we may have thought, the immediate object of that apprehension is "ideas," not external objects. But that's not an explanation of how it is that perception ensues upon physical and physiological events. It's at best – to say it again – a new analysis of what transpires in perception.[3] "Why therefore should we be led, by a theory which is neither

---

[3] As noted earlier, Reid's own view as to what is required of something if it is to count as an explanation is that "the causes assigned" "ought to be true, to have a real existence, and not to be barely conjectured to exist without proof," and "they ought to be sufficient to produce the effect" (EIP II, iii [250a]). His argument against the Way of Ideas as an explanation of perception and memory is that it satisfies neither of these two conditions.

grounded on evidence, nor, if admitted, can explain any one phenomenon of perception, to reject the natural and immediate dictates of those perceptive powers, to which, in the conduct of life, we find a necessity of yielding implicit submission?" (EIP II, xiv [302a]).[4]

Before we move on, one additional observation about how Reid was thinking of explanation is in order. Reid regards laws of nature as laws concerning necessities of nature; but he does not think that a knowledge of necessities concerning the relationships among phenomena is a scientific explanation. A scientific explanation illuminates certain necessities by appealing to other necessities; but one can recognize the existence of certain necessities without having a scientific explanation of them. Indeed, ultimately it must be thus.

supposing gravitation to be accounted for, by an etherial elastic medium for instance, this can only be done, 1st, by proving the existence and the elasticity of this medium; and 2ndly, by showing, that this medium must necessarily produce that gravitation which bodies are known to have. Until this be done, gravitation is not accounted for, nor is its cause known; and when this is done, the elasticity of this medium will be considered as a law of nature, whose cause is unknown. The chain of natural causes has, not unfitly, been compared to a chain hanging down from heaven: a link that is discovered supports the links below it, but it must itself be supported; and that which supports it must be supported, until we come to the first link, which is supported by the throne of the Almighty. Every natural cause must have a cause, until we ascend to the first cause which is uncaused, and operates not by necessity, but by will. (EIP II, vi [261b])

The relevance of this point to the purposes at hand is that we know various laws of nature concerning the physical circumstances under which perception arises. Here is one such law: "that we perceive no external object, but by means of certain bodily organs which God has given us for that purpose" (EIP II, i [246a]). Here's another: "that we perceive no object, unless some impression is made upon the organ of sense, either by the immediate application of the object, or by some medium which passes

---

[4] Reid is here alluding to his theses that the Way of Ideas contradicts Common Sense, that whoever wishes to contradict Common Sense bears the burden of proof in the argument, and that the Way of Ideas has not succeeded in bearing that burden. I discuss these theses in Chapter IX.

between the object and the organ" (EIP II, ii [247a]). And here's a third: "that in order to our perceiving objects, the impressions made upon the organs of sense must be communicated to the nerves, and by them to the brain" (EIP II, ii [247b]).[5] To know such laws, however, is not to have explained why things behave thus.

This, so far, is one of the ways in which Reid makes his point that the "explanation" of perception offered by the Way of Ideas theorists is no explanation at all. Now, for the second: What one would expect, out of an explanation of perception, is an account of why physical and physiological events of a certain sort give rise to the sorts of sensations and perceptions to which they do in fact give rise, rather than to sensations and perceptions of quite a different sort – why pressure on the skin gives rise to tactile rather than to olfactory sensations, why images on the retina give rise to visual rather than gustatory sensations, and so forth. But no such explanation is forthcoming from the Way of Ideas theorist. (Reid readily concedes that he too has no account to offer; but then, he never suggested that he did!) Over and over Reid makes the point; here's just one passage:

No man can give a reason, why the vibration of a body might not have given the sensation of smelling, and the effluvia of bodies affected our hearing, if it had so pleased our Maker. In like manner, no man can give a reason, why the sensations of smell, or taste or sound, might not have indicated hardness, as well as that sensation, which, by our constitution, does indicate it. (IHM V, ii [120b–121a; B 57])[6]

When he says here that "no man can give a reason," Reid quite clearly means not only that no man of his day could give such a

---

[5] In addition to these connections, it's important that there be the following: "as the impressions on the organs, nerves, and brain, correspond exactly to the nature and conditions of the objects by which they are made; so our perceptions and sensations correspond to those impressions, and vary in kind, and in degree, as they vary. Without this exact correspondence, the information we receive by our senses would not only be imperfect, as it undoubtedly is, but would be fallacious, which we have no reason to think it is" (EIP II, ii [248b]).

[6] Here's a passage in which Reid makes a similar point concerning physical "impressions" and our neurological response: "The rays of light make an impression upon the optic nerves; but they make none upon the auditory or olfactory. The vibrations of the air make an impression upon the auditory nerves; but none upon the optic or the olfactory. The effluvia of bodies make an impression upon the olfactory nerves; but make none upon the optic or auditory. No man has been able to give a shadow of reason for this" (EIP II, iii [253a]).

reason, but that no one will ever be able to give such a reason. The explanation is forever beyond us. His thought is this: We have explained certain laws pertaining to the behavior of water by discovering that it belongs to the nature of water to expand when freezing; we have explained certain laws pertaining to the behavior of material bodies by discovering that it belongs to the nature of material bodies that they be gravitationally attracted to each other; we have explained certain laws pertaining to human illness by discovering that it belongs to the nature of certain bacteria and the nature of the human body for the body to become ill when those bacteria invade the body and succeed in evading or overcoming the immune system; and so forth. Success in offering explanations of laws of nature (necessary correlations) requires discovering the natures of things.[7] It appears not to belong to the nature of the human being, however, that there are the particular hook-ups that in fact there are between "impressions" of physical objects and neural responses, on the one hand, and mental events, on the other; if so, that's why we cannot give a reason for (i.e., explain) the laws of nature which we know to hold. The point is clear in the following passage:

[It is] likewise a law of our nature, that we perceive not external objects, unless certain impressions be made by the object upon the organ, and by means of the organ upon the nerves and brain. But of the nature of those impressions we are perfectly ignorant; and though they are conjoined with perception by the will of our Maker, yet it does not appear that they have any necessary connection with it *in their own nature* [italics added], far less that they can be the proper efficient cause of it. We perceive, because God has given us the power of perceiving, and not because we have impressions from objects. We perceive nothing without those impressions, because our Maker has limited and circumscribed our powers of perception, by such laws of nature as to his wisdom

---

[7] That seems to me the force of a passage (73b–74a) in Reid's letter to James Gregory of July 30, 1789. Admittedly there are other passages in which Reid would appear to be of the view that a causal law (law of nature) is explained just in case it is subsumed under a more general law, whether or not that more general law gets at the natures of things. Clearly that is not the view coming to expression in the passage quoted in the text above; Reid's thought in this passage is that the reason we cannot explain the laws which do hold is that our Maker might have established different lawful connections between *our* sensory organs and *our* sensory experience – not different lawful connections between sensory organs and sensory experience in creatures who are not human beings, but different connections in creatures who are *human* beings, that is in creatures with *our* natures.

seemed meet, and such as suited our rank in his creation. (EIP II, iv [257b])

Though Reid judged himself and his predecessors "perfectly ignorant" of the nature of the impressions made upon sensory organs, nerves, and brain in perception, that ignorance might well be dispelled in the future; in principle it would be possible to discover the nature of these impressions and thus to account for the laws describing their workings. Not so for the connection of those to the mental act of perception. It does not appear that these impressions "have any necessary connection with it [i.e., perception] in their own nature." The nature of the brain and that of the mind remaining what they are, the hook-ups might have been different.[8]

NO CAUSAL EFFICACY IN NATURE

In the passage last quoted, Reid, having remarked that the necessary connection between brain states and acts of perception appears not to be grounded in the nature of those states and those acts, adds that it's even less plausible to suppose that those brain states are the "proper efficient cause" of acts of perception. The point he has in mind is more provocatively expressed in the following passage: "When I look upon the wall of my room, the wall does not act at all, nor is capable of acting; the perceiving it is an act or operation in me" (EIP II, iv [254b]).[9]

---

[8] More radically yet: "No man can show it to be impossible to the Supreme Being to have given us the power of perceiving external objects without such organs. We have reason to believe, that when we put off these bodies, and all the organs belonging to them, our perceptive powers shall rather be improved than destroyed or impaired. We have reason to believe, that the Supreme Being perceives everything in a much more perfect manner than we do, without bodily organs. We have reason to believe that there are other created beings endowed with powers of perception more perfect and more extensive than ours, without any such organs as we find necessary. We ought not, therefore, to conclude, that such bodily organs are, in their own *nature* [italics added] necessary to perception; but rather, that, by the will of God, our power of perceiving external objects is limited and circumscribed by our organs of sense. . . ." (EIP II, i [246a–b]). Of course, it's also by virtue of the will of God that there is such a substance as water. But the point is that God cannot create a substance which is water that does not expand when freezing; it's of the *nature* of water to expand when freezing. By contrast, God can create beings with a human nature in which the hook-ups of physiology to the mind are different from how they are in fact.

[9] Cf. EIP II, xiv [301a–b]: "An object, in being perceived, does not act at all. I perceive the walls of the room where I sit; but they are perfectly inactive, and therefore act not upon the mind."

Two points, actually, are being made in this last passage: that a wall neither acts nor is capable of acting; and that perceiving is an *act* of the perceiver. Let me save the latter point for later, and say a few things here about the former.

What's coming to the surface here is Reid's occasionalism. Reid's attack on the Way of Ideas, as completely failing to explain what it set out to explain, does not depend on this occasionalism; the issue of what, if anything, is capable of exercising causal efficacy plays no role in his charge that the Way of Ideas doesn't explain what it set out to explain. Nonetheless, a glance at his thought on the matter will explain how he himself was thinking of the laws of nature to which he does make reference in his attack.

We have to begin with Reid's understanding of what he calls "active power." Reid remarks that he does not think it possible to give an informative definition of the concept of power that he has in mind. One can say, quite rightly, that "The exertion of active power [is what] we call *action*." Likewise one can say, quite rightly, that "That which produces a change by the exertion of its power [is what] we call the *cause* of that change; and the change produced, the *effect* of that cause" (EAP I, i [515a]). But it's most unlikely that anyone who lacked the concept of active power before these things were said would have acquired it from the saying of these things.

Reid's inability to offer a definition is no great misfortune, however. For everybody already possesses the concept in question; a definition isn't necessary. What's relevant is "some observations that may lead us to attend to the conception we [already] have of [active power] in our own minds" (EAP I, i [512b]).

The concept of power Reid wishes us to attend to is the concept used when we say such things as these: "I had it in my power to turn my thoughts to Reid's claims about causal efficacy." "I do not have it in my power to run the mile in a minute." "I have it in my power to raise my arm and scratch my nose." The sort of power to which these sentences refer is the capacity to bring something about, to cause it to happen – when causing it to happen is up to the agent. What lies behind that last clause is the fact that, to use Reid's words, "power to produce an effect [pre]supposes power not to produce it: otherwise it is not power but necessity, which is incompatible with power taken in the strict sense" (letter to

James Gregory of June 14, 1765 [65b]).[10] If I have it in my power
to raise my hand, I have it in my power not to do so as well. By
contrast, though the piece of chalk falls when I release it, it does
not have it *in its power* to fall, since my releasing it necessitates its
falling. It isn't up to the chalk whether to fall.

What reason is there to suppose that there are any active powers
anywhere? Reid's answer is that "there are many operations of
mind common to all men who have reason, and necessary in the
ordinary conduct of life, which imply a belief of active power in
ourselves and in others" (EAP I, ii [517a–b]). For example,

All our volitions and efforts to act, all our deliberations, our purposes
and promises, imply a belief of active power in ourselves; our counsels,
exhortations, and commands, imply a belief of active power in those to
whom they are addressed.

If a man should make an effort to fly to the moon; if he should even
deliberate about it, or resolve to do it, we should conclude him to be
lunatic; and even lunacy would not account for his conduct, unless it
made him believe the thing to be in his power.

If a man promises to pay me a sum of money tomorrow, without believing that it will then be in his power, he is not an honest man; and, if I
did not believe that it will then be in his power, I should have no depen-
dence on his promise. . . .

It is evident, therefore, that without the belief of some active power,
no honest man would make a promise, no wise man would trust to a
promise. . . .

The same reasoning may be applied to every instance wherein we give
counsel to others, wherein we persuade or command. As long, therefore, as mankind are beings who can deliberate, and resolve, and will;
as long as they can give counsel, and exhort, and command, they must
believe the existence of active power in themselves, and in others. (EAP
I, ii [517b])

The background to Reid's claim here, that to perform such an
action as to deliberate whether or not to do something is to imply
the belief that one has it in one's power to do or not to do it, is
Reid's doctrine of Common Sense. When we consider it within that
context, however (see Chapter IX), it becomes clear that it would
be better for Reid to say that in performing such actions as he cites,
we *take for granted* the existence of active powers in ourselves and
others. In promising to meet you tomorrow for lunch I take for

---

[10] "Power to produce any effect implies power not to produce it" (EAP I, v [523a]).

granted that it will be in my power to bring it about that I meet you tomorrow for lunch; and you, in accepting and acting on this promise, likewise take for granted that that will be in my power.

Suppose we do all believe, with more or less awareness, that there are active powers in ourselves and others; how did we acquire the concept? For without having the concept, we cannot hold the belief.

We did not acquire it by first having acquaintance with active powers and then performing one and another mental operation on the object of acquaintance so as to arrive at the concept. For we have no such acquaintance. Powers are not the sort of entities that can be objects of our acquaintance.

Power is not an object of any of our external senses, nor even an object of consciousness. That it is not seen, nor heard, nor touched nor tasted, nor smelt, needs no proof. That we are not conscious of it, in the proper sense of that word, will be no less evident, if we reflect, that consciousness is that power of the mind by which it has an immediate knowledge of its own operations. Power is not an operation of the mind, and therefore no object of consciousness. Indeed, every operation of the mind is the exertion of some power of the mind; but we are conscious of the operation only, the power lies behind the scene; and though we may justly infer the power from the operation, it must be remembered, that inferring is not the province of consciousness, but of reason. (EAP I, i [512b–513a])[11]

Given that active powers cannot be objects of acquaintance, the only way we can get a mental grip on some particular active power – the power of moving my arm, say – is by thinking of it under a singular descriptive concept of the form, *that power which is exercised in such-and-such action* (alternatively, that power which *would be* exercised in such-and-such action).

Our conception of [active] power is relative to its exertions or effects. Power is one thing; its exertion is another thing. It is true, there can be

---

[11] Cf. this passage from an undated letter to James Gregory: "you speak of our having a consciousness of independent activity. I think this cannot be said with strict propriety. It is only the operations of our own mind that we are conscious of. Activity is not an operation of mind; it is a power to act. We are conscious of our volitions, but not of the cause of them. I think, indeed, that we have an early and a natural conviction that we have power to will this or that; that this conviction precedes the exercise of reasoning; that it is implyed in all our deliberations, purposes, promises, and voluntary actions; and I have used this as an argument for liberty. But I think this conviction is not properly called consciousness" (82b–83a).

no exertion without power; but there may be power that is not exerted. Thus a man may have power to speak when he is silent; he may have power to rise and walk when he sits still.

But though it be one thing to speak, and another to have the power of speaking, I apprehend we conceive of the power as something which has a certain relation to the effect. And of every power we form our notion by the effect which it is able to produce. (EAP I, i [514a–b])

The question remains, though, how we get the general concept of *a power*. Getting a particular power in mind by using a singular descriptive concept of the form, *that power which is exercised in such-and-such action*, presupposes that I have in my conceptual repertoire the general concept of *a power*. How did I acquire that concept?

Though I know of no passage in which Reid addresses in precisely this way the origin of our concept of an active power,[12] he does consider the origin of our concept of a *faculty*; and faculties are regarded by him as active powers. Reid steers a middle road between his empiricist forebears and his contemporary, Kant. Our concept of a faculty is not derived from experience by abstraction, generalization, or any other such process; on the other hand, it's also not an element of the indigenous structuring function of the mind. For while not derived from experience, it is nevertheless evoked by experience. It "is impossible to show how our sensations and thoughts can give us the very notion and conception either of a mind or of a faculty"; nonetheless, this is what they do. "The faculty of smelling is something very different from the actual sensation of smelling; for the faculty may remain when we have no sensation. And the mind is no less different from the faculty; for it continues the same individual being when the faculty is lost. Yet this sensation suggests to us both a faculty and

---

[12] A qualification: he does address the precise question in an undated latter to James Gregory (at 78a). I judge it not to be a carefully composed passage, however. He says that "We get the notion of active power, as well as of cause and effect . . . , from what we feel in ourselves. We feel in ourselves a power to move our limbs, and to produce certain effects when we choose. Hence, we get the notion of power, agency, and causation, in the strict and philosophical sense; and this I take to be our first notion of these three things." Presumably "feel" is here a synonym for what I have been calling *acquaintance*. Elsewhere Reid makes clear his view that though we have acquaintance with *acts of choosing to do* one thing and another, we do not have acquaintance with the *powers to do* those things which are *actualized* in those acts of choosing.

a mind; and not only suggests the notion of them, but creates a belief of their existence" (IHM II, vii [110b; B. 37]).[13]

Now for the question we wanted to get to. Why does Reid doubt that there are active powers in nature? And why, correspondingly, does he doubt that there is agency in nature – agency understood as the exercise of active power? Well, says Reid, suppose I have it in my power to carry out some promise I made. What would activate this power? My *deciding* to do that which I promised to do is what would activate it. That, and that alone. And in general, for all those active powers that we possess, the one and only way available to us for activating them is deciding to do that which it is in our power to do. In Reid's words, "we find in ourselves [the active power] to give certain motions to our bodies, or a certain direction to our thoughts; and this power in ourselves can be brought into action only by willing or volition" (EAP I, v [523a]). From which of course it follows that "if we had not will, and that degree of understanding which will necessarily implies, we could exert no active power, and consequently could have none: for power that cannot be exerted is no power" (ibid.).

A stronger point can be made. Not only do we not find in ourselves any other way of activating an active power to do something than by the volition to do it. We don't have even so much as an idea of another way of activating an active power. It is "from the consciousness of our own activity [that there is] derived, not only the clearest, but the only conception we can form of activity, or the exertion of active power" (EAP I, v [523b]) – from which it follows that we are able to "conceive no way in which [active] power may be determined to one [alternative] rather than the other, in a being that has no will" (EAP I, v [523a]).

So what's to be concluded? That nature might well be filled with active powers that get activated in ways of which we have no intimation? Hardly. For the concept of *volition* is not related to the concept of *active power* as some sort of addendum, so that we can first think of active powers and then raise the question of whether those powers might be activated in ways other than the way with which we are familiar, namely, by volition. Being activated by

---

[13] At the end of this chapter we will see how Reid was thinking in regarding faculties as powers. And in Chapter VI we will return to his doctrine of concept formation.

volition belongs to the very concept of an active power. "The only distinct conception I can form of active power," says Reid, is that it "is an attribute in a being by which he can do certain things if he wills. . . . The effect produced, and the will to produce it, are things different from active power, but we can have no conception of it, but by its relation to them" (EAP I, v [524b]). It follows that "the active power, of which only we can have any distinct conception, can be only in beings that have understanding and will." "If any man . . . affirms, that a being may be the efficient cause of an action, and have power to produce it, which that being can neither conceive nor will, he speaks a language which I do not understand" (EAP I, v [525a]).[14]

Unlike our ancient predecessors, few of us are inclined toward animism.[15] So we come round to the point with which we began this exposition:

From the course of events in the natural world, we have sufficient reason to conclude the existence of an eternal intelligent First Cause. But whether he acts immediately in the production of those events, or by subordinate intelligent agents, or by instruments that are unintelligent, and what the number, the nature, and the different offices of those agents or instruments may be; these I apprehend to be mysteries placed beyond the limits of human knowledge. We see an established order in the succession of natural events, but we see not the bond that connects them together. (EAP I, v [522b])

Many times Reid remarks that "There is nothing more ridiculous than to imagine that any motion or modification of matter should produce thought" (EIP II, iv [253b]). Not even "savages" hold the absurd view "that the impressions of external objects upon the machine of our bodies, can be the real efficient cause of thought and perception" (ibid.). It's now evident that Reid had

[14] Cf. letter to Lord Kames of Dec. 16, 1780: "I am not able to form any distinct conception of active power but such as I find in myself. I can only exert my active power by will, which supposes thought. . . . I can reason about an active power of that kind I am acquainted with – that is, such as supposes thought and choice, and is exerted by will. But, if there is anything in an unthinking inanimate being that can be called active power, I know not what it is, and cannot reason about it" (59a–b).

[15] Reid speculates that the origin of the "loose and popular" sense of "cause," according to which we apply active verbs to inanimate objects ("the sun shines") and speak of them as "causing" things ("the sun causes the warmth of the earth"), lies in the fact that when the animism which originally grounded that way of speaking eroded, the way of speaking continued. See the passage in an undated letter to James Gregory at 78a.

two reasons for saying this. Mental events would not be the sorts of things that bodies, if they were causal agents, were capable of bringing about; but more fundamentally, it makes no sense to say that bodies devoid of intelligence and volition have it in their power to bring things about.

As we have already seen, Reid was definitely not an antagonist of the new science coming to birth in his century and the century preceding. He joined everyone else in admiration of Galileo and Newton; "the grandest discovery ever made in natural philosophy," he says, "was that of the law of gravitation, which opens such a view of our planetary system, that it looks like something divine" (EAP I, vi [527a]). But if the discoveries of the new science are not discoveries of the causes of things, of what then are they the discoveries?

They *are* discoveries of the causes of things; but not in the sense of "cause" which we have been discussing – that being the "strict and proper" sense, as Reid calls it.[16] They are discoveries of causes in the "lax and popular" sense of the term. Here is Reid's explanation of the distinction:

a cause, in the proper and strict sense (which, I think, we may call the metaphysical sense.) signifies a being or mind that has the power and will to produce the effect. But there is another meaning of the word cause, which is so well authorized by custom, that we cannot always avoid using it, and I think we may call it the physical sense; as when we say that heat is the cause that turns water into vapour, and cold the cause that freezes it into ice. A cause, in this sense, means only something which, by the laws of nature, the effect always follows. I think natural philosophers, when they pretend to shew the causes of natural phenomena, always use the word in this last sense; and the vulgar in common discourse very often do the same. (Letter to James Gregory of Sept. 23, 1785 [67a])

Reid speaks here of heat as the cause of water turning into vapor and of cold as the cause of water freezing. From other passages it becomes clear that causation in this lax and popular sense is a relation between events. Reid's lax and popular sense of "cause" is what is nowadays called "event causation." It's the *event* of heat

---

[16] Cf. undated letter to James Gregory, 77a: "In the strict and philosophical sense, I take a cause to be that which has the relation to the effect which I have to my voluntary and deliberate actions. ... In this sense, we say that the Deity is the cause of the universe."

being applied to the water that causes the *event* of the water turning into vapor.

In a good many passages, some of them cited earlier, Reid makes clear that event causation is necessitation of a certain sort; a condition of the application of the heat causing the boiling of the water is that the application necessitate the boiling.[17] The first great challenge confronting the natural scientist is to discriminate causation from coincidence – that is, to single out, from all the pairs of types of events, those such that the occurrence of an example of the one type necessitates the occurrence of an example of the other type. To discover such a pair of event types is to have discovered a law of nature. The second great challenge of the natural scientist is to apply such natural laws as he has discovered to *account* for some phenomenon of nature – to explain the phenomenon. And the third great challenge is to explain, in turn, such laws of nature as he has discovered.[18]

Lastly, how are event causation, and the laws of nature presupposed by event causation, related to what we were speaking of earlier, namely, causal agency? Reid's answer is that laws of nature are a blend of descriptions of the behavior of things as determined by their natures plus the rules in accord with which the causal agents operative in nature, whatever those be, do their work. The necessity of the laws is a consequence of the necessi-

---

[17] "I admit that, for anything I know to the contrary, there may be such a nature and state of things which have no proper activity, as that certain events or changes must necessarily follow. I admit that, in such a case, that which is antecedent may be called the physical cause, and what is necessarily consequent, may be called the effect of that cause" (Letter to James Gregory of July 30, 1789 [73b]).

[18] He does this, says Reid in a letter to Lord Kames of Dec. 16, 1780, by "searching for a more general law, which includes that particular law . . . (57b–58a). If my earlier conclusion is correct, Reid's full view is that explanation of some law of nature is not achieved simply by subsuming it under a more general law; the explanation must also appeal to the natures of the entities under discussion.

   What Reid does consistently emphasize is that natural philosophy (natural science, as we would call it) does not traffic in efficient causes. "Efficient causes, properly so called, are not within the sphere of natural philosophy. Its business is, from particular facts in the material world, to collect, by just induction, the laws that are general, and from these the more general, as far as we can go. And when this is done, natural philosophy has no more to do. It exhibits to our view the grand machine of the material world, analysed, as it were, and taken to pieces, with the connexions and dependencies of its several parts, and the laws of its several movements. It belongs to another branch of philosophy to consider whether this machine is the work of chance or of design . . ." (same letter to Lord Kames [58a]). Reid ascribes this way of thinking of natural science (natural philosophy) to Newton; see undated latter to James Gregory, 76a.

ties embedded in the natures of things plus the resoluteness of those agents.[19]

PHILOSOPHICAL EXPLANATIONS OF MENTAL ACTIVITY

We have by now so often heard Reid pronouncing one and another mental phenomenon inexplicable that one naturally wonders whether it's his view that explanation, no matter of what sort, is out of the question when it comes to the life of the mind – that the activity of philosophers and scientists, when it comes to mental phenomena, will never attain to anything more than description. In fact that's not his view.

Reid is always operating, sometimes explicitly, but more often implicitly, with the distinction between what he calls "original operations" of the mind and "derived" or "acquired" operations – that is, nonoriginal. "Original" here means innate, indigenous. It's by virtue of the indigenous workings of the mind that, when I press my hand against some hard object, I gain an apprehension of its hardness and come to believe, about it, that it presently exists as an external entity. By contrast, it's not by virtue of the indigenous workings of the mind that, when I smell a particular fragrance wafting through the air, I acquire an apprehension of it as *the smell of a rose* and believe, about it, that it presently exists as an external entity. The formation of this latter conception and belief requires learning on my part. In addition to analyzing and describing the life of the mind, the philosopher and scientist can explain the nonoriginal operations of the mind by reference to its original operations. Whenever Reid claims that some operation of the mind is inexplicable, it's some *original* operation that he is speaking of – or, more cautiously, some operation that he believes to be original.[20]

---

[19] With his eye on the latter of these two sources of necessity, Reid says, in his letter to James Gregory of June 14, 1785, that "A law of nature is a purpose or resolution of the author of nature, to act according to a certain rule – either immediately by himself or by instruments that are under his direction" (66a–b). That Reid does indeed regard the necessity of causal laws (laws of nature) as having the two sources indicated, is clear from his letter to James Gregory of July 30, 1789, 73b–74a.

[20] "If the power of perceiving external objects in certain circumstances, be a part of the original constitution of the human mind, all attempts to account for it will be vain. No other account can be given of the constitution of things, but the will of Him that made them" (EIP II, v [260b]). What Reid here formulates as a supposition is, on his view, in fact the case: "The body and mind operate on each other, according

What is apt to give one the impression that Reid is simply opting out of explanation is that, compared to his predecessors, he thinks there are considerably more original operations of the mind that they did. "I believe," he says, that "the original principles of the mind, of which we can give no account, but that such is our constitution, are more in number than is commonly thought. But we ought not to multiply them without necessity" (EIP IV, iv [387a]). Whereas his predecessors thought, for example, that our acceptance of testimony can be entirely explained by reference to our disposition to form inductive beliefs (and dispositions), he thought it could only be explained by appealing to an original "credulity" disposition.

What makes the project of explaining phenomena in the life of the mind by reference to its original operations so challenging is that, by the time one begins to philosophize, not only are the acquired operations of one's mind thoroughly intermingled with the original operations but one has no memory of any time when it was otherwise. Discerning which of the operations are original is thus often an exceedingly difficult task, and the conclusions to which one comes, often controversial. Witness the controversy over the matter just mentioned: what accounts for our acceptance of testimony. Here is how Reid makes the point:

> If the original perceptions and notions of the mind were to make their appearance single and unmixed, as we first received them from the hand of nature, one accustomed to reflection would have less difficulty in tracing them; but before we are capable of reflection, they are so mixed, compounded and decompounded, by habits, associations and abstractions, that it is hard to know what they were originally. The mind may in this respect be compared to an apothecary or a chymist, whose materials indeed are furnished by nature; but for the purposes of his art, he mixes, compounds, dissolves, evaporates, and sublimes them, till they put on a quite different appearance; so that it is very difficult to know what they were at first, and much more to bring them back to their original and natural form. (IHM I, ii [99a; B 14])

If it were only by the performance of "deliberate acts of mature reason" that the life of the mind was fleshed out beyond the original faculties and their yield, the explanatory endeavor of the

to fixed laws of nature; and it is the business of a philosopher to discover those laws by observation and experiment: but, when he has discovered them, he must rest in them as facts, whose cause is inscrutable to the human understanding" (EIP III, vii [354b–355a]).

philosopher would not be especially difficult; we would be able to recollect how things went. But this "fleshing out" is not, for the most part, accomplished by mature reasoning "but by means of instincts, habits, associations and other principles, which operate before we come to the use of reason." It's for that reason that "it is extremely difficult for the mind to return upon its own footsteps, and trace back those operations which have employed it since it first began to think and to act" (IHM I, ii [99a; B 14–15]). In short, it requires

great caution, and great application of mind, for a man that is grown up in all the prejudices of education, fashion, and philosophy, to unravel his notions and opinions, till he finds out the simple and original principles of his constitution, of which no account can be given but the will of our Maker. This may be truly called an *analysis* of the human faculties; and till this is performed, it is in vain to expect any just *system* of the mind; that is, an enumeration of the original powers and laws of our constitution, and an explication [i.e., explanation] from them of the various phenomena of human nature. (IHM I, 11 [99a–b; B 15])

THE PRINCIPLES UNACCEPTABLE

I have noted, several times over, that on Reid's account it was not just the attempt to explain the occurrence of perception and memory that accounted for the emergence of the Way of Ideas, but that attempt combined with the criteria accepted by the Way of Ideas theorists for a satisfactory explanation. Those criteria were these two principles:

(1) The immediate object of an act of apprehension must be identical with the immediate cause thereof,

and

(2) There is no immediate causal action at a spatial or temporal distance.[21]

---

[21] I noted, in the last chapter, that Reid accepts this second principle. In light of the preceding discussion, however, one wonders how Reid is understanding it when he says he accepts it. What does he take "causal action" to be? The answer is clearly that he accepts it as a principle of causal agency, not as a principle concerning event-causation. This is what he says: "That nothing can act immediately where it is not, I think, must be admitted; for I agree with Sir Isaac Newton, that power without substance is inconceivable. It is a consequence of this, that nothing can be acted upon immediately where the agent is not present" (EIP II, xiv [301a]). Reid must be thinking of the principle as a principle concerning the causal agency of creatures, however – since certainly he would not hold that it applies to God.

From these two there follows the crucial principle that

(3) The location of the immediate object of an act of apprehension must be spatially contiguous with the location of the act of apprehension.

I observed in the preceding chapter that (3) sounds exceedingly strange to us. Brain states presumably have locations, of a sort, but acts of apprehension don't, nor do mental images. Accordingly, the concept of contiguity is simply not applicable to the relation of brain events to mental events. Admittedly a thoroughgoing reductionist of mental states to brain states would have no trouble on this count. But none of the eighteenth-century theorists was a reductionist of this sort. And I dare say that even a reductionist would find it odd, to say the least, to think of the occurrence of an image in the brain as one event, to think of the acquaintance therewith as a second event in the brain, and then to hold that the former is spatially contiguous to, and the cause of, the latter.

Wacky or not, it's clear that the eighteenth-century theorists did hold these principles. (See the passages cited by Reid in *Essays on the Intellectual Powers* II, xiv – a few of which I quoted near the end of our preceding chapter.) What's equally clear is that Reid, rather than trying to devise an alternative hypothesis which satisfies the principles, rejects them. More precisely, though he accepts the principle that is second in my ordering, he rejects the first, and hence, the third. Why assume, he asks, that the immediate object of an act of apprehension – even of an act of *acquaintance* – is identical with the immediate cause thereof? More radically yet: Why assume that the immediate object of an act of apprehension, be it an act of acquaintance or not, has any causal role whatsoever in the occurrence of that act?

Before we consider what Reid has to say directly against the principles, we should look briefly at his diagnosis of why it is that his predecessors supposed (1), and hence (3), to be true. For it was this question that absorbed the bulk of Reid's attention; he seems to have regarded the principles themselves as so patently false that it wasn't worth spending much time showing this.

Why were his predecessors attracted to the identity principle – the principle which says that the immediate cause of an act of apprehension is identical with the immediate object thereof? And why, accordingly, did they find it acceptable to use the causal principle – that there is no immediate causal action at a spatial or temporal distance – in determining the immediate object of the act of apprehension which is ingredient in perception, in reminiscence, and in intellection? Reid's diagnosis is that his predecessors were misled by analogies drawn from the physical realm.[22] In the first place, they used the word "impression" as a general name for the explanatory processes to be found in nature: "Whether it be pressure, or attraction, or repulsion, or vibration, or something unknown, for which we have no name, still it may be called an impression" (EIP II, ii [248a]). They then assumed, by analogical thinking, that an entity's being apprehended by the self is a case of an entity's making an impression on something. And from this they drew their conclusions.

This notion, that, in perception, the object must be contiguous to the percipient, seems, with many other prejudices, to be borrowed from analogy. In all the external senses, there must, as has been before observed, be some impression made upon the organ of sense by the object, or by something coming from the object. An impression supposes contiguity. Hence we are led by analogy to conceive something similar in the operations of the mind. Many philosophers resolve almost every operation of mind into impressions and feelings, words manifestly borrowed from the sense of touch. And it is very natural to conceive contiguity necessary between that which makes the impression, and that which receives it; between that which feels, and that which is felt. (EIP II, xiv [302a])[23]

[22] "There is no subject in which men have always been so prone to form their notions by analogies . . . as in what relates to the mind. We form an early acquaintance with material things by means of our senses, and are bred up in a constant familiarity with them. Hence we are apt to measure all things by them; and to ascribe to things most remote from matter, the qualities that belong to material things. . . . Though we are conscious of the operations of our own minds when they are exerted, and are capable of attending to them, so as to form a distinct notion of them; this is so difficult a work to men, whose attention is constantly solicited by external objects, that we give them names from things that are familiar, and which are conceived to have some similitude to them; and the notions we form of them are no less analogical than the names we give them. . . . Because bodies are affected only by contact and pressure, we are apt to conceive, that what is an immediate object of thought, and affects the mind, must be in contact with it, and make some impression upon it" (EIP I, iv [237b]).

[23] Cf. EIP II, iv [254b]: "philosophers have an avidity to know how we perceive objects; and conceiving some similitude between a body that is put in motion, and a mind that is made to perceive, they are led to think, that as the body must receive some impulse to make it move, so the mind must receive some impulse or impression to make it perceive. This analogy seems to be confirmed, by observing that we perceive objects only when they make some impression upon the organs of sense, and upon the nerves and

But "if we conceive the mind to be immaterial, of which I think we have very strong proofs," says Reid, "we shall find it difficult to affirm a meaning to *impressions made upon it* (EIP II, iv [254a])."[24] And difficult to affirm a meaning to entities being adjacent to the mind, or adjacent to such acts of the mind as apprehension. "When we lay aside those analogies, and reflect attentively upon our perception of the objects of sense, we must acknowledge, that, though we are conscious of perceiving objects, we are altogether ignorant how it is brought about: and know as little how we perceive objects as how we were made" (EIP II, xiv [302a]).

Having offered his diagnosis of what led his predecessors to subscribe to their particular criteria for a satisfactory explanation of perception and memory – in particular, what led them to subscribe to the identity thesis – Reid goes on to offer what he regards as counterexamples to the identity thesis. And there are plenty of counterexamples; any act of introspective acquaintance will do. The relation of one's dizziness to one's introspective acquaintance with the dizziness is surely not a causal relation, nor is the relation of some belief one has to one's acquaintance with the belief a causal relation. But for reasons unclear to me, the cases Reid immediately cites as counterexamples to the identity thesis are not these obvious ones but others that are either surprising or of dubious polemical effectiveness. (As we will see in subsequent chapters, perception and recollection, on Reid's analysis, also constitute counterexamples.)

Let's begin with a case cited by Reid as a counterexample that most of us, I dare say, find surprising. Among the individual objects that he can directly conceive [apprehend], says Reid, is

brain; but it ought to be observed, that such is the nature of body that it cannot change its state, but by some force impressed upon it. This is not the nature of mind." Men would never "have gone into this notion, that perception is owing to some action of the object upon the mind, were it not, that we are so prone to form our notions of the mind from some similitude we conceive between it and body. Thought in the mind is conceived to have some analogy to motion in a body: and as a body is put in motion by being acted upon by some other body; so we are apt to think the mind is made to perceive, by some impulse it receives from the object. But reasonings, drawn from such analogies, ought never to be trusted. They are, indeed, the cause of most of our errors with regard to the mind (EIP II, xiv [301b]).

[24] Behind this comment is Reid's dualism; he thought of the human person as composed of body and mind. But rejecting the dualism doesn't make the fundamental point any less compelling: nobody has discovered any "mechanism" that explains why sensory experience and perception occur under the physical conditions that they do occur under.

St. Paul's church in London. I have an idea of it; that is, I conceive it. The immediate object of this conception is four hundred miles distant; and I have no reason to think that it acts upon me, or that I act upon it; but I can think of it notwithstanding. I can think of the first year, or the last year of the Julian period. (EIP IV, ii [374b])

Why would Reid cite this as a counterexample to the identity thesis? Surely every Way of Ideas theorist would concede that one can get St. Paul's church in mind when four hundred miles distant.

It's not clear that they would. The crucial word is "immediate": the *immediate* object of this conception [apprehension] is four hundred miles distant. Recall, once more, the central thought of the Way of Ideas theorists: the only entities of which we have immediate apprehension are those which are the immediate cause of the act of apprehension. The only way for any other entity to be apprehended is for one's apprehension of it to be mediated by an immediate apprehension of a representation of that entity – a representation which images that entity in the way that a mountain's reflection in a lake images the mountain. Reid's thought is that nothing of that sort takes place when I get St. Paul's Church in mind by the apprehensive use of the singular concept, *St. Paul's Church*. I don't fetch out of my memory a certain church image, allow that image to cause immediate beliefs about itself in me, then draw inferences from those beliefs about the image to propositions about the external world and its relation to the cause, and thus get St. Paul's Church in mind. Conceptual apprehension of something is more like apprehending it by acquaintance than it is like apprehending it through the mediation of a reflective image of itself: it's a manner, a mode, of getting something in mind immediately, that is, without intervening imagistic representations.[25] We'll be discussing these issues

---

[25] That this is how the passage should be interpreted is confirmed, I judge, by the following passage: "it is very natural to ask, Whether it was Mr. Locke's opinion, that ideas are the only objects of thought? or, Whether it is not possible for men to think of things which are not ideas in the mind?

"To this question it is not easy to give a direct answer. On the one hand, he says often, in distinct and studied expressions, that the term *idea* stands for whatever is the object of the understanding when a man thinks, or whatever it is which the mind can be employed about in thinking. . . . These, and many other expressions of the like import, evidently imply, that every object of thought must be an idea, and can be nothing else.

"On the other hand, I am persuaded that Mr. Locke would have acknowledged, that we may think of Alexander the Great, or of the planet Jupiter, and of numberless things,

in more detail in Chapter VI. But surely we can say here that Reid is right about this; the case he cites is indeed a counterexample to the identity thesis of the Way of Ideas theorists.

Forward, then, to the counterexamples whose polemical effectiveness seems dubious. Consider, says Reid, any case of acquaintance with a universal – any case of grasping a universal. Universals have no causal powers whatsoever; and our grasping of them is not mediated by imagistic representations of themselves.[26] Q.E.D.: An entity can be the immediate object of an act of immediate apprehension – of acquaintance, even – without being the immediate cause thereof.

The argument is sound, in my judgment. The reason it would nonetheless almost certainly have been polemically ineffective is that the Way of Ideas theorists denied that there are universals, or any other sort of abstract entity. Hence it won't do for Reid to cite our acquaintance with universals as apprehensions whose immediate objects are not identical with their immediate causes; the Way of Ideas theorist denies that we have any apprehension whatsoever of universals. What should be added is that one of the principal reasons for this denial was that it would have been incompatible with the identity thesis to admit that there are universals and that we have acquaintance with them – given that universals would lack causal powers.[27]

which he would have owned are not ideas in the mind, but objects which exist independent of the mind that thinks of them.

"How shall we reconcile the two parts of this apparent contradiction? All I am able to say upon Mr. Locke's principles to reconcile them, is this, That we cannot think of Alexander, or of the planet Jupiter, unless we have in our minds an idea, that is, an image or picture of those objects. The idea of Alexander is an image, or picture, or representation of that hero in my mind; and this idea is the immediate object of my thought when I think of Alexander. That this was Locke's opinion, and that it has been generally the opinion of philosophers, there can be no doubt" (EIP II, ix [277b–278b], 160–1).

[26] For Reid's argument on this latter point, see EIP IV, ii [373].

[27] Reid readily concedes that he himself has no explanatory account to offer of our acquaintance with universals: "As to the manner how we conceive universals, I confess my ignorance. I know not how I hear, or see, or remember, and as little do I know how I conceive things that have no existence. In all our original faculties, the fabric and manner of operation is, I apprehend, beyond our comprehension, and perhaps is perfectly understood by him only who made them.

"But we ought not to deny a fact of which we are conscious, though we know not how it is brought about. And I think we may be certain that universals are not conceived by means of images of them in our minds, because there can be no image of an universal" (EIP V, vi [407b–408a]).

Let it be said that the Way of Ideas theorists were and are far from peculiar in this regard. It remains a standard objection to the claim that there are universals that since they lack causal power, we could never have acquaintance with them; and if no acquaintance, how could we ever get them in mind? The implicit assumption is obviously the identity principle – or some close variant thereon. The polemical force of Reid's examples, by themselves, is only to point out that one must choose between being a realist concerning universals and subscribing to the thesis that the immediate object of an act of acquaintance, or apprehension more generally, is identical with the immediate cause thereof.

Admittedly Reid does more in this connection than just cite as counterexamples to the identity thesis what he regards as cases of acquaintance with universals; he argues, albeit briefly, that that is what they are, cases of acquaintance with universals. And ironically, the alternative analysis offered by Way of Ideas theorists of what Reid regards as cases of acquaintance with universals has the consequence that those cases, on their analysis, are as much in violation of the identity thesis as they are on Reid's analysis. In all such cases, it was said, it is not universals with which we have acquaintance but "ideas" of a certain sort – we would nowadays call them *concepts*. The Way of Ideas theorists all tried to adhere to a conceptualist account of universals – not very successfully, it must be said. And acquaintances with concepts were taken by them to be special cases of acquaintance with one's mental states; that is, special cases of consciousness (Kant's "inner sensibility"). The tacit assumption was that a concept can be the cause of acquaintance therewith. But can it? When I actively grasp a concept, is the relation between my concept and my grasping thereof a *causal* relation? That seems dubious indeed.

In spite of the fact that Reid's counterexamples would most likely have been polemically ineffective against the Way of Ideas theorists, it's nonetheless worth looking briefly at his analysis – both because it's interesting in its own right and because I, along with Reid, have been assuming and will continue to assume that we do have acquaintances with abstract entities such as universals. The language Reid uses to argue that intellection provides us with counterexamples to the identity thesis tends to conceal from view that this is what he was arguing. Accordingly, I shall have to mingle exposition with a defense of the accuracy of my interpretation.

Reid says repeatedly that "everything that really exists is an individual" (EIP V, vi [407a]). A natural inference is that Reid is a nonrealist concerning universals. But the inference would be mistaken. In his discussion "Of General Conceptions formed by Analyzing Objects" (EIP V, iii), Reid distinguishes between what he calls "qualities" and what he calls "attributes." Qualities, as earlier noted, are what the medievals called *qualia* – abstract particulars; each can inhere in just one subject. As examples, Reid cites the whiteness of that sheet of paper on which he was writing and the whiteness of another sheet. By contrast, attributes are the sorts of entities that are "really common to many individuals" (EIP V, iii [395a]). They are, in that way, universals; and our conceptions of them are what Reid calls *general conceptions.*[28] Now since, as a matter of fact, "there are innumerable attributes that are really common to many individuals, . . . we may affirm with certainty, that there are such universals" as the schoolmen called *universale a parte rei* (EIP V, iii [395a]), says Reid.

Reid goes on to cite, in addition to the above, the following difference between qualities and universals: a conception [apprehension] of a quality is of "an individual really existing," whereas the conception of whiteness "implies no existence; it would remain the same, though every thing in the universe that is white were annihilated." Though it "may be predicated of every thing that is white, and in the same sense," it "implies no existence" (EIP V, iii [395a–b]). The point is of course general: "universals have no real existence" (EIP V, vi [407a]). For if a universal were "a thing that exists, . . . then it would be an individual; but it is a thing that is conceived without regard to existence" (EIP V, iv [398a]).[29] It's true that we sometimes ascribe "existence" to certain universals. But when we do, we are not to be understood as ascribing "an existence in time or place, but existence in some individual subject; and this existence means no more but that they are truly attributes of such a subject. Their existence is nothing

---

[28] "It ought to be observed, that they [i.e., general conceptions] take this denomination, not from the act of the mind in conceiving, which is an individual act, but from the object, or thing conceived, which is general" (EIP V, ii [391b]).

[29] Hence it is that Reid says, "we may conceive or imagine what has no existence, and what we firmly believe to have no existence. . . . Ever man knows, that it is as easy to conceive a winged horse or a centaur, as it is to conceive a horse or a man" (EIP I, i [223a]).

but predicability, or the capacity of being attributed [truly] to a subject. The name of predicables, which was given them in ancient philosophy, is that which most properly expresses their nature" (EIP V, vi [407a–b]).

So it's clear that Reid, in spite of linguistic appearances, was not a nominalist: there are universals. But universals are not individuals; their reality consists entirely in their predicability – in their being attributes. And they are not to be found within the causal order. Reid's way of putting these points is to say that they do not exist – adding that "if we can conceive objects which have no existence, it follows, that there may be objects of thought which neither act upon the mind, nor are acted upon by it; because that which has no existence can neither act or be acted upon" (EIP IV, ii [369a]).

What must be added is that, on Reid's view, acquaintance with universals is far more pervasive in our mental lives than one might suppose. Reid is discussing fictional entities:

> There are conceptions [apprehensions] which may be called fancy pictures. They are commonly called creatures of fancy, or of imagination. . . . Such was the conception which Swift formed of the island of Laputa, and of the country of the Lilliputians; Cervantes of Don Quixote and his Squire; Harrington of the Government of Oceana; and Sir Thomas More of that of Utopia. We can give names to such creatures of imagination, conceive them distinctly, and reason consequentially concerning them, though they never had an existence. They were conceived by their creators, and may be conceived by others, but they never existed. (EIP IV, i [363b])

To those of us who have read Alexius Meinong, the language of the passage – and of a good number of others – suggests that Reid was a Meinongian before Meinong. That is to say, the passage suggests that Reid was of the view that among all the "substances" that there are, some exist and some do not: the president of my university not only has being but also existence, whereas Don Quixote has being without existence. And of course if Reid were a Meinongian, he would have lots of counterexamples to the principles he is trying to unseat: If I imagine Don Quixote, then there is something with which I am acquainted in the imagining mode; namely, Don Quixote. But Don Quixote does not and never did exist. He lacks causal powers. Ergo, the object of an act of acquaintance need not be the immediate cause thereof. It need not be a cause at all, neither of acts of acquaintance with itself nor of anything else.

However, when other passages are brought into the picture it becomes amply clear that Reid was not a Meinongian; I see no evidence that he even so much as entertained the thought that the substances that exist might constitute a subset of those that have being. Fictional characters, fictitious beasts, plans for unbuilt buildings – all are, on his view, not nonexistent particulars but complex universals – person-types, animal-types, building-types, etc.[30] To imagine Don Quixote is to be acquainted, in the imagination mode, with a certain person type. Not a particular person of a certain type but a particular person type. Bare conceptions of things that don't exist – imaginings of such things – are just special cases of *general conceptions*:

> Some general conceptions there are, which may more properly be called *compositions* or *works* than mere combinations. Thus one may conceive a machine which never existed. He may conceive an air in music, a poem, a plan of architecture, a plan of government, a plan of conduct in public or in private life, a sentence, a discourse, a treatise. Such compositions are things conceived in the mind of the author, not individuals that really exist; and the same general conception which the author had may be communicated to others by language.
>
> Thus, the Oceana of Harrington was conceived in the mind of its author. The materials of which it is composed are things conceived, not things that existed. . . . And the same may be said of every work of the human understanding. (EIP V, iv [399a])[31]

THE MIND AS ACTIVE

Perception is not itself a case of *something's being effected*, nor are apprehension, of whatever mode, and belief. "All that we know about" the mind, says Reid, "shows it to be in its nature living and active, and to have the power of perception in its constitution, but still within those limits to which it is confined by the laws of

---

[30] As it happens, this is the view I myself developed, quite a few years before I ever read Reid. See my *Works and Worlds of Art* (Oxford: Clarendon Press, 1980).

[31] Cf. EIP V, iv [399b]: "such works are indeed complex general conceptions. . . . Nature has given us the power of combining . . . simple attributes, and such a number of them as we find proper; and of giving one name to that combination, and considering it as one object of thought." See also EIP IV, i [367b].

nature" (EIP II, iv [254b]).[32] Perception may well have an efficient cause; indeed, it must. But it is the act of perceiving that is
effected by the cause. Perceiving itself is an act of the mind. Perceiving is not an instance of the causal receptivity of the mind.

Yet perception is also not the activation of some active power;
for perception as such is not in one's power; it's not one's volition that brings about perception. Perceiving is the activation of
one of one's *intellectual* powers. Speaking of sensation, but obviously ready to make the same point about perception, Reid says
that "we cannot raise any sensation in our minds by willing it; and
on the other hand, it seems hardly possible to avoid having the
sensation, when the object is presented" (IHM II, x [114b; B 44]).
That's not to deny that volition does play a considerable role in
determining what we sense and perceive: "in proportion as the
attention is more or less turned to a sensation, or diverted from
it, that sensation is more or less perceived and remembered.
Whether therefore there can be any sensation where the mind is
purely passive, I will not say; but I think we are conscious of having
given some attention to every sensation which we remember,
though ever so recent" (ibid.).

Though sensation and perception are not brought about
by one's volition, something must bring them about; Reid took it
to be a necessary truth that perception has an efficient cause.
Accordingly, if the act of perception is to occur, the mind must
be receptive to the causal agency of *something* other than itself.
Only when something activates the capacity in me for perception
do I perform the act of perceiving. Reid was always unwilling to
speculate, let alone commit himself, as to what the active cause,
or causes, of our acts of perception might be, other than to say

[32] "It deserves our notice, that the various modes of thinking have always, and in all languages, as far as we know, been called by the name of *operations* of the mind, or by names
of the same import. To body we ascribe various properties, but not operations, properly so called; it is extended, divisible, moveable, inert; it continues in any state in which
it is put; every change of its state is the effect of some force impressed upon it. . . . These
are the general properties of matter, and these are not operations: on the contrary, they
all imply its being a dead inactive thing, which moves only as it is moved, and acts only
by being acted upon.
"But the mind is from its very nature a living and active being. Every thing we know
of it implies life and active energy; and the reason why all its modes of thinking are
called its operations, is, that in all, or in most of them, it is not merely passive, as body
is, but is really and properly active" (EIP I, i [221a]).

that ultimately it was God. Of course acts of perception don't occur "out of the blue." As we have seen, there are "laws of nature" for their occurrence. But these laws must ultimately be understood as the rules in accord with which the agent (or agents) of perception does its (do their) work.

Comparison to John McDowell's thought, in *Mind and World,* [33] may be helpful. Pervading McDowell's discussion is the Kantian contrast between, on the one hand, the passivity and receptivity of sensibility, and, on the other hand, the spontaneity of conceptualizing and reasoning. While assuming that sensibility fits into the causal order of nature, McDowell argues that conceptualizing and reasoning do not. What he tries to do, then, is develop an expanded notion of *natural* so that, in spite of the fact that they do not fit into the causal order, conceptualizing and reasoning are nonetheless fully natural activities of that entirely natural being which is the human being.

Where Reid differs is in rubbing out that heavy Kantian line between acquaintance, on the one hand, and conceptualizing and reasoning, on the other. Acquaintance and conceptualizing fall on the same side of the line. Both are modes of mental activity – both are manifestations of spontaneity. Both are the actualization of powers that we have, capacities that we possess. We are no better able to explain why we have powers of acquaintance and why those get actualized when they do than why we have powers of conceptualizing and why those get actualized when they do. It is indeed appropriate to think of acquaintance as reality being present to us – conversely, of us as being open to reality. But conceptualizing also incorporates acquaintance: acquaintance with universals. And *contra* Kant and his ilk, being open to reality does not consist of reality acting upon us. Reality acts on all kinds of things that are never acquainted with it, never open to it. Being open to reality consists of the actualization of one of our powers. Being acquainted with things, being open to them, having them present to us, is activity on our part, not passivity. The accomplishment is caused, no doubt. But it is the *act* of perceiving that is caused, this act being the exercise of an intellectual power. Perceiving is not the being-affected.

---

[33] Cambridge, Mass.: Harvard University Press, 1994.

CHAPTER IV

The Attack Continues:
There's Not the Resemblance

The Way of Ideas theorists argued that only if we concede that "ideas" are the sole immediate objects of apprehension can we explain how a sequence of physical and neurological events could cause perception. Reid's polemic against this argument, as I have presented it thus far, came in two parts. First he argued that perception is not in fact explained by hypothesizing ideas. And second, he objected to the principles that the Way of Ideas theorists accepted for a satisfactory explanation. The crucial principle was the one I have been calling "the identity principle": The immediate object of an act of apprehension is identical with the immediate cause thereof. Reid's response was that there is no good reason whatsoever to accept this principle; quite to the contrary, there are good reasons for rejecting it.

Reid has a bit more to say about the failure of the Way of Ideas theory to explain what it set out to explain; it also fails to explain the belief component of perception. But before we get to that, let's look at another aspect of Reid's argument against the claims of the Way of Ideas theorists concerning the conception (i.e., apprehension) which is ingredient in perception. Specifically, let's look at what he says concerning the claim of the Way of Ideas theorists that in perception the immediate object of apprehension is a sense datum that represents the external object perceived, and that the way to think of these mental representations is on the model of reflective images.[1]

---

[1] It's on this point especially that Descartes does not fit the stereotype of the Way of Ideas with which Reid is working; from Chapter VI of the *Meditations* it's clear that Descartes is not working with the model of reflective images. Of course Reid would have many objections to raise against the rather inchoate theory of perception that Descartes does articulate there.

AGAINST USING REFLECTIVE IMAGES AS THE MODEL FOR THINKING ABOUT PERCEPTION

Let's be clear about the force of the argument Reid will be giving. Reid himself holds that perception usually has sensory experience as one of its components. In addition, he agrees that there are laws of nature connecting events in the brain with those sensory experiences – and, in turn, laws of nature connecting those events in the brain with prior neurological and physical events. Further, he holds that "as the impressions on the organs, nerves, and brain, correspond exactly to the nature and conditions of the objects by which they are made; so our perceptions and sensations correspond to those impressions, and vary in kind, and in degree, as they vary. Without this exact correspondence, the information we receive by our senses would not only be imperfect, as it undoubtedly is, but would be fallacious, which we have no reason to think it is" (EIP II, ii [248b]).

Perception, on Reid's view, is an "information processing" activity of a special sort. For that activity to occur, earlier stages in the process must transmit information to later stages; a condition of such transmission is that later stages "correspond" to the earlier stages. What we hope and expect from scientists is that they will discover the details of these correspondences. Reid's argument, then, will not be against sensations as correspondences to perceived objects. His argument will be that it is a mistake to use the model of reflective images, and of our interpretation of such images, in our analysis of how such correspondence works.

Though in the passage quoted Reid speaks of "correspondences" between sensations, on the one hand, and impressions on the organs, nerves, and brain, on the other, far more often he speaks of sensations as "natural signs" – or simply "signs" – of external objects. Rather than the sensory experience involved in perception being an imagistic representation of the external object perceived, it is a *natural sign of* the object; it *naturally signifies* it. Speaking, for example, of the relation of tactile sensations to primary qualities, Reid says that the tactile sensations "are natural signs, and the mind immediately passes to the thing signified, without making the least reflection upon the sign" (IHM

V, v [124a; B 63]).[2] When the mind passes from the sensation which is a natural sign of an external object to a conception of, and belief about, the thing signified, Reid will often speak of the sign as "suggesting" the thing. The transition can be thought of, he says, as a species of *interpretation*:

> The signs in original perception are sensations, of which nature hath given us a great variety, suited to the variety of the things signified by them. Nature hath established a real connection between the signs and the things signified; and nature hath also taught us the interpretation of the signs; so that, previous to experience, the sign suggests the things signified, and creates the belief of it. (IHM VI, xxiv [195a; B 190])

I will be saying more, in the next two chapters, about Reid's use of the word "sign" at this juncture. Here we are still considering Reid's polemic against the Way of Ideas. Let us have the relevant part of the Way of Ideas before us one more time. To understand how we get a mental grip on, and form beliefs about, the nonmental, best to use as model, the Way of Ideas theorists said, the cognitive use that we make of images that objects cause of themselves in reflective media. Consider a mountain's image of itself in a lake. We can get a mental grip on the mountain by thinking of it under the causal particular description, *that which is causing this reflective image*. Then, by inference from beliefs about the image gotten by gazing at it, we can form beliefs about the mountain: that it is largely white, that it has such-and-such a contour, etc. In good measure the inferences will be made on the assumption that, in various respects, the reflective image resembles the mountain. All this we can do without ever glancing up and looking at the mountain.

As we saw in Chapter II, the Way of Ideas theorists sometimes spoke of the images involved in perception as images in the brain.

---

[2] In a general discussion about signs in *Inquiry* V, iii [121b–122b; B 58–61], Reid observes that what we customarily call "causes" in nature are really signs. See also *Inquiry* VI, xxiv [199a; B 198]: ". . . *effects* and *causes*, in the operations of nature, mean nothing but signs and the things signified by them. We perceive no proper causality or efficiency in any natural cause; but only a connection established by the course of nature between it and what is called its effect." Thus Reid speaks approvingly of Bacon's calling natural science "an interpretation of nature." What lies behind this, in Reid's case, is of course his occasionalism.

On this view, "the mind, being seated in the brain as its chamber of presence, immediately perceives those images only, and has no perception of the external object but by them" (EIP II, iv [254b]).[3] Reid's response to this suggestion is whimsical mockery: "the brain has been dissected times innumerable by the nicest anatomists; every part of it examined by the naked eye, and with the help of microscopes; but no vestige of an image of any external object was ever found. The brain seems to be the most improper substance that can be imagined for receiving or retaining images, being a soft moist medullary substance" (EIP II, iv [256b]). And further, "how shall we conceive an image of [the] colour of [an external object] where this is absolute darkness?" (EIP II, iv [257a]). To this he adds, "We are so far from perceiving images in the brain, that we do not perceive our brain at all; nor would any man ever have known that he had a brain, if anatomy had not discovered, by dissection, that the brain is a constituent part of the human body" (EIP II, iv [257a]).

The standard version of the Way of Ideas theory – the version that held that the images ingredient in perception are *mental* images – occupied much more of Reid's time. Reid was of the view that the objects of perception fall into a number of distinct ontological categories: individuals such as ducks and rabbits, liquid and solid substances such as water and iron, qualities such as hardnesses and whitenesses, powers of individuals and substances, and more besides. It was also his view, however, that our perceptions of qualities have a certain developmental priority amid the whole range of perceptions. Quality perceptions, so he argued, are *original*, whereas our perceptions of everything else (and of some qualities) are *acquired* perceptions. In the next chapter I will explain what Reid had in mind with this claim. In the meantime I'll follow in Reid's footsteps and take, as my examples of perception, examples of quality perception.

Let's begin with what Reid has to say about sensory experience in general. Reid was a resolute proponent of what has since come to be called the adverbial analysis of sensation; he was, to the best of my knowledge, the first to offer such an analysis. It seems plausible to suppose that when I feel warm, dizzy, or hungry, there's

[3] At EIP II, iv [256a], Reid quotes Locke as speaking thus.

not some object – be it mental or whatever – to which I bear the relation of *feeling* it. These experiences don't seem to have the ontological structure of self/feeling/object. Among the various modes of acquaintance with entities – perceptual, memorial, on so on – there's not this additional one: the mental-feeling mode. The experiences cited seem to be nothing else than diverse manners of feeling: adverbial modifiers of the intransitive act of feeling, to use a linguistic metaphor. Feeling warm is a *way* of feeling. "How do you feel?" we ask. "Warm," comes the answer. We sometimes refer to a particular hungry feeling, a particular dizzy feeling, a particular warm feeling, as a "sensation." The sensation in question just is – to use contemporary colloquial English – a "feel," of which one is then introspectively aware. The intuitional/presentational content of one's introspective mode of acquaintance, in such a case, is just a feeling of a distinct phenomenal character. A sensation of dizziness is a dizzy-sensation. One has introspective acquaintance with one's feeling; that act of acquaintance has a subject/act/object structure. But the feeling with which one has introspective acquaintance does not in turn have a subject/act/object structure.[4]

Reid's thesis was that the same is true for sensory experiences of the sort that are ingredient in perception. Take the sensory experience that is ingredient within one's perception of something green. It's not the case that the sensory experience consists of the act of being acquainted with a green sense datum – of which package, in turn, one has acquaintance in the introspective mode. The sensory experience does not consist of the sense datum's greenness being the object of an act of mental acquaintance. Rather, green is a feature of the phenomenal character of the experience. It's a green-sensation, in the same way that something is a dizzy-sensation.

Reid goes beyond arguing for similarities of this sort between feeling dizzy and having a sensory experience of green to suggest that the sensory experiences ingredient in perception just are a species of feeling. They just are "feels." The claim that there is an

---

[4] "The form of the expression, *I feel pain*, might seem to imply, that the feeling is something distinct from the pain felt; yet in reality, there is no distinction. As *thinking a thought* is an expression which could signify no more than *thinking*, so *feeling a pain* signifies no more than *being pained*. What we have said of pain is applicable to every other mere sensation" (IHM VI, xx [183a; B 168]). Cf. EIP I, i [229 a–b].

"object" distinct from *acquaintance* with the "object" is an empty claim. A sensation "can be nothing else than it is felt to be. Its very essence consists in being felt; and when it is not felt, it is not. There is no difference between the sensation and the feeling of it; they are one and the same thing. It is for this reason, that we before observed, that, in sensation, there is no object distinct from that act of the mind by which it is felt; and this holds true with regard to all sensations" (EIP II, xvi [310a]).[5] Concerning a proposal to analyze some state of mind into self, act, and object: if the purported object of acquaintance has some independence of this act of acquaintance – either it can exist independently of this act of acquaintance therewith or it is not fully present to this act of acquaintance – then there's some basis for the analysis. Otherwise, not. That basis is lacking in the case of sensory experience. By contrast, it's present in the case of, say, beliefs; beliefs are not just "feels."

Given this analysis of sensory experience, the conclusion Reid has been aiming at is right at hand. Sensory experiences, being one and all mental "feels" of one sort and another, bear no significant resemblance whatsoever to the qualities of external objects. A touch sensation of mine bears a close resemblance to one of my dizzy feelings, and to one of your touch sensations; all are mental "feels." But the qualities of external objects – their hardnesses, their shapes, on so on – are obviously not mental "feels"; accordingly, to such qualities sensory experiences bear no significant resemblance whatsoever. Reid attributes the point to Berkeley: "Bishop Berkeley gave new light to this subject, by shewing, that the qualities of an inanimate thing, such as matter is conceived to be, cannot resemble any sensation; that it is impossible to conceive any thing like the sensations of our minds, but the sensations of other minds. Everyone that attends properly to his sensations must assent to this" (IHM V, viii [131b; B 74]).

But suppose the Way of Ideas theorist sticks to his guns. When Reid said, in the passage quoted above, that the "very essence" of

---

[5] Cf. IHM VI, xxi [187a; B 175–6]: "It is essential to a sensation to be felt, and it can be nothing more than we feel it to be." There is an excellent critical discussion of the adverbial analysis of sensory experience in Chapter 3 of Frank Jackson, *Perception: A Representative Theory* (Cambridge: Cambridge University Press, 1977).

a sensory experience "consists in being felt," one of the contrasts he had in mind was with such mental phenomena as beliefs, judgments, and emotions. Though my anger at someone, when I am actively feeling it, no doubt has a "feel" component (a mental intuitional component), it's not *just* a "feel." There's more to it than that. The "essence" of an emotion does not consist just in a mental intuitional component. There's also an object of the anger, and beliefs of a certain sort about that object. Furthermore, the anger can be, as it were, stored; it can be out of consciousness for a time. Suppose that the Way of Ideas theorist concedes all these differences but insists that it does not follow that sensory experience lacks a self/act/object structure. It's compatible with Reid's observations concerning (as opposed to his analysis of) sensory experience to hold that such experience does have a self/act/object structure, but that the object in such experience is of a very distinct sort. The sense datum exists only when it's the object of this act of acquaintance; and there's nothing more to it than what is present to this act of acquaintance. Hence Reid is wrong to hold that sensory experience consists just of having a feeling of a sensory sort of which one is then conscious; it consists of being conscious of a mental object, a sense datum.

Most Way of Ideas theorists would go further and offer the same analysis for "feels" and sensations in general. Feeling dizzy likewise does not consist just of feeling in a certain manner; it consists of consciousness of a certain internal object – with the agent in turn being conscious of that whole package of self, act, and object. And though being angry, by contrast, consists of more than a momentary state of feeling, the feeling that is ingredient within it is also to be analyzed as consciousness of a certain internal object.

Now if a sense datum is confusedly amalgamated with the consciousness therewith into a "feel" of a certain sort, then of course one will conclude that there is no significant resemblance between sensory experience and the qualities of external objects. But let's keep sharply before us, says the Way of Ideas theorist of the Lockean sort, the distinction between sense datum and consciousness thereof. When looking for resemblances between sensory experiences and the qualities of external objects, we're to look at *sense data*. It's among those that we will find entities resembling external qualities. We won't find significant resemblance if we look at the whole of those ontologically complex entities that are *consciousness of sense data*. If that's what we're looking at, then we'll join Berkeley in exclaiming: "What could less resemble the qualities of external objects than acts of the understanding!"

Reid does not respond by introducing additional considerations in support of his adverbial analysis of sensory experience; instead he launches a line of argument against the Way of Ideas which applies just as much if one adopts the sense-datum analysis of sensory experience as if one adopts the adverbial analysis. The line of argument descends from the level of total generality and looks at cases.

It's always been typical of Way of Ideas theorists to conduct their argument in terms of visual perception and then to announce or assume that perception in the other sensory modes has the same structure. The innovative and decisive step on Reid's part was to begin instead with touch. Let me, however, enter Reid's line of thought by starting with a case of proprioceptive, rather than tactile, perception.[6]

While now sitting here at my desk I perceive, proprioceptively, the position of my left leg. If I were paralyzed from waist down and lying flat on a bed, strapped down, covered with blankets, I would have to ask someone to tell me the position of my left leg if I wanted to know it. That is not my present condition. I perceive the position of my left leg proprioceptively.

The central thesis of the Way of Ideas theorist, as it applies to

---

[6] Reid recognized that his attack on the account of perception of secondary qualities offered by the Way of Ideas theorists would have to be different from that on their account of perception of primary qualities; here it is his attack on the latter that is in view. "Locke saw clearly," he says, "and proved incontestably, that the sensations we have by taste, smell, and hearing, as well as the sensations of colour, heat and cold, are not resemblances of any thing in bodies; and in this he agrees with Des Cartes and Malebranche. Joining this opinion with the hypothesis, it follows necessarily, that three senses of the five are cut off from giving us any intelligence of the material world, as being altogether inept for that office. Smell, and taste, and sound, as well as colour and heat, can have no more relation to body, than anger or gratitude; nor ought the former to be called qualities of body, whether primary or secondary, any more than the latter. For it was natural and obvious to argue thus from that hypothesis: if heat, and colour, and sound, are real qualities of body, the sensations, by which we perceive them, must be resemblances of those qualities: but these sensations are not resemblances; therefore those are not real qualities of bodies" (IHM VI, vi [141a–b; B 92–3]).

this case, is that the acquaintance which is ingredient in my perception of my leg's position consists of my introspective acquaintance with a certain internal object, namely, a sense datum that is a reflective image of my leg's position; it's by inference from beliefs about that sense datum, formed in me by acquaintance with that mental entity, that I come to have knowledge of my leg's position. Recall the model: By looking at the reflective image of a mountain in a lake I come to know the mountain's contour – because the mountain's contour resembles the reflective image's contour. That is to say, the quality that is *the contour of the mountain* resembles that quality that is *the contour of the reflective image*.

The suggestion is preposterous! I'm aware of a mental image that exhibits a quality resembling that quality which is my leg's being bent at the knee? What would such a mental image be? Would it be an image with a bent-at-the-knee contour? No; because that would be a visual image whereas my perception of the position of my leg is proprioceptive. The very idea of a proprioceptive image seems incoherent.[7] Nothing in the argument depends on the sense of the word "image," however. Let's use a neutral word, "simulacrum." I proprioceptively perceive my leg's being bent at the knee; and that, so it is said, is because I'm introspectively aware of having a sense datum that is a simulacrum of that quale of my leg. The proposal seems just wacky!

Now for an example of the sort Reid was fond of. I'm presently perceiving, by touch, the hardness of the chair I'm sitting at – its considerable resistance to deformation. Of course its hardness is not as great as that, say, of a stone; and beyond a certain point on the gamut of relative hardness I have to use other strategies than merely touching to make discriminations. But I can tell that the chair is (relatively) hard by touch. There are lots of other hardnesses of objects that I have in mind (apprehend) only by means of a singular concept. But of the hardness of my chair I presently have a perception. And let's be clear, says Reid, that hardnesses

---

[7] Cf. Reid, EIP II, iv [257a]: "As to objects of sight, I understand what is meant by an image of their figure in the brain. . . . As to all other objects of sense, except figure and colour, I am unable to conceive what is meant by an image of them. Let any man say, what he means by an image of heat and cold, an image of hardness or softness, an image of sound, of smell, or taste. The word *image*, when applied to these objects of sense, has absolutely no meaning."

and softnesses are "real qualities" of objects "before they [are] perceived by touch, and continue to be so when they are not perceived: for if any man will affirm, that diamonds were not hard till they were handled, who would reason with him?" (IHM V, ii [120a; B 55])

As his opening move Reid joins with his opponents in affirming that "there is no doubt a sensation" – he means, a sensory experience – "by which we perceive a body to be hard or soft. This sensation of hardness may easily be had, by pressing one's hand against the table, and attending to the feeling that ensues, setting aside, as much as possible, all thought of the table and its qualities, or of any external thing" (IHM V, ii [120a; B 55–6]). In that sentence Reid seamlessly runs together the having of the sensory experience with the attending to it. Immediately, however, he goes on to say that "it is one thing to have the sensation, and another to attend to it, and make it a distinct object of reflection. The first is very easy; the last, in most cases, extremely difficult. We are so accustomed to use the sensation as a sign, and to pass immediately to the hardness signified, that, as far as appears, it was never made an object of thought, either by the vulgar or by philosophers; nor has it a name in any language. . . . There are indeed some cases wherein it is no difficult matter to attend to the sensation occasioned by the hardness of a body; for instance, when it is so violent as to occasion considerable pain: then nature calls upon us to attend to it, and then we acknowledge that it is a mere sensation, and can only be in a sentient being" (IHM V, ii [125a; B 64]). Of course we can call the sensory experience in question a "tactile sensation"; but I take Reid's point to be that in our extant language we don't have the vocabulary for distinguishing between the sort of tactile sensation we have when touching a hard object and the sort we have when touching a soft, or a rough, object.

Though he thinks it will be difficult, Reid asks us now to attend carefully to the tactile sensation we have when perceiving something's hardness. And then to consider this question: Does this tactile sensation, or anything therein, resemble the hardness of the object? The tactile sensation is to be analyzed ontologically – so says the Way of Ideas theorist – into a sense datum and the act of acquaintance that has the sense datum as its object. OK. Is that sense datum hard? Is hardness one of its phenomenal qualities? Is there such a quality as the sense datum's hardness? If there is, then of course that quality will resemble, with more or less closeness, that quality that is the object's hardness. But is there any such quality as the sense datum's hardness? Is there anything at all in sensory experience that is hard?

Reid answers with a resounding No: "Let a man attend distinctly to [his tactile sensation and to the hardness of the object], and he will perceive them to be as unlike as any two things in nature. The one is a sensation of the mind, which can have no existence but in a sentient being; nor can it exist one moment longer than it is felt; the other is in the table, and we conclude without any difficulty, that it was in the table before it was felt, and continues after the feeling is over. The one implies no kind of extension, nor parts, nor cohesion; the other implies all these. Both indeed admit of degrees; and the feeling, beyond a certain degree, is a species of pain; but adamantine hardness does not imply the least pain" (IHM V, v [125a; B 64]). In short, the hardness "of a body, is no more like that sensation by which I perceive it to be hard, than the vibration of a sonorous body is like the sound I hear ..." (IHM V, ii [120b; 57]).

I find Reid's argument compelling. Neither the experience as a whole nor any ingredient therein has the property of being hard. There is no such quality as the sensory experience's hardness – none such as the sense datum's hardness. There couldn't be. Sense data, if there are such entities, aren't the sort of things that could be hard. There couldn't possibly be a quality present in the sense datum which resembles the hardness of the object in that both are hardnesses.

Isn't this much too easy? Can a theory of perception which held so powerful a grip for so long on the imagination of so many intelligent philosophers, and which to a considerable extent still does, be subject to so briskly decisive a refutation as this appears to be? One does indeed hesitate for this very reason; but I think the answer has to be: Yes, the refutation is decisive. Of course – to repeat a point made in opening this discussion – to argue that the sensory experiences ingredient in perception are not images of the objects perceived is not to argue that in no way do they "correspond" to those objects; in some way they must if they are to play a role in processing information about the external world.

The relative hardnesses of things were classified by Reid and his predecessors as primary qualities. And the Way of Ideas theorists held that when it came to the primary qualities of objects, sensory experiences, or the sense data therein, resemble those primary qualities. Resemblance comes in respects; so the appropriate question to put to the Way of Ideas theorist is this: *In what respect*, on your theory, does the sense datum resemble an object's hardness? Since everything resembles everything in some respect or other, the Way of Ideas theorist will always be able to point to some respect or other in which there's resemblance between the sense datum and the object's hardness. But that's not enough for his purposes. The Way of Ideas theorist proposed that we use reflective images, and our cognitive interaction with those, as our model for understanding how perception works. The reflective image of a mountain in a lake really does have a whiteness and a specific contour; and it's appropriate to infer that the mountain has a color *like that image's whiteness* and a contour *like that image's contour*. By contrast, the sense datum which is supposedly ingredient in a touch sensation does not have a hardness nor anything remotely like one.

But if the refutation is really this easy, then at least we need an explanation of why the Way of Ideas theorists failed to notice the absurdity of their position. Reid's diagnosis is that they failed to do so because they failed to distinguish sharply and consistently between perception of objects and the subjective sensory experience that is ingredient in perception. "All the systems of philosophers about our senses and their objects have split upon this rock, of not distinguishing properly" sensory experience from the perception of external objects (IHM V, viii [130b; B 72]).

I dare say Reid is right in speculating that it was their failure to make and keep in mind the distinction between sensation and perception that concealed from the Way of Ideas theorists the absurdity of their position. But I doubt that that is the whole explanation. I suggest that another factor that contributed to the absurdity going unnoticed is that when people speak of "a sensation of hardness" they often fail to see, consistently and clearly, that such a sensation, whatever it might be, is not a hard sensation. A third factor – I am inclined to think that this is the major one – is the habit of philosophers of concentrating on vision when developing theories of perception and offhandedly assuming that the other senses work pretty much the same way.[8] In the case of vision there is some plausibility to the resemblance assumption. Many an after-image, for example, really does have a contour and a color; one can sketch out the contour on a piece of paper and color it in. After-images are like reflective images in that respect. Unfortunately for the Way of Ideas theory they are also like reflective images in the respect which Reid so insistently calls to our attention: though mountains are hard, reflective images of mountains in lakes are not! That's why the model is of no use for developing a general theory of perception.

The devastation wreaked by Reid's argument extends well beyond the Way of Ideas. It extends to all phenomenalist theories of perception – makes no difference whether they be of the Humean or of the Kantian sort. Humean phenomenalism (as I understand Hume – all interpretations are controversial!) holds that "external" objects – tables, ducks, etc. – just are collections, of a certain sort, of sense data. There are lots of collections of sense data that it would be patently absurd to identify with external objects. Hence the great looming challenge for the Humean phenomenalist has always been to pick out, from among all the collections of sense data, those about which he wants to say: These are the physical objects. The challenge has never been met. And if the proposal is that the collections are *sets*, then one can see that no matter what collections of sense data the Humean phenomenalist eventually picks out, those can't be external objects. For their modal properties will always be wrong. It's impossible that a set should have any other members than those it does have – on pain of no longer being that set. An external object can always have had different perceptible qualia from those it has: If it's green, it might have been blue, and so on. What's fascinating about Reid's argument is that it provides us with a decisive argument of quite a different sort against phenomenalism: Lots of external objects are hard, perceptibly so; among their perceptible qualia are their hardnesses. But nowhere within the realm of

---

[8] This is true, for example, of Frank Jackson's *Perception: A Representative Theory* (Cambridge: Cambridge University Press, 1977).

sense data is there a hardness to be discovered – hence, none that resembles the hardness of my desk in being a hardness.[9]

Phenomenalism of the Kantian sort fares no better. Kant, like the theorists of the Way of Ideas, begins with experience; that is, with the subjective effect of reality's impact on us. That is the intuitional given. He further held that the totality of the manifold of a person's *Anschauungen* is conceptualized as (and hence represented to the person as) states of self, and that some of that very same manifold can also be conceptualized as (and hence presented to the person as) external objects and qualities thereof. Thus, not an ontological duality of types of entities (subjective states vs. external objects and qualities) but a duality of ways in which the intuitional given is conceptualized as, and presented to, a person (as subjective states of self vs. as objective entities). Reid's argument shows why – in spite of its ingenuity – Kant's proposal will also not work. If some segment of my intuitional experience (i.e., of my manifold of *Anschauungen*) is veridically conceived and presented to me as one of my pressure sensations, then it cannot also be veridically conceived and presented to me as some object's hardness. It's important here to recall that Kant most certainly did not hold that anything in intuitional experience can be veridically conceived and presented under any old concept whatever; the manifold of intuition is not totally plastic. If I veridically conceive and am presented with something as an elephant, then I cannot also veridically conceive and be

---

[9] Keith de Rose, in "Reid's Anti-Sensationalism and His Realism" (*Philosophical Review* XCVIII, No. 3 [July 1989]: 313–48), suggests that Berkeley's phenomenalism may have been different from that which, above, I attribute to Hume. Perhaps it was Berkeley's view that "when we are thinking of a sphere," we are thinking of "what sensations we would have if it were in front of us and if we were to move our hands in such-and-such a way" (340). As to hardness, the view would be that "the only content there is in thinking of a body as being such that it cannot easily be made to change its figure [i.e., thinking of it as hard, on Reid's analysis of our concept of hardness] is the sensations one thinks *would* be had if, for example, he were to push against the object" (341). But in the first place, what, on this view, is the force of thinking of the sensations we would have if *it* were in front of us? What is that *it*? And second, if hard objects were only resistant to deformation by *us*, then de Rose's articulation of Berkeley's proposal for what it is to think of a hard object would have some plausibility. But hard objects are also resistant to deformation by other objects.

There is an excellent discussion in de Rose of how the assumption functioned, in the argumentation of Hume, that we cannot conceive of anything except as resembling our mental states, and in the argumentation of Berkeley, that we cannot conceive of anything except as resembling our mental states *or ourselves*.

presented with it as an apple. Reid forces us to notice that, contrary to Kant's general thesis, if I can veridically conceive and be acquainted with some intuition as a pressure sensation, then it will resist veridical conception and acquaintance as a hardness quality.

REID'S ARGUMENT AGAINST THE ACCOUNT
OF PERCEPTUAL BELIEFS OFFERED BY
THE WAY OF IDEAS

Perception of external objects regularly induces the formation of beliefs about the objects perceived. Often those beliefs are not only true, but well grounded; there's good evidence for them. On this much, Reid and the Way of Ideas theorists agree. The Way of Ideas theorists go beyond this bare-bones description to offer an explanation of the formation of such beliefs. Reid tacitly concedes that, on this point, what they offer counts as an explanation; it is, however, fatally flawed.

The theorists of the Way of Ideas held that the process of forming perceptual beliefs has two stages, the first of these consisting in the formation of beliefs about sensations. The acquaintance with sense data that is ingredient in perception immediately evokes in me beliefs about the phenomenal qualities belonging to those sense data; it also justifies the beliefs thus formed – that is, it constitutes evidence for them. For example, my acquaintance with a certain sensation (sense datum) immediately evokes in me and justifies the belief, about that sensation, that it is green – that it has a greenness as one of its qualities. To say that such beliefs about sensations are "immediately evoked" – or "immediate," for short – is to say that they are not formed by inference from other beliefs. They are formed by some process other than inference.

One's perceptual beliefs about external objects are, by contrast, *mediate* beliefs formed by inference from immediate beliefs about one's sensations. First, from my sensation belief I infer that there exists some external object by which the sensory experience is caused and of which that sensory experience is an imagistic representation. That places me in the position of being able to get a mental grip on that external entity with the causal particular concept, *that external object which is the cause of this sense datum and of which the sense datum is an imagistic representation.* Once I have that entity in mind in that way, I then form beliefs about its qualities by inference from my beliefs about the qualities of my sense datum – the assumption being that in fundamental respects the external object resembles the sense datum.

Reid objects to both stages in the explanation. Concerning the first stage, he holds that typically we form no beliefs at all about our sensations. In the case of tactile perception, for example, unless one's contact with the object produces pain, one's attention is focused so exclusively on the object perceived that one seldom has any awareness at all of the sensation. "We are so accustomed to use the sensation as a sign, and to pass immediately to the hardness signified, that, as far as appears, it was never made an object of thought, either by the vulgar or by philosophers. . . . There is no sensation more distinct, or more frequent; yet it is never attended to, but passes through the mind instantaneously, and serves only to introduce that quality in bodies, which, by a law of our constitution, it suggests" (IHM V, ii [120a; B 56]).

Concerning the second stage, Reid poses the question: what "principle of human nature that hath been admitted by philosophers" could account for this supposed inference from beliefs about sensations to perceptual beliefs?" (IHM V, iii [122b; B 61]). As Berkeley and Hume already observed, ordinary deductive inference won't do the trick; "we cannot, by reasoning from our sensations, collect the existence of bodies at all, far less any of their qualities" (ibid.). The reason is that there aren't the necessary connections requisite for such inference. Is it "self-evident," Reid asks, "from comparing the ideas, that such a sensation could not be felt, unless such a quality of bodies existed?" (IHM V, ii [121a; B 58]). Obviously not. Our reason cannot "perceive the least tie or connection between them; nor will the logician ever be able to show a reason why we should conclude hardness from this feeling, rather than softness, or any other quality whatsoever. . . . The sensation of heat, and the sensation we have by pressing a hard body, are equally feelings: nor can we by reasoning draw any conclusion from the one, but what may be drawn from the other" (IHM V, v [125a; B 64–5]).

If there were a logically necessary connection between pressure sensations of a certain sort and hardness qualities, then the correlations between these could not be different from what they actually are: Pressure sensations of this sort could not be correlated with anything other than hardness qualities; nor, conversely, could hardness qualities be correlated with anything other than pressure sensations of this sort. But as we saw in the previous chapter, Reid over and over presses the point that, human nature remaining what it is, the correlations could be different. It's logically possible that a touch on the skin would occasion auditory experiences and that activation of the nerves in the ear would occasion olfactory sensations.

What then about the alternative possibility, that the inferences are based on our knowledge of contingent laws of nature? I have noticed a correlation between pressure sensations and the presence of hardnesses; now upon having a pressure sensation I infer that there exists a hardness. Perhaps I recall the correlation and quite consciously make the inference; alternatively, perhaps I make the inference by virtue of a habit that has been formed in me. Or perhaps the correlation is not one that I myself have noticed but one that I have been told about.

But how are we to gain knowledge of such correlations? To discern the relevant correlations I have to be able to pick out both pressure sensations and hardnesses. Picking out pressure sensations is no problem on the Way of Ideas account. But what about the hardnesses? By hypothesis I do not have acquaintance with them. If I'm to pick them out, it has to be by the use of singular concepts. "The hardness of this chair," "the hardness at the end of my fingertips," etc. But that presupposes that I have the concept of *hardness*. How, on the Way of Ideas account, could I come by this concept?

As we saw in Chapter II, the thesis of the Way of Ideas concerning concept formation is that all our concepts are formed by first taking note of the qualitiess of the objects of our acquaintance, then forming concepts of those by abstraction, and then forming additional concepts by operating on those basic concepts with the activities of generalization, combination, and division. The concept of a hardness cannot be a basic concept, derived from our sense data by abstraction, sincc no state or act of mind is hard. It has to be a derivative concept formed from basic concepts by generalization, combination, or division. But what might be those basic concepts from which it is formed? It's hard to see what else the Way of Ideas theorist could propose than that the concept of a hardness is composed, by one or another operation, out of concepts of the phenomenal features of pressure sensations. But this proposal won't go anywhere for the reason we've already canvassed: Hardnesses are no more like the phenomenal qualia of pressure sensations than like the phenomenal qualia of countless other sensations: they're radically unlike all of them (IHM V, vi [123b–125b; B 65–6]).

Let us suppose, however, that I have somehow acquired the concept of a hardness. How am I to go about establishing correlations between the occurrence of a pressure sensation in my mind and the existence of an external hardness in contact with some part of my body? Since hardnesses are not entities with which I can have acquaintance, I need some line of argumentation to establish that the concept of a hardness is instantiated when it is. But what line of argumentation could that possibly be? Presumably it would have to be a deductive inference. But as already observed, it's not a matter of logical necessity that when I'm having a pressure sensation some hard object is in contact with that part of my body in which I feel the pressure sensation. We "might have been so made as to taste with our fingers, to smell with our ears, and to hear by the nose" (IHM VI, xxi [187b; B 176]). In short, there's no way of even getting started on the establishing of correlations.

The inferences that we make from sensation beliefs to perceptual beliefs, on the Way of Ideas account, cannot be based on our knowledge of logical necessities because there aren't any relevant logical necessities. But neither can they be based on our knowledge of laws of nature, because, on the account offered, it's impossible that we should even grasp such laws, let alone know that they hold. The "connection between our sensations and the conception and belief of external existence can neither" be based on reason, says Reid, nor on "habit, experience, education, or any [other] principle of human nature that hath been admitted by philosophers" (IHM V, iii [122b; B 61]).

Yet it's obviously "a fact, that such sensations are invariably connected with the conception and belief of external existences." Accordingly we must conclude, says Reid, "that this connection is the effect of our constitution, and ought to be considered as an original principle of human nature, till we find some more general principle into which it may be resolved" (ibid.). Being an original principle of our nature, it cannot be explained. All we can do is describe its workings – and use it to explain other "principles" of our nature.

CHAPTER V

Reid's Analysis of Perception: The Standard Schema

Reid never doubted that sensations are an ingredient of perception.[1] The having of sensations is not sufficient for perception, however. In Reid's words, "if nature had given us nothing more than impressions made upon the body, and sensations in our minds corresponding to them, we should in that case have been merely sentient, but not percipient beings." Hinting at his own analysis of perception, Reid continues: "We should never have been able to form a conception of any external object, far less a belief of its existence" (IHM VI, xxi [187b; B 176]). As we saw earlier, Reid is convinced that "All the systems of philosophers about our senses and their objects have split upon this rock, of not distinguishing properly sensations which can have no existence but when they are felt, from the things suggested by them" (IHM V, viii [130b–131a; B 72–3]).[2]

Perception occurs when one's environment is represented to one as being a certain way – *perceptually* represented, of course.[3]

---

[1] This is the general rule; in the next chapter we'll be seeing an exception.

[2] The distinction between sensation and perception is so important for Reid's purposes that it is worth citing one more passage in which he details the distinction. "When I smell a rose, there is in this operation both sensation and perception. The agreeable odour I feel, considered by itself, without relation to any external object, is merely a sensation. It affects the mind in a certain way; and this affection of the mind may be conceived, without a thought of the rose, or any other object, This sensation can be nothing else than it is felt to be. Its very essence consists in being felt; and when it is not felt, it is not. There is no difference between the sensation and the feeling of it; they are one and the same thing. . . .

"Let us next attend to the perception which we have in smelling a rose. Perception has always an external object; and the object of my perception, in this case, is that quality in the rose which I discern by the sense of smell. . . . This quality in the rose is the object perceived; and that act of my mind, by which I have the conviction and belief of this quality, is what in this case I call perception" (EIP II, xvi [310a–b]).

[3] I am borrowing this use of the word "represented" from the articulators of the so-called New Theory of Representation. For an introduction, see the essays in Tim Crane, ed., *The Contents of Experience* (Cambridge: Cambridge University Press, 1992).

It occurs when one's experience is *objectivated* – to use terminology from Kant's *Prolegomena*. In perception one leaves behind the confines of one's own mind and brings one's spatial environment into the picture. One brings it into mind not by drawing inferences about it but by representing it as being a certain way – or better by *its* being represented *to one* as being a certain way.

What do we want out of a theory – that is, an analysis – of perception? Several things, no doubt. But one thing we want is some account of what it is for one's environment to be represented to one as being (or appearing) a certain way. We want some account of what objectivation consists of. That is, in fact, the central question that Reid seeks to answer in his analysis of perception – along with, as the reader will by now expect, an answer to the question as to which are the original faculties at work in bringing it about that one's environment is perceptually represented to one as being (or appearing) a certain way.

In my discussion, in Chapter I, of Reid's use of the word "conception," I argued that when Reid speaks, say, of having a conception of a cat, he never means what we mean when we say that we have a concept of cat. He almost always means what he himself says he will mean, namely, an *apprehension* of *some particular cat.* The exceptions are those cases in which he means, instead, some *belief* about some particular cat.[4] I also observed that Reid uses "conception" to cover three very different types of apprehension: nominative apprehension, conceptual apprehension (i.e., apprehension by means of a singular concept), and presentational apprehension (i.e., apprehension by acquaintance).

Reid's concept of *conception* will be on center stage in his account of perception: In perception, the sensation evoked by the perceived object in turn evokes a conception of that object. A question that naturally comes to mind is this: What type of conception does Reid have in mind? Does perception yield us only conceptual apprehension of the external object, or does it yield us presentational apprehension? Reid never directly tells us.

I find that surprising. My guess is that Reid was not clear on the matter in his own mind, rather than that he failed to make his thought clear to us, his readers. And the reason for that, I surmise,

---

[4] He himself observes that this latter is a common use of the word: See EIP I, i [223a], and EIP IV, i [361a].

was twofold. For one thing, Reid would insist that whether it be presentational or conceptual apprehension that is ingredient in perception, either way, it is *direct, immediate* apprehension. Reid saw that claim as marking the decisive difference between his account and that of the Way of Ideas theorists. They held that apprehension of external objects is always indirect; that is to say, given Reid's use of "indirect" in this context, that it's always *by way of* our apprehension of something else that imagistically represents the external object – in the way in which a reflective or photographic image of some object imagistically represents that object. Reid denied that thesis; and that denial was far more central in his mind than the issue I have pressed, of whether our apprehension of the external object, in perception, is presentational or conceptual. A second factor, so I judge, is that Reid took over from his predecessors their habit of not keeping firmly in mind the distinction between these two modes of apprehension, presentational and conceptual. Not until Kant made systematic use of his distinction between concepts and intuitions was the habit broken.

I propose expounding Reid's thought in this chapter without pressing the issue of the type of conception of the external object that Reid thinks is ingredient in perception; I'll follow Reid's practice and speak simply of conception (and apprehension), leaving the issue open. Then, with the main outlines of Reid's theory in hand, I'll discuss the issue in the next chapter.

OBJECTIVATION

A preliminary point. As mentioned earlier, Reid was of the view that the objects of perception fall into a number of distinct ontological categories: individuals such as ducks and rabbits, liquid and solid substances such as water and iron, qualities (abstract particulars) such as hardnesses and whitenesses, powers of individuals and substances, and more besides. It was also his view, however, that our perceptions of qualities have a certain developmental priority amid the whole range of perceptions. Perceptions of qualities, so he argued, are original, whereas our perceptions of everything else (and of some qualities) are acquired perceptions. Later I'll explain what he has in mind by this distinction between original and acquired. For the time being, let me follow in his footsteps and concentrate on our perceptions of qualities.[5]

Let's begin with a rather good statement from Reid himself of the main elements of his analysis:

> The external senses have a double province; to make us feel, and to make us perceive. They furnish us with a variety of sensations, some pleasant, others painful, and others indifferent; at the same time they give us a conception, and an invincible belief of the existence of external objects. This conception of external objects is the work of nature. The belief of their existence, which our senses give, is [also] the work of nature; so likewise is the sensation that accompanies it. This conception and belief which nature produces by means of the senses, we call *perception*. The feeling which goes along with the perception, we call *sensation*. The perception and its corresponding sensation are produced at the same time. In our experience we never find them disjoined. (EIP II, xvii [318b])

A couple of additions and a clarification are in order. Though he doesn't happen to mention it in this passage, Reid held that the belief about the perceived entity, that it exists objectively, is produced *immediately*[6]; he's disagreeing at this point with the Way of Ideas theorists, who held that the belief of the existence of the external object is inferred from a belief about a sense datum, this latter belief being formed immediately. To make inferences about external objects is not to perceive them. One might well draw inferences about one's environment from one's feeling of dizziness; but that doesn't catch up one's feeling of dizziness into an objectivated experience. Objectivated experience occurs when one finds oneself immediately and ineluctably believing, about something in one's environment, that it exists as external. Even

---

[5] At one point, Reid says flatly that "The objects of perception are the various qualities of bodies" (EIP II, xvii [313b]). Later he explains what he means: "the things immediately perceived are qualities, which must belong to a subject; and all the information that our senses give us about this subject, is, that it is that to which such qualities belong. From this it is evident, that our notion of body or matter, as distinguished from its qualities, is a relative notion . . ." (EIP II, xix [322b]). His main discussion concerning the ontology of qualities, and the distinction between qualities and attributes, occurs at EIP V, iii [394b ff.].

[6] "this conviction [which is ingredient in perception] is not only irresistible, but it is immediate; that is, it is not by a train of reasoning and argumentation that we come to be convinced of the existence of what we perceive" (EIP II, v [259b]).

the word "believing" is perhaps not quite right; it makes it sound too self-conscious. It's more like *finding oneself taking* something to be external.[7]

Second, a striking feature of Reid's analysis – connected with the first point – is that there is no mention at all of a conception of, and belief about, the sensation. It was Reid's view, in contrast to the Way of Ideas theorists, that typically in perception there is no such conception and belief; we're not sufficiently aware of the sensation to get it in mind and form a belief about it. Getting it in mind so as to have beliefs formed about it requires attention; and typically that attention is lacking.[8] One cannot have sensations of which one is not conscious; but one can be conscious of some sensation without attending to it.

Third, the "belief of the existence of" the external object is a *de re*/predicative belief about the external object; and what is believed about it is that it exists as a component of one's environment – or something that entails that. One doesn't just believe *that* there exists some external object; one believes *about* some particular external object, namely, the one perceived, that *it* exists as external.[9]

Fourth, when Reid says that "in our experience we never find them disjoined," he must be understood as having two qualifications in mind. In cases of hallucination, a sensation that would

[7] Reid thinks of judgment as an act, and belief as an enduring state produced by that act; thus, he will sometimes say that the central ingredient in perception is judgment, and sometimes, that it is belief. In an interesting passage he wonders, however, whether "judgment" is quite the right word for what takes place in perception (I know of no passage in which he wonders similarly about the propriety of "belief"): "it is certain that all of them [perception, memory, consciousness] are accompanied with a determination that something is true or false, and a consequent belief. If this determination be not judgment, it is an operation that has got no name; for it is not simple apprehension, neither is it reasoning; it is a mental affirmation or negation; it may be expressed by a proposition affirmative or negative, and it is accompanied with the firmest belief. These are the characteristics of judgment; and I must call it judgment, till I can find another name to it" (EIP VI, i [414b]).

[8] "Nature intended them [i.e., sensations of various sorts] only for signs; and in the whole course of life they are put to no other use. The mind has acquired a confirmed and inveterate habit of inattention to them; for they no sooner appear than quick as lightning the thing signified succeeds, and engrosses all our regard. . . . although we are conscious of them when they pass through the mind, yet their passage is so quick, and so familiar, that it is absolutely unheeded; nor do they leave any footsteps of themselves, either in the memory or imagination" (IHM VI, iii [135b; B 82]).

[9] "We may observe, that the laws of perception, by the different senses, are very different. . . . In all of them the object is conceived to be external, and to have real existence, independent of our perception . . ." (IHM VI, xii [158b; B 124]).

normally occur within the process of perceiving an object occurs without perception. And second, as we shall see in the next chapter, Reid thought that in our perception of visible figure and magnitude, there is no sensation functioning as a sign of that figure and magnitude; the perception occurs without any corresponding sensory experience.

Last, Reid regards the sensation as functioning both as a "sign of" the perceived object, that is, an *indicator* of the object; and as "suggesting" a conception of the object, that is, *causing* a conception of the object. Hence he says that in perception "the mind, either by original principles or by custom, passes from the sign [which is the sensation] to the conception and belief of the thing signified [which is the external object]" (IHM VI, xxiv [194b; B 190]).

Let me put the core of Reid's analysis in my own words. Perceiving one's environment to be a certain way consists of a belief being immediately and ineluctably formed in one, about some item of the external environment, that it presently exists as an item of the external environment. That's what the objectivation, which constitutes the core of perception, consists of: the formation of an immediate belief, about some item in one's environment, that it exists as an external object. (One can now see why Reid thinks that belief lies at the very foundation of human existence!) But one cannot have a *de re*/predicative belief about some item in one's environment unless one somehow apprehend that item – somehow gets it in mind. What's required in addition then is that one have an apprehension of that external object. Last, that apprehension must be evoked by that object.

We human beings are so constituted that perception, thus understood, occurs only when a sensation that is caused by an external object and is a sign thereof suggests the conception of, and belief about, the object. I perceive the hardness of some object when the object's hardness causes in me a tactile sensation of a sort that is a sign or indicator of the hardness, and when that in turn causes a conception of that hardness and a belief, about it, that it exists as an external object (or a belief about it which entails that.) "Suggests" means *causes*. The reason Reid doesn't simply say "causes" is that he wishes to do whatever he can to prevent us from thinking that the sensation is an *efficient* cause of the apprehension and belief. Tactile sensations are not the sorts of entities that could be efficient causes.

This formulation of Reid's theory, along with almost all of Reid's own general formulations, must be understood as presenting only what I shall call Reid's *standard schema* for perception. As already mentioned, Reid thought that perception of visible figure and magnitude occurs without any corresponding sensation. In this present chapter I will be discussing Reid's standard schema; in the next we will look at the exception to the standard schema.

Note that perception does not consist of believing, about one's sensory experiences, that *they* presently exist as components of one's spatial environment. It consists of believing immediately, *about some item in one's spatial environment*, that *it* exists as external. Perception occurs when "a sensation . . . instantly make[s] us conceive and believe the existence of an external thing altogether unlike it" (IHM V, viii [131b; B 74]). That we human beings do this is extraordinary; he has no explanation for it, says Reid. All he means to do is "express a fact, which every one may be conscious of; namely, that by a law of our nature, such a conception and belief constantly and immediately follow the sensation" (ibid.).

Sometimes we sufficiently attend to some of our sensations as to have our attended-to consciousness of them immediately evoke beliefs in us *about them*. And some of our sensations or feelings, no matter how carefully we attend to them, never do anything more than that; one's feeling of dizziness does not evoke objectivation. But some of our sensations, whether attended to or not, have this extraordinary power of immediately evoking beliefs in us about things "altogether unlike" those sensations themselves; namely, beliefs about external objects. That is extraordinary and not to be explained, only to be remarked and described. How do "the sensations of touch, of seeing and hearing, [which] are all in the mind, and can have no existence but when they are perceived . . . constantly and invariably suggest the conception and belief of external objects?" It's not surprising that such sensations would evoke conceptions and beliefs about themselves, when they do. What is surprising is that they would evoke objectivating beliefs How do they do that? "No philosopher can give any other answer to this, but that such is the constitution of our nature" (IHM VI, xii [159a; B 124]).

Kant's view, by contrast, was strikingly different. A sensory intuition of a certain sort can be conceptualized either as one's pressure sensation or as the presentation of an object's hardness. The objectivated character of perception, which makes it essentially different from sensation, is the consequence of applying to one's sensory intuitions the conceptual scheme of objectivity, with the result, in this case, that one apprehends one's intuition under the concept of *a hardness*. Reid had of course not read Kant; but had he done so, he would have found this suggestion perplexing if not preposterous. Short of confusion bordering on madness, one cannot be acquainted with any of one sensory intuitions under the concept of hardness; one cannot be acquainted with them as hard. For they are not hard; sensory intuitions don't satisfy the concept of hardness.

Those of us who have been inducted into contemporary analytic epistemology regularly attempt to give explicit formulation to necessary and sufficient conditions for one thing and another. Reid did not use this rhetorical mode, nor did anybody else in the seventeenth and eighteenth centuries. Nonetheless, there's probably no harm in trying to capture his standard schema for perception in such a formula. The formula would go something like this:

S perceives external object O *if and only if* O affects one's sensory organs in such a way as to cause in S a sensory experience which is a sign (indicator) of O, which sensation in turn causes in S an apprehension of O, and an immediate belief about O whose predicative content is or implies that O exists as an entity in S's environment.

There can be little doubt that Reid regarded what's expressed by the right-hand side of this formula as a necessary condition of perception on the standard schema (I say this, pending a revision to be introduced when we discuss his way of handling hallucinatory phenomena). But whether what's expressed by the right-hand side is also a sufficient condition is something that, so far as I can see, Reid never gave any sustained thought to. Might there be certain sorts of causal paths from an external object to a sensory experience that is an indicator of that object, and then to an apprehension of and belief about that object, such that cases of this sort of causal path do not constitute perception of the object? Reid never addresses the question.[10]

Though Reid would regard what's expressed by the right-hand side of the formula as a necessary condition of perception on the standard schema, what must at once be added is that he would regard it as a blend of logically necessary and causally necessary conditions. What's logically necessary to the occurrence of perception is that objectivation take place – this being analyzed by Reid as consisting in the immediate formation of *de re*/predicative beliefs about external objects to the effect that they exist as external (or beliefs entailing that). Over and over one finds Reid saying this: "If . . . we attend to that act of our mind which we call the perception of an external object of sense, we shall find in it these three things. *First*, Some conception or notion of the thing perceived. *Secondly*, A strong and irresistible conviction and belief of its present existence. And, *thirdly*, That this conviction and belief are immediate, and not the effect of reasoning" (EIP II, v [258a]).[11] Reid acknowledged the implication that infants are probably not capable of perception. "The belief of the existence of any thing seems to suppose a notion of existence; a notion too

---

[10] In his "Externalist Theories of Perception" (*Philosohy and Phenomenological Research*, Vol. L, Supplement, Fall 1990), William P. Alston argues forcefully that attempts to find the right sort of causal path are hopeless.

[11] Cf. EIP II, xx [326a]: "there are two ingredients in this operation of perception: 1st, the conception or notion of the object; and, 2ndly, the belief of its present existence." Whereas objectivating belief thus constitutes the essence of perception (and a corresponding sort of belief, the essence of recollection), the same is not true for consciousness. Consciousness, if accompanied with *attention*, evokes beliefs about the objects of consciousness; but those beliefs do not *constitute* consciousness. Hence Reid observes that "No philosopher has attempted by any hypothesis to account for his consciousness of our own thought, and the certain knowledge of their real existence which accompanies it" (EIP VI, v [443a]). Belief *accompanies* consciousness (when attention is adequate); it does not constitute it.

In the passage quoted just above, from EIP II, xx, and in a good many others, Reid speaks of judgment or belief as not just logically necessary to perception, but as ingredients of perception; indeed, belief, and the conception it presupposes, are said to be *the* ingredients. But there are a few perplexingly atypical passages in which Reid declines to say that judgment (and belief) are ingredients of perception: "whether judgment ought to be called a necessary concomitant of these operations [e.g., perception], or rather a part or ingredient of them, I do not dispute" (EIP VI, i [414b]). I have no idea what Reid, in composing this passage, might have thought were the ingredients of perception if belief (and presumably conception) are not that. Sensation? As we shall see in the next chapter, he holds that perception of visible figure has no accompanying sensations. In any case, Reid never wavers from his conviction that conception and belief are *logically necessary* to perception.

abstract, perhaps, to enter into the mind of an infant" (EIP II, v [260a]). A good many of Reid's generalizations about perception must thus be understood as intended only for "the power of perception in those that are adult, and of a sound mind" (ibid.).[12]

What about the role of sensory organs in perception? Is that logically necessary or only causally? What's clear is that our *present* sensory organs, and their proper functioning, is no more than a causal condition of the occurrence of perception. Reid regularly puts the point in terms of what God could have done differently: God could have created us so that light shining on the skin produced visual sensations, sound entering the nose produced auditory sensations; and so forth. More radically:

No man can show it to be impossible to the Supreme Being to have given us the power of perceiving external objects without such organs. We have reason to believe, that when we put off these bodies, and all the organs belonging to them, our perceptive powers shall rather be improved than destroyed or impaired. . . . We ought not, therefore, to conclude, that such bodily organs are, in their own nature, necessary to perception; but rather, that, by the will of God, our power of perceiving external objects is limited and circumscribed by our organs of sense; so that we perceive objects in a certain manner, and in certain circumstances, and in no other. (EIP II, i [246a–b])

What does Reid mean? Does he mean that God, for our future state, will give us quite different sensory organs for perception from those we presently have, or that God will make it possible for us to perceive *without any sensory organs*? The passage leaves that unclear. I think it's clear from the following passage, however, that Reid's view was the latter: "For any thing we know, we might have been so made as to perceive external objects, without any impressions on bodily organs, and without any of those sensations which invariably accompany perception in our present frame" (EIP II, xx [327a]).

It's not a logically necessary condition of the occurrence of

---

[12] Shortly, when considering what Reid has to say about hallucination, we will see the force of the qualifier, "and of a sound mind." A good many of Reid's generalizations about mental activity in general have to be understand as pertaining only to normal adults. At EIP VI, i [414a–b], for example, Reid observes that infants and "some idiots" may not only be incapable of making judgments concerning existence, but incapable of making any judgments at all. He says that in what follows he accordingly wishes to be understood as speaking only about "persons come to the years of understanding," that is, "persons who have the exercise of judgment."

perception that sensory organs play any role; that seems to be Reid's thought. But what about the presence of sensory experience? Is it also logically possible for perception to occur without any corresponding sensory experience? The passage just cited clearly indicates that it's logically possible for sensory experiences to evoke quite different conceptions and beliefs of external objects from those they do; over and over Reid makes that point against the Way of Ideas theorists. It's not by virtue of our knowledge of logical necessities that we make the transition from sensations to beliefs about the external world; in particular, perception can and does occur without *resemblances* between sensations and the inferred objects. But can perception occur without any corresponding sensations whatsoever? Reid thinks of perception, as it presently occurs, as a special sort of information processing. In perception, our conceptions and beliefs concerning external objects retrieve information about the external world from our sensations, that information having been transmitted to our sensations from our sensory apparatus and our brains. The sensory apparatus – and presumably the brain – is not a logically necessary part of the information processing that constitutes perception. Presumably the thought is that external objects could directly transmit information to our sensations without the mediation of nerves and brain. But is it also logically possible that they would directly evoke conceptions and beliefs about themselves without the mediation of sensory experience? And if so, would that be perception?

On this point, I find Reid not clear. The final clause of the passage quoted above doesn't help one way or the other: "without any of those sensations which invariably accompany perception in our present frame." We don't know what force to give that final phrase, "in our present frame." When Reid tells us what perception is, as distinguished from the conditions under which it (presently) occurs, he invariably mentions only the objectivating conceptions and beliefs. Might that indicate that he thinks sensory experience is not necessary to perception?[13] Reid always

---

[13] Here's an example, in addition to the one cited above from EIP II, v: "This conception of external objects is the work of nature. The belief of their existence, which our senses give, is the work of nature; so likewise is the sensation that accompanies it. This conception and belief which nature produces by means of the senses, we call *perception*" (EIP II, xvii [318b]).

assumes, so far as I can tell, that perception must have some non-conceptual intuitional content; perception is not mere thought about objects. Might that content have been something other than sensations? Might it have been the perceived object itself – as it is in the case of our perception of visible figure and magnitude? Was Reid perhaps thinking that it's logically possible that all our perception would have been like that – no sensations whatsoever, just acquaintance with the external object? Possibly.

For our purposes here it won't matter much matter, however, that Reid's distinction between what he regards as the essence of perception and what he regards as its causal conditions remains somewhat hazy. He himself introduces and uses the distinction to make certain polemical points against the Way of Ideas theorists; those polemical purposes don't require that he get clear on the points I have been pressing. For the rest, Reid's interest lies in analyzing how perception does in fact work, not in how it might possibly work instead. We'll be following him in that analysis. We are so constituted that, as a matter of fact, perception does not occur without the perceived object making an "impression" on our sensory organs, and without that, in turn, evoking a signifying sensation – with the exception of our perception of visible figure and magnitude.

Just now I have spoken of Reid as offering an "analysis" of perception. In speaking thus I am using Reid's own word for what he sees himself as doing. He's offering us a schematic analysis of perception. He's not offering us an explanation.[14] Nor is he merely giving us a description. And he is certainly not giving us a compilation of "common sense" thoughts about perception. Though ultimately grounded in Common Sense, philosophy is not merely the summation of Common Sense. "The vulgar" do not distinguish – not much, anyway – between the qualities of objects and the sensory experiences they have when perceiving those qualities; seldom is there anything in one's experience that invites one to make the distinction. Almost everything works against one's

---

[14] Reid says that "though I have endeavoured to show, that the theories of philosophers on this subject are ill-grounded and insufficient, I do not attempt to substitute any other theory in their place" (EIP II, xv [307b]). I have already remarked that it is this refusal to offer an explanatory theory that makes it seem to some readers that Reid is opting out of philosophy rather than engaging in it. We like imaginative conjectures. What Reid is actually doing, of course, is challenging our preconceptions concerning the task of philosophy.

making it. The transition from sensory experience to conception and belief of external object is swift, smooth, immediate, and ineluctable; and for the most part, our interest is entirely in the qualities perceived, not in the sensory experience. It is philosophical analysis and argumentation, not ordinary experience, that leads to the unraveling of sensation from perception.

> Sensation, taken by itself, implies neither the conception nor belief of any external object. It supposes a sentient being, and a certain manner in which that being is affected; but it supposes no more. Perception implies an immediate conviction and belief of something external; something different both from the mind that perceives, and from the act of perception. Things so different in their nature ought to be distinguished; but by our constitution they are always united. Every different perception is conjoined with a sensation that is proper to it. The one is the sign, the other the thing signified. They coalesce in our imagination. They are signified by one name, and are considered as one simple operation. The purposes of life do not require them to be distinguished.
>
> It is the philosopher alone who has occasion to distinguish them, when he would analyze the operation compounded of them. (EIP II, xvi [312b])

Reid is of the view that his philosophical predecessors had done a very poor job of unraveling sensation from perception, and that this accounts for a great deal of their confusion. When one perceives the hardness of some object upon having a tactile sensation, "so naturally and necessarily does the sensation convey the notion and belief of hardness, that hitherto they have been confounded by the most acute inquirers into the principles of human nature" (IHM V, iii [122b; B 60]).

One more point must be made in this section. I have spoken of the Way of Ideas theorists as using reflective images as a model for understanding how we get non-mental entities in mind and form beliefs about them – in particular, for understanding how we do that in perception and memory. By contrast, I have spoken of Reid as proposing a schema. My reason is this: The Way of Ideas theorists did not think that the mind, or brain, contains what are *literally* reflective images; sense data are no more than analogous to reflective images. Their proposal was that we allow reflective images to serve as a sort of template in our analysis of perception. By contrast, Reid thought that sensations are literally signs.

The full import of what he had in mind in calling sensations *signs* will slowly unfold itself. But it may help to call attention to three aspects of that import here. Reid indicates that his choice of the word "sign" was far from casual: "Because the mind passes immediately from the sensation to that conception and belief of the object which we have in perception, in the same manner as it passes from signs to the things signified by them, we have therefore called our sensations *signs of external objects*; finding no word more to express the function which nature hath assigned to them in perception, and the relation which they bear to their corresponding objects" (IIIM VI, xxi [188a; B 177]).

The sentence indicates that Reid's choice of the word "sign" was inspired by two considerations.[15] Looking in the one direction, toward their antecedents, sensations are "indications" (IHM VI, ii [135a; B 81]) of external objects – *signs* in that sense. They carry information about external objects. They are signs in the way in which, for example, tracks in the snow are signs, indications, of what sort of animal came by in the night. For this, "a real connection between the sign and the thing signified [must] be established, either by the course of nature, or by the will and appointment of men" (IHM VI, xxi [188a; B 177]). Looking in the other direction, toward their interpretation, sensations are signs in the way in which, for example, road indicators are signs: they immediately, noninferentially, evoke beliefs in us about the road before us. Requisite "to our knowing things by signs," says Reid, "is, that the appearance of the sign to the mind, be followed by the conception and belief of the thing signified. Without this, the sign is not understood or interpreted; and therefore is no sign to us, however fit in its own nature for that purpose" (ibid.). Furthermore, it's characteristic of many signs that they evoke in us the relevant conception and belief without our attending with any care whatsoever to the sign itself.[16]

In the same passage from which these citations have been drawn, Reid indicates that there was also a third consideration

---

[15] He acknowledges, in IHM VI, ii [135a; B 82], that he is adapting the term from Berkeley's use of it.

[16] In perception, "the mind passes instantly to the things signified, without making the last reflection upon the sign, or even perceiving that there is any such thing. It is in a way somewhat similar, that the sounds of a language, after it is become familiar, are overlooked, and we attend only to the things signified by them" (IHM VI, ii [135a; B 81–2]).

going through his mind when he chose the word "sign". In general, "there is no necessity of a resemblance between the sign and the thing signified." The use by the Way of Ideas theorists of the model of reflective images for understanding the relation of mind to world required postulating imagistic representations in the mind of nonmental entities; Reid's use of the concept of a sign requires nothing of the sort.

Perception, as Reid understands it, is at bottom an act of information processing concerning the external world; he argues that the processing involves neither inference nor images of the external world as media. We are hard wired to perform some of such processing; and by the use of various parts of our hard wiring we acquire habits that enable us to engage in more elaborate processing. Reid needs a word for the role of sensations in this process. The best he can think of, he says, is "sign": sensations function as signs in the information processing that constitutes perception. We are today flooded with a great variety of different sorts of artificially constructed devices for information processing. Would Reid be able to find a better word for his purposes from the language we have created for describing these various devices?

I'll leave it to others to answer that question.

DIFFERENCE BETWEEN PRIMARY AND SECONDARY QUALITIES

Reid follows his predecessors in distinguishing – albeit in his own way – between primary and secondary qualities. We'll get a better insight into how he was thinking of perception if we follow him as he makes the distinction. Start with primary qualities. Primary qualities "involve" – to speak loosely for the moment – dispositions in external objects to cause sensations of certain sorts in perceivers. Hardness, for example, "involves" the disposition to produce certain pressure sensations in perceivers. The primary quality is not to be identified with the disposition, however; rather, it's the physical basis of the disposition. Hardness, which is the primary quality, *possesses* the disposition to cause certain pressure sensations in perceivers.

Not only is the essence of a primary quality not to be identified with a disposition to produce sensations of certain sorts in perceivers; the dispositions of this sort which primary qualities possess are not essential to them. As Reid observes, it was possible for God to attach the disposition of objects to produce pressure sensations in perceivers to some other physical basis than that to which it is attached. "No man can say, but that effluvia, or the vibration of the parts of a body, might have affected our touch, in the same manner that hardness now does, if it had so pleased the Author of our nature" (IHM V, iv [123a; B 62]).

An additional mark of primary qualities is that "we know what they are" (EIP II, xvii [314a]). That is to say, we know their essences, not just "barely what relation they bear to something else" (ibid.); indeed, our concepts of them are of their essences. We gain this knowledge we have of their essences from perception. We don't have to consult science to learn what it is in an object that accounts for its causing particular kinds of pressure sensations in us; we know that it's the object's hardness. And by perception we know, in turn, what that is. Science might eventually succeed, says Reid, in offering explanatory accounts of the primary qualities of things. What it cannot do is inform us as to the essences of the primary qualities themselves, nor as to which primary qualities cause which sensations, since we already know these things before we consult science – know them "by our senses" (EIP II, xvii [314b]), that is, by perception. Of hardness, for example, "we have as clear and distinct a conception as of any thing whatsoever. The cohesion of the parts of a body with more or less force, is perfectly understood, though its cause is not. We know what it is, as well as how it affects the touch. It is therefore a quality of a quite different order from . . . secondary qualities . . . , whereof we know no more naturally, than that they are adapted to raise certain sensations in us" (IHM V, iv [123a; B 61]). If hardness were a secondary quality, like color,

it would be a proper inquiry for philosophers, what hardness in bodies is? and we should have had various hypotheses about it, as well as about colour and heat. But it is evident that any such hypothesis would be ridiculous. If any man should say, that hardness in bodies is a certain vibration of their parts, or that it is certain effluvia emitted by them which affect our touch in the manner we feel: such hypothesis would shock common sense; because we all know, that if the parts of a body adhere strongly, it is hard, although it should neither emit effluvia, nor vibrate. (IHM V, iv [123a; B. 61–2])

Secondary qualities also "involve" – to speak loosely again – dispositions to cause sensations of certain sorts in perceivers. And of course these dispositions have a physical basis. As in the case of primary qualities our initial question, then, is whether secondary qualities are to be identified with those dispositions or with the physical basis of those dispositions. Unfortunately, Reid's attention is so much focused on other points in his analysis that he doesn't speak consistently on the matter. In the *Inquiry* he says, for example, that color "is a certain power or virtue in bodies" (VI, iv [138a; B 87]; cf. II, ix [114a; B 43]), whereas in the *Essays* he says that "smell in the rose is an unknown quality or modification" in the rose (II, xvii [314b]; cf. IHM V, i [119b; B 54]). If green were a disposition in things to cause certain sensations under certain conditions and not the physical basis of that disposition, we would know what it was.

A way to highlight the difference is to consider a counterfactual situation. Just as it was possible for God to attach the disposition to cause pressure sensations to a different physical basis from that to which this disposition is in fact attached, so also it was possible for God to attach the disposition to cause "green-type" sensations to a different physical basis. So suppose God had done so. In that alternative world, would the greenness of objects have a different physical basis, or would the greenness of objects no longer have the disposition to cause "green-type" sensations in perceivers? Were Reid to choose the former of these alternatives, that would show that he was thinking of secondary qualities as identical with certain dispositions – no matter what the physical basis of those dispositions. Were he to choose the latter, that would show that he was thinking of secondary qualities as certain physical bases, no matter what the dispositions attached to those bases.

My own view is that reflection on this counterfactual situation makes it pretty clear that colors are the dispositions, not the physical bases which those dispositions happen to have in our world; and that secondary qualities are, in this way, significantly different from primary qualities. It's my impression that most of the time, though by no means always, Reid instead thinks of secondary qualities as the physical bases, since he regularly says that we know not what they are. The inconsistency, while regrettable, seldom if ever makes any difference to the points he's concerned to make; his attention, as I said, is elsewhere than on this issue. For convenience of exposition, though, a choice must be made. Because it appears to me that Reid's dominant tendency is to think of secondary qualities as the physical bases rather than as the dispositions, let me henceforth speak in that fashion. It would not be difficult to reformulate everything along the lines of the alternative understanding.

A point Reid does emphasize is that while in vision, for example, certain aspects of our sensations function as indicators of those qualities that are the colors of the perceived objects, it is those objective qualities that are the colors, not our subjective sensations nor any qualities thereof. This is true, at least, if we are using words in the ordinary way. By color, he says,

all men, who have not been tutored by modern philosophy, understand, not a sensation of the mind, which can have no existence when it is not perceived, but a quality or modification of bodies, which continues to be the same, whether it is seen or not. The scarlet rose, which is before me, is still a scarlet rose when I shut my eyes, and was so at midnight when no eye saw it. The colour remains when the appearance ceases: it remains the same when the appearance changes. . . . The common language of mankind shows evidently, that we ought to distinguish between the colour of a body, which is conceived to be a fixed and permanent quality in the body, and the appearances of that colour to the eye, which may be varied a thousand ways, by a variation of the light, of the medium, or of the eye itself. (IHM VI, iv [137a–b; B 85–6])

We can now see more than we could before of what Reid has in mind when he speaks of the sensory experiences ingredient in perception as "signs" of the perceived entities – in particular, of perceived qualities. The color of my desk blotter is green. It retains that color whether or not I'm looking at it – whether anybody is looking at it. Likewise it retains that color when it's in the dark, and throughout different colors of light being shone upon it. Lastly, several of us can see the color of the blotter. The sensory experience I have when perceiving the blotter is very different: It does not abide as the color of the blotter abides, nor can anybody else see it. It's odd even to speak of me as "seeing" it. So what then is the relation of the sensory experience I have when perceiving the color of the blotter, to that color itself? Well, it's an *indicator* of the color, a *sign* of the color – an indicator which, of course, is caused by the color itself.[17] Could we also speak of the sensation as an *appearance* of the blotter's color? Yes, Reid speaks of it that way too; later we'll see why.[18]

As already indicated, Reid holds that an important feature of secondary qualities, distinguishing them from primary ones, is that we do not know by perception what they are. If we are ever to know, science will have to teach us:

If you ask me, what is that quality or modification in a rose which I call its smell, I am at a loss to answer directly. Upon reflection I find, that I have a distinct notion of the sensation which it produces in my mind. But there can be nothing like to this sensation in the rose, because it is insentient. The quality in the rose is something which occasions the sensation in me; but what that something is, I know not. My senses give me no information upon this point. The only notion therefore my senses give is this, that smell in the rose is an unknown quality or modification, which is the cause or occasion of a sensation which I know well. The relation which this unknown quality bears to the sensation with which nature has connected it, is all I learn from the sense of smelling: but this is evidently a relative notion. (EIP II, xvii [314a–b])[19]

---

[17] "Such an immense variety of sensations of smell, taste, and sound, surely was not given us in vain. They are signs, by which we know and distinguish things without us; and it was fit that the variety of the signs should in some degree correspond with the variety of the things signified by them" (IHM IV, i [117a; B 49]). What secondary qualities definitely are *not* is resemblances of external qualities: "although colour is really a quality of body, yet it is not represented to the mind by an idea of sensation that resembles it; on the contrary, it is suggested by an idea which does not in the least resemble it" (IHM VI, vi [140a; B 90]).

[18] "When I see an object, the appearance which the colour of it makes, may be called the *sensation*, which suggests to me some external thing as its cause" (IHM VI, viii [145a; B 99]).

[19] Cf. EIP II, xvii [313b–314a]: "there appears to me to be a real foundation for the distinction [between primary and secondary qualities]; and it is this: that our senses give us a direct and distinct notion of the primary qualities, and inform us what they are in themselves: but of the secondary qualities, our senses give us only a relative and obscure notion. They inform us only, that they are qualities that effect us in a certain manner, that is, produce in us a certain sensation; but as to what they are in themselves, our senses leave us in the dark. . . .

"I observed further, that the notion we have of primary qualities is direct, and not relative only. A relative notion of a thing, is, strictly speaking, no notion of the thing at all, but only of some relation which it bears to something else. . . .

"Thus I think it appears, that there is a real foundation for the distinction of primary from secondary qualities; and that they are distinguished by this, that of the primary we have by our senses a direct and distinct notion; but of the secondary only a relative notion, which must, because it is only relative, be obscure; they are conceived only as the unknown causes or occasions of certain sensations with which we are well acquainted."

It is, of course, the relation of distinct secondary qualities to distinct sorts of sensory experiences that enables us to pick them out – to get distinct secondary qualities in mind. We get a grip on them by the use of "relative notions"; this is the only way we can get a mental grip on them. "The blotter is green," I say. The quality that I thereby pick out and attribute to the blotter is that quality in objects which is the physical basis of the disposition to cause "green-type" sensations in properly functioning percipients in standard conditions. (Alternatively, it's that disposition itself not its physical basis.)

When we think or speak of any particular colour, however simple the notion may seem to be, which is presented to the imagination, it is really in some sort compounded. It involves an unknown cause, and a known effect. The name of *colour* belongs indeed to the cause only, and not to the effect. But as the cause is unknown, we can form no distinct conception of it, but by its relation to the known effect. . . . When I would conceive those colours of bodies which we call *scarlet* and *blue*, if I conceived them only as unknown qualities, I could perceive no distinction between the one and the other. I must therefore, for the sake of distinction, join to each of them, in my imagination, some effect or some relation that is peculiar. And the most obvious distinction is, the appearance which one and the other makes to the eye. (IHM VI, iv [138a; B 86–7])

ORIGINAL AND ACQUIRED PERCEPTIONS

A question suggested ineluctably by the preceding discussion, as by the text of Reid himself, is this: "*Which* conception and *which* belief?" Over and over we've been told that perception of an object occurs when a sensation that is an indicatory effect of the object evokes a conception of the object and a belief, about the object, that it exists as external – or a belief that implies that. This is Reid's account of that experiential objectivation that lies at the heart of perception.

"Which conception?" we want to know, and "Which belief?" The answer is: It doesn't matter. It doesn't matter what one believes, about the object about which one believes something, just provided that one believes about it that it exists as external (or believes what implies this). And it doesn't matter what is the mental grip one gets on the object, just provided one gets a firm enough grip on it for one to have a belief about it. The most rudimentary conceptual apprehensions will presumably be by means of such singular concepts as *the thing I'm smelling, the thing I'm tasting, the thing I'm feeling.* Sometimes I get some external object in mind with the singular concept, *the thing I'm presently seeing,* and believe about that object that it is a green blotter; sometimes I get that same object in mind with the singular concept, *the blotter I'm seeing,* and believe about it that it is green. It makes no difference.

That is by no means the extent of what Reid wants to say about the evoked beliefs, however. For recall, the sensations ingredient in perception are signs, indicators, of the objects that cause them; and we get our knowledge of the external world by reading those signs, interpreting those indicators. Normally my sensory experience does not just evoke in me the utterly rudimentary thought, about what I'm seeing, that it is external; it evokes in me the belief, say, that what I'm seeing is a green blotter, or that the blotter I'm seeing is green. Reid introduces his distinction between original and acquired perceptions in his attempt to tell us something more about what accounts for the way we interpret our sensory experience – something more about what accounts for why sensory experiences evoke the objectivating beliefs that they do evoke.

Recall that, for Reid, one of the fundamental goals of an analysis of mental life is to discover the original principles of the human mind – the "hard wiring"; and then, by reference to those, to explain the other workings of the mind. Of the workings of our original principles we can give no explanation – other than to declare that things work that way because that's how our Creator makes them work. A good deal of Reid's disagreement with the Way of Ideas theorists was over the identification of the original principles of the mind – the identification of our hard wiring. When one surveys the whole of Reid's view and compares it to the Way of Ideas, it's obvious that Reid regarded our hard wiring as much more elaborate than the Way of Ideas theorists were willing to concede. In other words, he thought much less could be explained than they thought.

Let's now have a passage before us in which Reid draws the distinction between original and acquired beliefs by citing examples:

Our perceptions are of two kinds: some are natural and original, others acquired, and the fruit of experience. When I perceive that this is the taste of cider, that of brandy; that this is the smell of an apple, that of an orange; . . . these perceptions and others of the same kind, are not original, they are acquired. But the perception which I have by touch, of the hardness and softness of bodies, of their extension, figure, and motion, is not acquired; it is original. . . . By [sight] we perceive originally the visible figure and colour of bodies only, and their visible place but we learn to perceive by the eye, almost every thing which we can perceive by touch. (IHM VI, xx [184b–185a; B 171])

At the ground level of perception there has to be some hard wiring connecting distinct sensory experiences with distinct conceptions and beliefs. Reid concedes that before this hard wiring can do its work some maturation must have taken place. One must possess the concept of existence, or be capable of having it evoked in one, if one is to believe, of the object of one's apprehension, that it exists. Since infants have presumably not yet matured to that extent, they are not capable of perception; they cannot perform the objectivation that constitutes the core of perception. Yet it is by virtue of the original principles of our constitution that certain tactile sensations evoke in us apprehensions of, and beliefs about, hardness, extension, figure, and motion, and that certain visual sensations evoke in us apprehensions of, and beliefs about, color.

What happens in the course of experience, then, is that sensations acquire powers of suggestion well behind those that they have by virtue of our hard wiring. That is to say, they acquire the disposition to evoke many other apprehensions and beliefs than those that they evoke by virtue of one's hard wiring. Certain perceptions also acquire such powers.[20]

The way sensations and perceptions acquire these additional powers is as follows: There is in all of us the disposition to acquire customs or habits. This is one of the original principles of our constitution (Reid calls it the "inductive" principle.) It's repetition of one sort and another that accounts for the activation of this disposition, and thus, for the acquisition of a particular habit

---

[20] "In original perception, the signs are the various sensations which are produced by the impressions made upon our organs. . . . In acquired perception, the sign may be either a sensation, or something originally perceived" (EIP II, xxi [332a]).

or custom. In the case before us, it's the repeated observation of a constant, or nearly constant, conjunction in nature that accounts for the formation of the relevant custom or habit. Many times over I smell this particular objective fragrance when I see that I am in the vicinity of a rose. Eventually a custom or habit is formed in me so that now, upon smelling that objective fragrance, I believe of it that it's the fragrance of a rose. (Alternatively, a custom or habit is formed in me so that now, upon having a certain olfactory sensation, I believe, of that objective fragrance which I'm smelling, that it's the fragrance of a rose. Nota bene: It's not about my olfactory sensation that I believe it's the fragrance of a rose; it's about that objective secondary quality that I'm smelling.)

Reid rather often describes the product of an acquired perception as if it were the perception of a fact; one of the examples he cites in the passage quoted above is the perception "that this is the taste of cider." But though that's a natural way of putting the point he has in mind, it's also somewhat misleading. Recall that in the example cited, the rose is absent. Hence I don't perceive the *fact* that this is the fragrance of a rose; I do that when I get up close to a rose and both see the rose and smell the fragrance – just as I perceive the fact that the clock shows one o'clock when I look at a clock showing one o'clock. Reid's thought, concerning the case we've been considering, is that the olfactory sensation evokes in me, by virtue of an original principle of the mind, an apprehension of that objective quality that I am smelling; and then, by virtue of the custom that I have acquired, I believe of it that it is the fragrance of a rose. I believe it to be the fragrance of a rose.

Why call this a "perception," Reid asks? Why say that I *perceive* this to be the fragrance of a rose? One consideration is that this is how we do in fact speak.[21] But there's also a systematic, or theoretical, consideration in favor of classifying these cases

---

[21] Cf. EIP II, xxii [336b]: "That [acquired perceptions] are formed even in infancy no man can doubt; nor is it less certain that they are confounded with the natural and immediate perception of sense, and in all languages are called by the same name. We are therefore authorized by language to call them perception, and must often do so, or speak unintelligibly. But philosophy teaches us in this, as in many other instances, to distinguish things which the vulgar confound. I have therefore given the name of acquired perception to such conclusions, to distinguish them from what is naturally, originally, and immediately testified by our senses."

under perception: They fit the analysis of perception Reid arrived at when he had his eye on original perceptions. Perception, he says,

> ought not only to be distinguished from sensation, but likewise from that knowledge of the objects of sense which is got by reasoning. There is no reasoning in perception, as hath been observed. The belief which is implied in it, is the effect of instinct. . . . There are many things, with regard to sensible objects, which we can infer from what we perceive; and such conclusions of reason ought to be distinguished from what is merely perceived. When I look at the moon, I perceive her to be sometimes circular, sometimes horned, and sometimes gibbous. This is simple perception, and is the same in the philosopher, and in the clown: but from these various appearances of her enlightened part, I infer that she is really of a spherical figure. This conclusion is not obtained by simple perception, but by reasoning. . . . Perception, whether original or acquired, implies no exercise of reason; and is common to men, children, idiots, and brutes. (IHM VI, xx [185a–185b; B 172–3])[22]

FROM APPEARANCE TO REALITY

The preceding section enriched our understanding of how sensory experience functions as sign and indicator of the objective world. When we first introduced Reid's notion of sensory experience as sign, the thought was that sensory experience, far from being identical with objective and abiding primary and secondary qualities, is but a subjective and transitory indicator of them. It's a source of information about them, on account of having been appropriately caused by them. Perception involves reading the signs, interpreting the indicators. Some of that interpreting occurs on account of our hard wiring; at the bottom of all our interpreting there must be some hermeneutic hard wiring.

---

[22] Reid concedes that it's sometimes "difficult to trace the line which divides" acquired perceptions from reasoning (IHM VI, xx [186a; B 173]). An additional point is this: though perception itself involves no reasoning, that leaves it open as to whether the acquisition of the habits which account for acquired perceptions involves reasoning. Reid indicates that though he has a view on the matter, it makes no difference for his main argument: "Whether this acquired perception is to be resolved into some process of reasoning, of which we have lost the remembrance, as some philosophers think, or whether it results from some part of our constitution distinct from reason, as I rather believe, does not concern the present subject" (EIP II, xxii [336b]). Whatever it may be that accounts for the acquisition of the custom or habit, the issue, when it comes to perception, is only whether, on account of the custom, the belief is formed immediately.

We have now seen, however, that most of that interpreting occurs on account of customs and habits that we have acquired. Our sensory experiences have vastly more potential as indicators than our hard wiring is equipped to interpret. It's only on account of our acquisition of the requisite customs that most of the informational potential of our sensations can be interpreted – in the perceptual way, not the inferential and theoretical way. This particular olfactory sensation is an indicator of the fragrance of brandy. It may be by virtue of my hard wiring that I interpret it as an indicator of an objective fragrance; it's certainly not by virtue of my hard wiring that I interpret it as an indicator of the fragrance of brandy.

Now, as we follow Reid's discussion on appearance and reality, our understanding of the indicative, signifying function of sensory experience will be yet further enriched. Let's start with a few examples that Reid gives of the phenomenon that he now wants to analyze. The phenomenon turns up mainly, though not exclusively, in vision.

A book or a chair has a different appearance to the eye, in every different distance and position; yet we conceive it to be still the same; and overlooking the appearance, we immediately conceive the real figure, distance, and position of the body, of which its visible or perspective appearance is a sign and indication.

When I see a man at a distance of ten yards, and afterward see him at the distance of a hundred yards his visible appearance in its length, breadth, and all its linear proportions, is ten times less in the last case than it is in the first: yet I do not conceive him one inch diminished by this diminution of his visible figure. Nay, I do not in the least attend to this diminution, even when I draw from it the conclusion, without perceiving that ever the premises entered the mind. A thousand such instances might be produced, in order to show that the visible appearances of objects are intended by nature only as signs or indications; and that the mind passes instantly to the things signified, without making the least reflection upon the sign, or even perceiving that there is any such thing. . . . the visible appearance of objects is a kind of language used by nature, to inform us of their distance, magnitude, and figure . . . . (IHM VI, ii [135a; B 81–2])

In the preceding section we saw that our ability to immediately interpret the information about the external world carried by sensory experience is vastly expanded by our acquisition of customs of the right sort. Now we see that sometimes the sensory experiences are indicators in a quite special way. They are *appearances* of objects, when the objects are other than how they appear.

If green things never produced in us anything other than greenlike sensory experiences, if cold things never produced in us anything other than cold sensations, and so forth, then we would have no use for the appearance/reality distinction in describing physical reality; our challenge as objectivating interpreters of our sensory experience would be confined to the challenges described earlier. But of course that's not how it is, and not how it could be, given various laws of nature. So a great deal of what goes into our immediate objectivating interpretation of experience is that, taking the signs to be appearances, we read off what the object is really like from how it is appearing to us.

This sort of interpretation, insofar as it is a component of perception, happens automatically – "immediately and ineluctably," in Reid's words. And Reid argues that because we so naturally, immediately, and ineluctably move from appearance to objectivating beliefs about the reality that is thus appearing, it's often difficult, and sometimes impossible, to note how the thing is actually appearing. That the north wall of the room appears to me somewhat darker than the west wall is something I could notice, though usually I don't; I just immediately believe, of the room I'm looking at, that its walls are all painted the same color. That the man farther away appears shorter than the one of the same size who's closer is something that most of us cannot manage to take note of – not, at least, without the removal of all those features that serve as cues that we're dealing with relative distance from the eye rather than with difference of size.

Reid observes that it's the artists among us who are most skilled at taking note of how things appear to us and not just rushing to judgment as to how they are. Their profession requires of them that they be skilled at this:

I cannot . . . entertain the hope of being intelligible to those readers who have not, by pains and practice, acquired the habit of distinguishing the appearances of objects to the eye, from the judgment which we form by sight, of their colour, distance, magnitude, and figure. The only profession in life wherein it is necessary to make this distinction, is that of painting. The painter hath occasion for an abstraction, with regard to visible objects somewhat similar to that which we here require: and this indeed is the most difficult part of his art. For it is evident, that if he could fix in his imagination the visible appearance of things, without confounding it with the things signified by that appearance, it would be as easy for him to paint from the life, and to give every figure its proper shading and relief, and its perspective proportions, as it is to paint from a copy. Perspective, shading, giving relief, and colouring, are nothing else but copying the appearance which things make to the eye. (IHM VI, iii [135b; B 82–3])

A final question here: What accounts for this capacity and disposition of ours to construe objective reality as *being* a certain way on the basis of sensory experiences which, as such, only present to us how things appear? Possibly a bit of hard wiring is involved; but Reid's view is that most of such objectivating interpretations are a special case of acquired perceptions.

To a man newly made to see, the visible appearance of objects would be the same as to us; but he would see nothing at all of their real dimensions, as we do. He could form no conjecture, by means of his sight only, how many inches or feet they were in length, breadth, or thickness. He could perceive little or nothing of their real figure; nor could he discern that this was a cube, that a sphere; that this was a cone, and that a cylinder. . . . The habit of a man or of a woman, which appeared to us of one uniform colour, variously folded and shaded, would present to his eye neither fold nor shade, but variety of colour. . . . [His eyes] would indeed present the same appearances to him as they do to us, and speak the same language; but to him it is an unknown language; and therefore he would attend only to the signs, without knowing the signification of them: whereas to us it is a language perfectly familiar; and therefore we take no notice of the signs, but attend only to the things signified by them. (IHM VI, iii [136b–137a; B 84–5])

Though Reid refers to illusions at various points in his discussion – optical, tactile, and so forth – he never takes the time to offer an analysis of such phenomena within the framework of his theory. So let me ask, on his behalf, what a Reidian style of analysis would look like for these special cases of appearance diverging from reality. Consider the Müller–Lyer illusion:

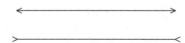

The relative length of the lines appears different from how it really is. The lines appear to be of different lengths when in reality they are of the same length. What makes this case an illusion, rather than an ordinary discrepancy between appearance and reality, is that our interpreting equipment doesn't do the corrective work that it does in those appearance/reality cases that are not illusions. If the sensory experience does immediately evoke in us a belief about the comparative length of the lines, it will be the belief that the lines are of unequal length; but this belief is false. Of course, lots of the beliefs immediately evoked by looking at the lines will be true ones. The fundamental objectivating belief that what I'm seeing is a component of my environment will be evoked; and that's true. But the belief, about the lines I'm seeing, that they are of unequal length, will be false.

So far, no problem for Reid's theory; the hard wiring along with the acquired customs which together account for our immediate interpretations of sensory experience don't always yield truth. The skeptic will seize on this sort of case as evidence for the unreliability of the senses; in Chapter VIII we'll see what Reid has to say to the skeptic. However, nothing in Reid's theory of perception requires that the immediately evoked interpretative beliefs always be true.

But let's look deeper. When I myself look at a case of the Müller–Lyer illusion, I'm not fooled. The illusion did, once upon a time, do its deceiving work on me; but it doesn't any more. I don't come out believing that the lines are of different length. Though the New Theory of Representation, to which I earlier referred, is Reidian in many respects, its representatives have used this particular fact to argue against a central point in Reid's own theory. The objectivation that lies at the core of perception cannot consist, so they argue, in the formation of beliefs about the external world; it has to consist in something else. For in the case of illusions that we have "seen through," our environment is represented to us as being a certain way without our believing that it is that way. Thus the phenomenon of one's environment being represented to one as being a certain way cannot be identified with the phenomenon of immediately believing about one's environment that it is a certain way.[23]

---

[23] See Christopher Peacocke, *Sense and Content* (Oxford: Clarendon Press, 1983), p. 6: "A man may be familiar with a perfect *trompe l'oeil* violin painted on a door, and be sure from his past experience that it is a *trompe l'oeil*: nevertheless his experience may continue to represent a violin as hanging on the door in front of him. The possibility of such independence is one of the marks of the content of experience as opposed to the content of judgment."

This is an argument that, if cogent, strikes at the heart of Reid's theory. But I do not find it compelling. The New Theorists hold that what remains constant, before and after I have "seen through" the illusion, is that my environment is represented to me – objectivated for me – as being a certain way; specifically, that my environment is represented to me as containing lines of different length. But I fail to see that that's what remains constant. What remains constant is how the lines appear to me; the sensory appearance continues to be of lines of different length. What has changed is that my objectivating interpretative equipment has been inhibited. The belief is no longer formed in me that the lines are of different lengths. The formation of that belief has been inhibited by my bringing to the experience my belief, about the Müller–Lyer illusion, that the lines are of the same length. This is a belief that I arrived at inferentially; I once took out a ruler and measured, and now remember having done that. I now hold the belief that they are of the same length independently of the interpretative workings of my hard wiring and acquired customs for this sort of sensory appearance. So do I now perceive them to be of the *same* length? No, not that either – at least not on Reid's account of perception. I *believe* that they are of the same length, but I don't *perceive* it; since the belief that they are of the same length is not evoked in me immediately by the appearance.[24]

In short, when looking at the Müller–Lyer illusion, after I have "seen through" it, my environment is not perceptually represented to me as containing lines of unequal length; though it continues to appear that way, it's no longer represented to me that way.

REID'S ANALYSIS OF HALLUCINATORY PHENOMENA

In Chapter II, section xviii of the *Intellectual Powers*, and again in Chapter II, section xxii, Reid describes certain "disorders" of the mind and brain that various writers of his day called "deceptions of the senses," and which they cited as evidence for "the falla-

---

[24] The following passage leads me to surmise that Reid would also handle illusions that we have "seen through" in the way I have suggested above: "A man who has had his leg cut off, many years after feels pain in a toe of that leg. The toe has now no existence; and he perceives easily, that the toe can neither be the place, nor the subject of the pain which he feels; yet it is the same feeling he used to have from a hurt in the toe; and if he did not know that his leg was cut off it would give him the same immediate conviction of some hurt or disorder in the toe" (EIP II, xviii [320b]).

ciousness of the senses." As one would expect, Reid disputes the conclusion: "We must acknowledge it to be the lot of human nature, that all the human faculties are liable, by accidental causes, to be hurt, and unfitted for their natural functions, either wholly or in part: but as this imperfection is common to them all, it gives no just ground for accounting any one of them fallacious more than another" (EIP II, xxii [338b]).[25] From a consideration of Reid's thought here my conclusion will be that if we give full interpretive weight to Reid's analysis of hallucinatory phenomena – and I'm not at all sure we should – we must slightly revise his analysis of perception as I have thus far expounded it

Begin with Reid's description of the sort of disorders he has in mind: "In a delirium, or in madness, perception, memory, imagination, and our reasoning powers, are strangely disordered and confounded. There are likewise disorders which affect some of our senses, while others are sound. Thus a man may feel pain in his toes after the leg is cut off. He may feel a little ball double, by crossing his fingers. He may see an object double, by not directing both eyes properly to it. By pressing the ball of his eye, he may see colours that are not real. By the jaundice in his eyes, he may mistake colours" (ibid.).

The first point Reid makes in his analysis is that the "disorder" or "fallacy" in such cases has to be located in the perception component of the experience, not in the sensation component: "for we are conscious of all our sensations and they can neither be any other in their nature, nor greater or less in their degree than we feel them. It is impossible that a man should be in pain, when he does not feel pain; and when he feels pain, it is impossible that his pain should not be real, and in its degree what it is felt to be: and the same thing may be said of every sensation whatsoever. . . . If, therefore, there be any fallacy in our senses, it must be in the perception of external objects . . ." (EIP II, xxii [335a]). The person suffering from hallucination represents his environment as being or appearing a certain way; if that weren't the case, there would be no hallucination. The disorder, the malfunction, has to be located in that representation, that objectivation. But how are we to describe what it is about that objectivation that is disordered?

---

[25] The point of the last clause is that it gives no reason to regard sensory perception as more fallacious than, say, reason and introspection.

Well, consider a person who, as we say, "feels pain in his toe" after his leg has been cut off. Reid says that the "deceit" in such a case is to be located "in the seeming perception he had of a disorder in his toe. This perception, which nature had conjoined with the sensation, was in this instance fallacious" (EIP II, xviii [320b]).

Located in the "seeming perception." What's that? What becomes clear as Reid proceeds is that a "seeming perception" is not something that seems to be a perception but is not; it's a perception that's *deceptive.* "Seeming" is a synonym for "deceptive." Immediately after the passage quoted, in which Reid speaks of a "seeming perception," he goes on to cite a variety of hallucinatory and illusionary phenomena; he then concludes by saying that "in these, and other like cases, the sensations we have are real, and the deception is only in the perception that nature has annexed to them" (ibid.).

We haven't made much of an advance. All we've learned is that Reid does not identify the disordering that takes place in hallucination with the *absence* of a perception and its replacement with something else; he identifies it with the *disordering* of perception. Perception still takes place; but it's disordered perception.

What exactly is the disorder? Well, given Reid's general analysis of perception, we expect him to locate the disorder in some abnormality of the conception or the belief. And so he does. Let's have the crucial passage before us:

Nature has connected our perception of external objects with certain sensations. If the sensation is produced, the corresponding perception follows even when there is no object, and in that case is apt to deceive us. In like manner, nature has connected our sensations with certain impressions that are made upon the nerve and brain: and, when the impression is made, from whatever cause, the corresponding sensation and perception immediately follows. Thus, in the man who feels pain in his toe after the leg is cut off, the nerve that went to the toe, part of which was cut off with the leg, had the same impression made upon the remaining part, which, in the natural state of his body, was caused by a hurt in the toe: and immediately this impression is followed by the sensation and perception which nature connected with it. (EIP II, xviii [320b–321a])

In hallucinatory perceptions there's no object of the perception – that is to say, there's no external object apprehended, and none about which one believes that it exists as external. That comes about like this: God has ordained that we human beings, in this present existence of ours, would only have a perception of an external object in the circumstance that that object causes neural impulses, which in turn cause a certain brain state, which in turn causes a certain sensation, which in turn – by virtue of inexplicable natural laws – causes a conception of, and belief about, that object. Now in hallucinations the brain state appropriate to the perception of an object occurs and causes the sensation, conception, and belief that it's been hard wired to cause, without itself being caused by an object. Thus in this case we have the sort of apprehension and the sort of belief appropriate to perception of an object, but they don't in fact attach to any object. Hence, perception without an object. Object-less perception. The disorder consists in the conception and belief lacking an object. That's how Reid is thinking.

One response that you and I are powerfully inclined to make, formed as we are by Wittgenstein and Oxford Language Philosophy, is that Reid is abusing the language. "Perception" is a success term: If I perceive, then there exists something such that I perceive it.

This objection would not just roll off Reid's back. It would sting him, for he prided himself on speaking with the vulgar. But it would not be decisive. Granted that he used the word "perception" in an aberrant way. No matter. His point is this: What happens in hallucination is that some sensation evokes the sort of conception and belief characteristic of perception without that conception and belief, in this case, having any object. The disorder lies in the lack of external object for conception and belief.

Let's reflect a bit on the proposal itself, not worrying about the use and abuse of language. Begin with the following ringing passage; many others making the same points could be cited instead:

Although there is no reasoning in perception, yet there are certain means and instruments, which, by the appointment of nature, must intervene between the object and our perception of it; and, by these our perceptions are limited and regulated. First, if the object is not in contact with the organ of sense, there must be some medium which passes between them . . . ; otherwise we have no perception. Secondly, there must be some action or impression upon the organ of sense, either by the immediate application of the object, or by the medium that goes between them. Thirdly, the nerves which go from the brain to the organ, must receive some impression by means of that which was made upon the organ; and probably, by means of the nerves some impression must be made upon the brain. Fourthly, the impression made upon the organ, nerves, and brain, is followed by a sensation. And, last of all, this sensation is followed by the perception of the object. (IHM VI, xxi [186a–b; B 174])

We've known for some time that Reid wants this passage to be read with the understanding that in good measure he is laying out causal necessities, not logical necessities. God could have created us with a different design plan for perception from that with which he did in fact create us; what's described here is just the design plan that we do in fact have. But now we learn that the passage is to be read with an important additional understanding. We are to read the passage as only describing how things go when we are functioning properly. They don't always go that way. One way in which we can function abnormally is that some brain state appropriate for perception may occur without the normal causal antecedents thereof occurring – those causal antecedents which, if things were working properly, would cause that sort of brain state. In such a case, the brain state may still do its downstream work, with the consequence that perception occurs, but without there being any object of the perception.

So far, no problem. But now let's look at those conceptions and beliefs that Reid identifies as lying at the very core of perception. I have all along interpreted Reid as using "conception" in such a way that if one has a conception, then there exists some entity of which one has that conception. I have likewise all along interpreted him as holding that the sort of belief that is ingredient in perception is a *de re*/predicative belief; and that some mental entity is a *de re*/predicative belief only if there exists some entity such that, in holding the belief, one believes something about that entity. In short, I have interpreted him as picking out, with the words "conception" and "belief," certain *relationships* between mind and reality. Then on the central issue I have interpreted him as contending that the objectivation that constitutes the essence of perception consists in believing, about something in one's environment, that it exists as external. This interpretation is powerfully suggested by a multitude of passages – for example, the one quoted earlier in this chapter: the perception of an external object consists of

First, Some conviction or notion of the object perceived. *Secondly,* A strong and irresistible conviction and belief of its present existence. And, *thirdly,* That this conviction and belief are immediate, and not the effect of reasoning. (EIP II, v [258a])

But these mind-to-world relationships are missing in the case of hallucination. There's no object, and hence no relationship of mind to world. All we have are two sorts of purely mental phenomena, two sorts of *noematic* phenomena (from the Greek: *noema* = thought), not two sorts of relationships of mind to world. The world isn't of the right sort for there to be the relationships – the relationship of the mind, to some external object, of apprehending it, and the relationship of the mind, to that same external object, of believing something about it. Of course the person suffering from the hallucination *believes* that there are those relationships; but she's wrong about that, there aren't.

So what to do? One thing to do would be to alter our interpretation of Reid: When he over and over uses the formula "conception and belief of an external object," to understand him as claiming that the objectivation that lies at the heart of perception consists of sensations immediately evoking mental phenomena that the person *believes to be* about entities in the environment and that are of such a sort that they *would be* about the environment if the environment were of the right sort.

That seems to me not the best course, however – for the reason that over and over Reid says that whereas we can conceive things that don't exist (namely, universals), we cannot perceive or be conscious of things that don't exist, nor remember things that never existed: "What never had an existence cannot be remembered; what has no existence *at present* cannot be the object of perception or of consciousness" (EIP I, i [223a]).[26] Given this repetitive claim on Reid's part, what he should have said about hallucination is that it *seems* to the person suffering the hallucination that he is having objectivated experience, when he is not – that is, his sensations are evoking in him mental phenomena

---

[26] To cite just one additional passage: "It seems to be admitted as a first principle by the learned and the unlearned, that what is really perceived must exist, and that to perceive what does not exist is impossible" (EIP II, viii [274b]).

which seem to him to be apprehensions of, and beliefs about, external objects, when they are not that. The world is not of the right sort for them to be that; and that comes about because the sensations which evoke these pseudo-apprehensions and these pseudo *de re* beliefs were brought about in an aberrant way. They were not in fact functioning to transmit information about the external world. What's abnormal about hallucination is that the person suffering the hallucination thinks that information processing is going on when it isn't. Our articulation of the standard schema should not be revised.

ON BEING UNCERTAIN WHEN ONE IS PERCEIVING

Let me close this discussion of Reid's theory of perception by reflecting on a puzzling passage:

In perception we not only have a notion more or less distinct of the object perceived, but also an irresistible conviction and belief of its existence. This is always the case when we are certain that we perceive it. There may be a perception so faint and indistinct, as to leave us in doubt whether we perceive the object or not. Thus, when a star begins to twinkle as the light of the sun withdraws, one may, for a short time, think he sees it, without being certain, until the perception acquires some strength and steadiness. When a ship just begins to appear in the utmost verge of the horizon, we may at first be dubious whether we perceive it or not: but when the perception is in any degree clear and steady, there remains no doubt of its reality; and when the reality of the perception is ascertained, the existence of the object perceived can no longer be doubted. (EIP II, v [258b])

There definitely seems something right about the point Reid is making here. Yet, on the theory of perception he has constructed it is puzzling. The heart of perception, he has told us, consists in immediate and ineluctable objectivation. Over and over he sounds the theme. "We are never said to *perceive* things, of the existence of which we have not a full conviction" (EIP I, i [322a]). Now he tells us that if we are uncertain as to whether we are perceiving, objectivation may well not occur. But what can this claim come to, on his theory: If I am certain that objectivation is taking place, then it is; but if I am in doubt, then it may not be. That is to say, given Reid's analysis of objectivation, if I am certain that my sensations have evoked an apprehension of, and an immediate belief about, some external object, then they have evoked those; whereas if I am in doubt on the matter, then possibly they have not evoked those. What sense does this make?

I think one can see what Reid was driving at. In some situations one is uncertain whether one's sensory experience is an indicatory effect of some external object; this will especially be the case when one's sensory experience is "faint and distinct." In such situations of uncertainty, objectivation will be inhibited; it will be inhibited even if, as a matter of fact, the sensory experience *is* an indicatory effect of an object. Admittedly this is not what Reid says. What he says is not that one's sensory experience is faint and indistinct but that one's *perception* is faint and indistinct. My interpretation assumes that Reid is speaking loosely here, not strictly.

Given my interpretation, I offer a correction on one small point. Reid appears to divide the cases into those in which one is certain, and those in which one is in doubt. I think the division should instead be between those cases in which one is in doubt and all the others. In the normal run of events, I don't hold with certainty the belief, about my sensory experience, that it is an indicative effect of some external object. The reason I don't hold it with certainty is that I don't hold it at all. I do indeed do something like *take the proposition for granted.*[27] But I don't believe it; it doesn't cross my mind. Perception occurs nonetheless. Objectivation doesn't require believing that one's sensory experience is an indicative effect of some external object; certainly it doesn't require believing it with certainty. All it requires is that I don't doubt that my sensory experience is an indicative effect of some external object. If I do doubt, *that doubt* then functions as an inhibitor on objectivation.

---

[27] We'll be talking more about this phenomenon of *taking for granted* in Chapters VIII and IX.

CHAPTER VI

An Exception (or Two) to
Reid's Standard Schema

We have been exploring the standard schema, as I called it, which Reid proposes for the analysis of what transpires in perception. The schema is this: The perceived entity evokes in the mind a sensation that is a sign of itself; this in turn evokes an apprehension of that entity and an immediate belief as to its external existence (or a belief which entails that). Here's how Reid himself states the schema in one passage: "The signs in original perception are sensations, of which nature hath given us a great variety, suited to the variety of the things signified by them. Nature hath established a real connection between the signs and the things signified; and nature hath also taught us the interpretation of the signs; so that, previous to experience, the sign suggests the things signified, and [immediately] creates the belief of it" (IHM VI, xxiv [195a; B 190]). Acquired perception differs from original perception in that whereas in the latter it's on account of an innate disposition that the sensation sign evokes the apprehension and belief, in the former it's on account of a disposition acquired in the course of experience.

One can thus think of perception, says Reid, as

a kind of drama, wherein some things are performed behind the scenes, one succeeding another. The impression made by the object upon the organ, either by immediate contact, or by some intervening medium, as well as the impression made upon the nerves and brain, is performed behind the scenes, and the mind sees nothing of it. But every such impression, by the laws of the drama, is followed by sensation, which is the first scene exhibited to the mind; and this scene is quickly succeeded by another, which is the perception of the object. (IHM VI, xxi [187b; B 176–7])

An important question about this schema that I postponed from the preceding chapter is this: What is the nature of that conception of the perceived entity that the entity evokes through the mediation of a sensation that is a sign thereof? Is it presentational apprehension – that is to say, is the perceived entity present to the mind? Or is it conceptual apprehension, that is, apprehension by means of a singular concept?

I observed that Reid gives us little assistance in answering this question; and that, I said, was surprising. Surprising because if it's his view that in perception on the standard schema our apprehension of external objects is only a conceptual, not a presentational, apprehension, then his view, on this point, would come perilously close to the Way of Ideas. A central thesis of the Way of Ideas theorists was that the intuitional component in perception is always and only a sense datum, never an external object. Reid would be saying very much the same, that the intuitional component in perception is always and only a sensation. Sensations would be just as much inputs from the world that are interfaces between us and the world as are sense data in the Way of Ideas. It would remain true that the role Reid assigns to sensations in his theory is significantly different from the role assigned to sense data in the Way of Ideas; so too, he disputes that sensations are sense data. Nonetheless, both sensations, on Reid's analysis, and sense data, on the analysis of the Way of Ideas, would be input interfaces; and it's at most with these that we have acquaintance, not with the world.

It's hard to believe that if Reid thought there was a difference between his theory and that of the Way of Ideas at this point, he would have been quiet about it; he would have told us emphatically that whereas the Way of Ideas theorists hold that we have no acquaintance with external objects, he, Reid, holds that we do. Reid says no such thing; nowhere does he say or suggest that there is this difference. I take that as rather good evidence, though not indeed decisive, that there isn't this difference – rather good evidence that Reid was thinking of the apprehension of an external object that we have in perception, on the standard schema, as conceptual apprehension.

But if that's right, what's the big argument about? It's clear what Reid thought the big argument was about. Over and over he located the fundamental point of dispute as the claim of the Way of Ideas theorists that neither in perception nor in any other mental activity do we have immediate apprehension of nonmental entities; our apprehension of nonmental entities, so they said, is always mediated. Only of mental entities do we have immediate apprehension.

But how was Reid thinking when he located this thesis as the core of the dispute? Isn't he himself of the view that our perceptual apprehension of, and belief concerning, external objects is mediated by neurological events, brain events, and sensations? And if he does in fact agree with the Way of Ideas theorists that the apprehension of an external object, which is ingredient in perception, is a conceptual apprehension, isn't he then tacitly of the view that our apprehension of that object is mediated by that singular concept? So how can he possibly locate the core dispute between his account and that of the Way of Ideas theorists in whether we can have immediate apprehension of external objects – and whether, in particular, perception affords us such apprehension? What else could immediate apprehension of some entity consist of but *acquaintance* with that entity? If Reid concedes that we do not have acquaintance with external objects, isn't he then perforce denying immediate apprehension of those entities?

Reid leaves no doubt as to how he would respond to this expression of perplexity. He concedes that one can identify, at various points in his account, what might properly be called "mediation." Any "kind of sign may be said to be the medium by which I perceive or understand the thing signified. The sign by custom, or compact, or perhaps by nature, introduces the thought of the thing signified" (EIP II, ix [278a]). The sign can be said to be a *representation* of the thing signified. But Reid has his eye throughout on one particular mode of mediation or representation, namely, that which lay at the core of the Way of Ideas: mediation by *imagistic* representations. He has his eye on the claim that cognitive contact with nonmental entities is mediated by mental entities that imagistically represent those nonmental entities – in the way that a reflective or photographic image of some entity imagistically represents that entity. When I use some singular concept to get some entity in mind, that concept is not a representation of that entity. And though it would not be wrong to describe our sensations as "representing" external entities, they do not represent them imagistically.

"Modern philosophers," says Reid, "as well as the Peripatetics and Epicureans of old, have conceived, that external objects cannot be the immediate objects of our thought; that there must be some image of them in the mind itself, in which, as in a mirror, they are seen. And the name *idea*, in the philosophical sense of it, is given to those internal and immediate objects of our thought. The external thing is the remote or mediate object; but the idea, or image of that object in the mind, is the immediate object, without which we could have no perception, no remembrance, no conception of the mediate object" (EIP I, i [226a–b]). Making the same point more metaphorically, he says in another passage that "Philosophers, ancient and modern, have maintained, that the operations of the mind, like the tools of an artificer, can only be employed upon objects that are present in the mind, or in the brain, where the mind is supposed to reside. Therefore, objects that are distant, in time or place, must have a representative in the mind, or in the brain; some image or picture of them, which is the object that the mind contemplates" (EIP II, ix [277b]).[1] And speaking in particular of those Way of Ideas theorists who were realists concerning the existence of external objects, Reid describes them as holding that, besides external objects, "there are immediate objects of perception in the mind itself; that, for instance, we do not see the sun immediately, but an idea. . . . This idea is said to be the image, the resemblance, the representative of the sun. . . . It is from the existence of the idea that we must infer the existence of the sun. . . . there are substantial and permanent beings called the sun and moon; but they never appear to us in their own person, but by their representatives, the ideas in our own minds, and we know nothing of them but what we can gather from those ideas" (EIP II, xiv [298b]).

This is a good place to bring into the discussion an argument that Reid offers against this way of thinking that we have not yet presented. In addition to all the objections already raised, it just "seems very hard, or rather impossible, to understand what is meant by an object of thought, that is not an immediate object of thought. A body in motion may move another that was at rest, by the medium of a third body that is interposed. This is easily understood; but we are unable to conceive any medium interposed

[1] "It is a very ancient opinion, and has been very generally received among philosophers, that we cannot perceive or think of such objects [i.e., external objects] immediately, but by the medium of certain images or representatives of them really existing in the mind at the time" (EIP VI, iii [431a]).

between a mind and the thought of that mind; and, to think of any object by a medium, seems to be words without any meaning." He then draws out the implication: "I apprehend, therefore, that if philosophers will maintain, that ideas in the mind are the only immediate objects of thought, they will be forced to grant that they are the sole objects of thought, and that it is impossible for men to think of any thing else" (EIP II, ix [279a]).

The comment is cryptic; how was Reid thinking? He doesn't elaborate; so let me offer a speculation. Keep in mind that though all sorts of things can be described as mediating between one thing and another, the mediating entities Reid has in view are imagistic representations. Suppose once again, then, that one is looking at a mountain's reflective image of itself in a lake. One can then get that mountain in mind with the causal particular concept, *that mountain of which this image is the reflection.* But that concept is not itself a reflective image, obviously; concepts are neither representations nor images. In the opening chapter I distinguished three ways in which we can get things in mind – three modes of apprehension: conceptual apprehension, nominative apprehension, and presentational apprehension. There's not a fourth mode of apprehension to be added to that list: imagistic representational apprehension. What would that be? I think this may well have been what Reid was thinking.

PERCEPTION OF VISIBLE FIGURE, MAGNITUDE, AND POSITION CONSTITUTES THE EXCEPTION

The question still on our docket is whether, on Reid's standard schema of perception, the conception of an external object that is ingredient in perception is a presentational apprehension of that object, or a conceptual apprehension. To answer that question it will be important to have in hand the last piece of Reid's full account of perception – his analysis of those cases of perception that, as he sees it, do not fit his standard schema; namely, perception of visible figure, magnitude, and position in the visual field.

It's easy to miss the fact that perception of visible figure, magnitude, and position, as analyzed by Reid, do constitute an exception to his standard schema; it's not a point he emphasizes. But that he did in fact understand such perception as an exception to the standard schema is clear from a passage in which he refers back to the passage in which the structure of the exception is developed. In this later passage Reid is advancing his standard claim that we human beings might have been so constituted that perception occurred under quite different circumstances from those under which it does in fact occur. After considering a variety of such alternatives, he concludes by saying: "Or, lastly, The perceptions we have, might have been immediately connected with the impressions upon our organs, without any intervention of sensations. This last seems really to be the case in one instance, to wit, in our perception of the visible figure of bodies, as was observed in the 8th section of this chapter" (IHM VI, xxi [187b; B 176]).[2]

If we then go back to the eighth section of the chapter (it's the chapter on visual perception), we find Reid saying that "there seems to be no sensation that is appropriated to visible figure, or whose office it is to suggest it. It seems to be suggested immediately by the material impression upon the organ, of which we are not conscious: and why may not a material impression upon the *retina* suggest visible figure?" (IHM VI, viii [146b; B 101]). "If it should be said," Reid remarks, "that it is impossible to perceive a figure, unless there be some impression of it upon the mind; I beg leave not to admit the impossibility of this, without some proof: and I can find none" (ibid.). The affinity with Kant's doctrine, that our intuitions of space are "pure" intuitions, is unmistakable. I perceive the wall before me as spread out in space; but I have no space *sensations*, only color and light sensations.

The core of Reid's account of the objectivation that occurs in perception remains in place: an apprehension of the object perceived is evoked in us by that object, along with an immediate belief, about the object, that it exists externally; what's different about this case is that the intervening sensation is deleted.[3] Furthermore, Reid will argue that even in this case, there's a sign that

---

[2] At EIP II, xvi [310a], Reid throws out a cryptic allusion to the same point: "Almost all our perceptions have corresponding sensations. . . ."

[3] This, at least, is how Reid presumably thinks of the situation. It's not at all clear to me, however, that he either does or can hold that in visual perception, objectivating beliefs get formed in us about visible figure, magnitude, and position. One of his insistent claims is that in ordinary life we never attend to visible figure, and that it is in fact extremely difficult to do so. Are beliefs about them nevertheless formed in us? That seems dubious. But Reid locates the objectivation inherent in perception in the formation of beliefs, about external objects, *that* they are external. Accordingly, if Reid is to acknowledge our ordinary cognitive contact with visible figure as a case of perception, he will have to adapt his standard schema more drastically than he ever acknowledges.

gets interpreted: visible figure, magnitude, and position in the visual field function as signs of real figure, magnitude, and position. In short, Reid's thought is clearly that his standard schema *in its essentials* applies just as much to our perception of visible figure, magnitude, and position as it does to other sorts of perception. It's for that reason that his emphasis falls not on the difference, but on the similarity, between perception that fits the standard schema and perception of visible figure, magnitude, and position.[4] The structure of our perception of visible figure, magnitude, and position is only a minor variant on the structure of perception generally.

As will become clear shortly, I think he's wrong about that. In perception of visible figure there's no sensation functioning, on the one hand, as a sign of an external object, and on the other, as an entity to be interpreted so as to extract from it the information it bears concerning the perceived object. Yet there is intuitional content. Hence the apprehension of the external object has to be, in this case, apprehension by acquaintance. In visual perception we enjoy acquaintance with visible figure and magnitude. That is by no means a minor difference between such perception and perception which fits the standard schema. For though visible figure is, in a way, an appearance of real figure, Reid leaves no doubt that nonetheless it is an external entity of some sort. With mock humility he begs off specifying its Aristotelian category[5]; but he has no doubt that the "visible figure of

---

[4] Here is what Reid himself says on the point: "The correspondence and connection which Berkeley shows to be between the visible figure and magnitude of objects, and their tangible figure and magnitude, is in some respects very similar to that which we have observed between our sensations, and the primary qualities with which they are connected. No sooner is the sensation felt, than immediately we have the conception and belief of the corresponding quality. We give no attention to the sensation; it has not a name; and it is difficult to persuade us that there was any such thing.

"In like manner, no sooner is the visible figure and magnitude of an object seen, than immediately we have the conception and belief of the corresponding tangible figure and magnitude. We give no attention to the visible figure and magnitude. It is immediately forgotten, as if it had never been perceived . . . the mind gets the habit of passing so instantaneously from the visible figure, as a sign to the tangible figure, as the thing signified by it, that the first is perfectly forgotten, as if it had never been perceived" (EIP II, xix [325a–b]).

[5] Visible figure is "neither an impression nor an idea. For, alas! it is notorious, that it is extended in length and breadth; it may be long or short, broad or narrow, triangular, quadrangular, or circular; and therefore, unless ideas and impressions are extended and figured, it cannot belong to that category. If it should still be asked, to what category of beings does visible figure then belong? I can only, in answer, give some tokens, by which

bodies is as real an external object to the eye, as their tangible figure is to the touch" (IHM VI, viii [146b; B 101]). In the case of color perception, by contrast, it is our sensations that are the appearances to us of colored objects; and these sensations are, of course, entirely subjective. As he says in a passage quoted earlier, "When I see an object, the appearance which the colour of it makes, may be called the *sensation*, which suggests to me some external thing as its cause" (IHM VI, viii [145a; B 99]).

What then is *visible figure?* Whereas "the real figure of a body consists in the situation of its several parts with regard to one another, so its visible figure consists in the position of its several parts with regard to the eye (IHM VI, vii [143b; B 96])."[6] For example, the visible figure of a coin placed obliquely to the eye is a two-dimensional ellipse; that of a rectangular object placed obliquely to the eye is a two-dimensional trapezoid. "Objects that lie in the same right line drawn from the centre of the eye, have the same position, however different their distances from the eye may be: but objects which lie in different right lines drawn from the eye's centre have a different position; and this difference of position is greater or less, in proportion to the angle made at the eye by the right lines mentioned" (IHM II, vii [143a–b; B 96]). The general principle is this: "the visible figure of all bodies will be the same with that of their projection upon the surface of a hollow sphere, when the eye is placed in the centre" (IHM VI, vii [143a; B 96]). The important point to note and keep in mind is that visible figure and magnitude is a *two-dimensional* entity.[7]

those who are better acquainted with the categories, may chance to find its place. . . . A projection of the sphere, or a perspective view of a palace, is a representative in the very same sense as visible figure is, and wherever they have their lodgings in the categories, this will be found to dwell next door to them" (IHM VI, viii [144b; B 98–9]).

[6] Here is perhaps the place to observe that in his discussion of our perception of visible figure, Reid regularly uses "visible figure" as short for "visible figure, magnitude, and position in the visual field"; and "real figure" as short for "real figure, magnitude, and position." Now and then I will do the same.

[7] Hence it is that Reid says: "The distance of the object, joined with its visible magnitude, is a sign of its real magnitude" – that is, visible magnitude is not such a sign by itself; "and the distance of the several parts of an object, joined with the visible figure, becomes a sign of its real figure." Visible figure is not such a sign by itself. "Thus, when I look at a globe, which stands before me, by the original powers of sight I perceive only something of a circular form, variously coloured. The visible figure hath no distance from the eye, no convexity, nor hath it three dimensions; even its length and breadth are incapable of being measured by inches, feet, or other linear measures" (IHM VI, xxiii [193b; B 187–8]).

As we have seen, Reid regularly insists that when it comes to color, "there is no resemblance, nor, as far as we know, any necessary connection, between that quality in a body which we call its *colour*, and the appearance which that colour makes to the eye" (IHM VI, vii [142b; B 95]). Things are quite otherwise when it comes to the relation between visible figure and real figure – both of which are objective, even though it would not be wrong to call the first an appearance of the second.

> There is certainly a resemblance, and a necessary connection, between the visible figure and magnitude of a body, and its real figure and magnitude; no man can give a reason why a scarlet colour affects the eye in the manner it does; no man can be sure that it affects his eye in the same manner as it affects the eye of another, and that it has the same appearance to him as it has to another man; but we can assign a reason why a circle placed obliquely to the eye, should appear in the form of an ellipse. The visible figure, magnitude, and position, may, by mathematical reasoning, be deduced from the real; and it may be demonstrated, that every eye that sees distinctly and perfectly, must, in the same situation, see it under this form, and no other. Nay, we may venture to affirm, that a man born blind, if he were instructed in mathematics, would be able to determine the visible figure of a body, when its real figure, distance, and position, are given. (IHM VI, vii [142b–143a; B 95])

Elaborating that last point just a bit, Reid observes that just as "he that hath a distinct conception of the situation of the parts of [a] body with regard to one another, must have a distinct conception of its real figure; so he that conceives distinctly the position of its several parts with regard to the eye, must have a distinct conception of its visible figure. Now, there is nothing surely to hinder a blind man from conceiving the position of the several parts of a body with regard to the eye, any more than from conceiving their situation with regard to one another; and therefore I conclude, that a blind man may attain a distinct conception of the visible figure of bodies" (IHM VI, vii [143b; B 96]).

But if a blind person can attain a distinct conception of the visible figure of bodies, why is he nonetheless incapable of *perceiving* visible figure? The core of what's missing is that the figure is not *present* to the blind person: "the blind man forms the notion of visible figure to himself, by thought, and by mathematical reasoning from principles; whereas the man that sees has it presented to his eye at once, without any labour, without any reasoning, by a kind of inspiration (IHM VI, vii [144a; B 97]).[8]

There's another difference as well. Visible figure functions for those who have sight as a sign of real figure; and the sign is interpreted not by reason but by some principle – an acquired principle, on Reid's view – which produces its effect, of conception and belief, immediately. Visible figure "leads the man that sees, directly to the conception of the real figure, of which it is a sign. But the blind man's thoughts move in a contrary direction. For he must first know the real figure, distance, and situation of the body, and from thence he slowly traces out the visible figure by mathematical reasoning. Nor does his nature lead him to conceive this visible figure as a sign; it is a creature of his own reason and imagination" (IHM VI, vii [144a; B 97–8]).[9]

---

[8] A possibility to consider is that Reid regarded the difference between our perception of visible figure and the blind man's knowledge of visible figure as located in the difference between immediately formed and inferentially formed beliefs about the figure. But that interpretation would not account for the words, in the passage cited, "has it presented to the eye. . . ."

[9] Reid cites an additional difference. "Visible figure is never presented [n.b.] to the eye but in conjunction with colour; and although there be no connection between them from the nature of the things, yet, having so invariably kept company together, we are hardly able to disjoin them even in our imagination." By contrast, the "blind man's notion of visible figure will not be associated with colour, of which he hath no conception" (IHM VI, vii [143b–144a; B 97]).

While on the topic of Reid's view concerning the relation of color perception to perception of visible figure, let me offer an interpretation of a passage which, on first reading, is very perplexing. A "material impression, made upon a particular point of the *retina*, by the laws of our constitution, suggests two things to the mind, namely, the colour, and the position of some external object. . . . And since there is no necessary connection between these two things suggested by this material impression, it might if it had so pleased our Creator, have suggested one of them without the other. Let us suppose, therefore, since it plainly appears to be possible, that our eyes had been so framed, as to suggest to us the position of the object, without suggesting colour, or any other quality: what is the consequence of this supposition? It is evidently this, that the person endued with such an eye, would perceive the visible figure of bodies, without having any sensation or impression made upon his mind. The figure he perceives is altogether external; and therefore cannot be called an impression upon the mind. . . . If we suppose, last of all, that the eye hath the power restored of perceiving colour, I apprehend that it will be allowed, that now it perceives figure in the very same manner as before, with this difference only, that colour is always joined with it. In answer, therefore, to the question proposed, there seems to be no sensation that is appropriated to visible figure, or whose office it is to suggest it. It seems to be suggested immediately by the material impression upon the organ, of which we are not conscious" (IHM VI, viii [146a–b; B 100–1]).

The objection that this passage brings to mind is this: How could we possibly perceive the visible figure, magnitude, and position of objects if we had no color perception?

To begin, let's be sure we understand the scenario that Reid is asking us to imagine. He's asking us to imagine that we retain perception of visible figure, and of real figure, but that we have lost color perception. As he puts it, we are to imagine an alteration in

In introducing his discussion of visual perception, Reid remarks that "we must distinguish the appearance the objects make to the eye, from the things suggested by that appearance; and again, in the visible appearance of objects, we must distinguish the appearance of colour from the appearance of extension, figure, and motion" (IHM VI, ii [133b; 79]). In the preceding chapter we saw that an appearance of the color of an object is a color sensation evoked by the object's color; with this appearance of the color we have acquaintance. The appearance, that is, the sensation, is a sign of the color of the object; our perceptual interpretation of the information the sign bears concerning the real color occurs immediately, by virtue of an acquired habit on our part.

By contrast, the visual appearance of the shape of an object is not a sensation; it is something objective. It's with that visual figure that we have acquaintance. There's no sensation involved at all that corresponds to that figure. Of course the perceiver will typically be having color sensations. The point is that there's no sensation that is a sign of the visible figure and whose information about the visible figure we extract immediately by virtue of some original or acquired disposition.[10] The visible figure is indeed a sign of the real figure – and typically we immediately interpret it as such. But there's not a sign, in turn, of the visible figure. That would be a sign too many. Here's the full passage of which a part was quoted earlier: "When I see an object, the

what is *suggested* to us by "material impressions" on our visual organs: the perception of visible figure still suggests real figure, but "color experiences" no longer suggest colors in objects. We still have those experiences; but they no longer evoke in us the conception and belief of an external entity, namely, a color. (There is, of course, another way of losing color perception than the way Reid is here asking us to imagine: one's sensations may be so altered that they lose all color contrasts while retaining contrasts of light and dark.)

But doesn't Reid say, in expounding his scenario, that the person "would perceive the visible figure of bodies, without having *any sensation or impression* made upon his mind" (my italics)? And how could one possibly lose all visual sensations and yet be capable of perceiving visible, and thereby real, figure?

Yes, he does say that. But once again, the scenario Reid is asking us to imagine is clearly one in which the *suggestive* powers of impressions made on the retina are altered. Thus he's not asking us to imagine a person who has no visual sensations. What he has in mind is more fully expressed in the next to last sentence quoted: there is "no sensation that is *appropriated* to visible figure, or *whose office* it is to suggest it" (my italics). The sentence in question, about there being *no* sensation or impression, is to be read like this: "the person endued with such an eye, would perceive the visible figure of bodies, without having any sensation or impression made upon his mind *whereby he perceives that figure.*"

[10] However, the signs of real distance from the eye are subjective sensations; see IHM VI, xxi [189a–b; B 180–1].

appearance that the colour of it makes may be called the *sensa-tion*, which suggests to me some external thing as its cause; but it suggests likewise the individual direction and position of this cause with regard to the eye. I know it is precisely in such a direc-tion, and in no other. At the same time, I am not conscious of any thing that can be called *sensation*, but the sensation of colour. The position of the coloured thing is no sensation, but it is by the laws of my constitution presented to the mind along with the colour, without any additional sensation" (IHM VI, viii [145a; B 99]).[11]

In Chapters III and IV we discussed Reid's handling of the argu-ments offered by the Way of Ideas theorists for their position. In addition to the arguments considered there, Reid discusses one additional argument; the argument, and Reid's response, fit nat-urally in this part of our discussion. It's an argument offered by Hume in these words:

> The table, which we see, seems to diminish as we remove further from it; but the real table, which exists independent of us, suffers no alter-ation. It was therefore nothing but its image which was present to the mind. These are the obvious dictates of reason; and no man who reflects, ever doubted that the existences which we consider, when we say, *this house*, and *that tree*, are nothing but perceptions in the mind, and fleet-ing copies and representations of other existences, which remain uniform and independent. (Quoted by Reid at EIP II, xiv [302b])

Reid's treatment of the argument is brisk and devastating. Distinguish, he says, between *real magnitude* and *apparent magni-tude* – apparent magnitude being what he calls, in the passages we have just been discussing, *visible* magnitude. Now "it is evident that the real magnitude of a body must continue unchanged, while the body is unchanged" (EIP II, xiv [303b]). But it is equally evident that the apparent magnitude need not remain unchanged while the body is unchanged. "Every man who knows any thing of mathematics can easily demonstrate, that the same individual object, remaining in the same place, and unchanged, must nec-essarily vary in its apparent magnitude, according as the point

---

[11] Let it be said again that in his account of visible figure Reid is obviously taking account, in his own way, of some of the same phenomena of which Kant was taking account when he introduced his doctrine of the "pure," i.e., nonsensory, intuition of space.

from which it is seen is more or less distant; and that its apparent length or breadth will be nearly in a reciprocal proportion to the distance of the spectator" (EIP II, xiv [304a]). So how could such variations in the apparent magnitude of the table, while its real magnitude remains the same, possibly be a ground for concluding that it wasn't a real table one saw? "Let us suppose, for a moment," says Reid, "that it is the real table we see. Must not this real table seem to diminish as we remove further from it? It is demonstrable that it must. How then can this apparent diminution be an argument that it is not the real table? When that which must happen to the real table, as we remove further from it, does actually happen to the table we see, it is absurd to conclude from this, that it is not the real table we see" (EIP VI, xiv [304b]).

Think of it like this. Take a table. Consider "demonstratively, by the rules of geometry and perspective, what must be its apparent magnitude, and apparent figure, in each of" the distances and positions in which it can be placed. Then place it "successively in as many of these different distances, and different positions, as you will, or in them all." Look at it in these various distances and positions. And now suppose that you "see a table precisely of that apparent magnitude, and that apparent figure, which the real table," according to your calculations, "must have in that distance, and in that position. Is this not a strong argument that it is the real table that you see?" (ibid.). Conversely, suppose that the apparent magnitude does not match your calculations. Would that not be a reason to suppose that something strange was going on – that perhaps you were not perceiving a real table?

DOES PERCEPTION YIELD ACQUAINTANCE WITH THE WORLD?

We are ready, finally, to address the issue we have been postponing: Does Reid think of the conception that is ingredient in perception on the standard schema as apprehension by acquaintance or as apprehension by singular concept? Does perception on the standard schema yield acquaintance with the world or does it not? Let me approach my answer a bit indirectly.

Reid analyzes tactile perception of primary qualities as a paradigmatic instance of his standard schema. Was that a mistake on his part? Should he have treated tactile perception of primary qualities as an exception to his standard schema, of the same sort as perception of visible figure? (Of course, the schema would then be on the way to no longer being standard!) The standard schema certainly appears to fit our tactile perception of such secondary qualities as heat and cold. May it be, accordingly, that the very same sort of complexity that confronts us in the case of visual perception confronts us also in the case of tactile perception? Vision informs us of both the secondary qualities of color and the primary qualities of visual figure; the standard schema fits only the former, however. Might it be that touch similarly informs us of both the secondary qualities of temperature and the primary qualities of hardness, figure, magnitude, and so forth, but that the standard schema fits only the former?

Let's begin by taking note of what Reid sees as a fundamental relation between visual and tactile perception. Visible figure is presented to us in vision; and it's *only* visible figure, never real figure, that's presented. The figured body is never presented to us "neat"; all that's ever presented to us is "the position of the several parts of a figured body, with regard to the eye," never just with respect to each other. Yet typically the visible figure that we see is perceptually interpreted by us as a sign of the object's real figure; in that way we perceive the real figure. Indeed, so compelling is this interpretation that normally it's extremely difficult for us to note the properties of the visible figure; we go immediately to the real figure.

Now in general it's the case that when something is perceptually interpreted by us as an appearance of something real, that happens on account of an acquired, rather than an original, disposition. Our perceptions of the real qualities of things are acquired perceptions. But for an acquired perception of some real quality to occur, one needs some conception of that quality – some apprehension of it, some cognitive grip on it. So if apparent figure, that is, visible figure, is perceptually interpreted by us as a sign of real figure, how do we come by our apprehension of that real figure?

Reid's answer is that touch provides us with what is necessary for our apprehension of real figure. Speaking of magnitude rather than of figure, but embracing the same account of both, he says that real magnitude "is an object of touch only, and not of sight; nor could we ever have had any conception of it, without the sense of touch; and bishop Berkeley, on that account, calls it *tangible magnitude*" (EIP VI, xiv [303b]).[12] But "though the real magnitude of a body is not originally an object of sight, but of touch,"

yet we learn by experience to judge of the real magnitude in many cases by sight. We learn by experience to judge of the distance of a body from the eye within certain limits; and from its distance and apparent magnitude taken together, we learn to judge of its real magnitude.

And this kind of judgment, by being repeated every hour, and almost every minute of our lives, becomes, when we are grown up, so ready and so habitual, that it very much resembles the original perceptions of our senses, and may not improperly be called *acquired perception*.

Whether we call it judgment or acquired perception, is a verbal difference. (EIP VI, xiv [304a])

Thus primarily tactile perception, and then secondarily, perception of visible figure, together lie at the foundation of our knowledge of the world about us – or strictly, of our knowledge of its primary qualities. Reid has an interesting passage in which he describes how children go about acquiring knowledge of the world. The theoretical account outlined above lies in the background.

From the time that children begin to use their hands, nature directs them to handle every thing over and over, to look at it while they handle it, and to put it in various positions, and at various distances from the eye. We are apt to excuse this as a childish diversion, because they must be doing something, and have not reason to entertain themselves in a more manly way. But if we think more justly, we shall find, that they are engaged in the most serious and important study; and if they had all the reason of a philosopher, they could not be more properly employed. For it is this childish employment that enables them to make the proper use of their eyes. They are thereby every day acquiring habits of perception, which are of greater importance than any thing we can teach them. (IHM VI, xxiv [200b; B 201])

[12] Reid is here referring to Berkeley's discussion in *An Essay towards a New Theory of Vision*, §§ 41–66. Reid's distinction between visible and tangible figure, and his use of the distinction, is an adaptation and elaboration of Berkeley's discussion. The revisions which go into the adaptation are much more thoroughgoing, however, than the above passage would suggest. Berkeley regarded tangible magnitude as a sensation (idea) of a certain sort. For Reid, by contrast, tangible magnitude is the magnitude of an external object. It's the *real* magnitude of the object. The point of calling it "tangible" magnitude is only that our primary access to this magnitude is by way of touch.

What's presupposed by Reid's account of our perception of primary qualities is that in touch there's nothing like the phenomenon of visible figure – that is to say, nothing like "the position of the several parts of a figured body, with regard to the eye." There's no geometry of tangibles as a counterpart to the geometry of visibles. Visible figure, though an objective phenomenon, is nonetheless an appearance of real figure. There's nothing like that appearance/reality distinction in the domain of touch.[13]

And now for the question: How does Reid understand the *conception* that, on his view, is an ingredient in our tactile perception of primary qualia? Is it apprehension by acquaintance or apprehension by way of some singular concept? Recall that Reid treats tactile perception of primary qualities as a paradigmatic instance of his general schema: The hardness of an object evokes in a perceiver a sensation that is a sign of itself; this in turn evokes a conception (apprehension) of that object's hardness and an immediate belief, about it, that it exists objectively. Are there two potential objects of acquaintance in such perception, namely, the sensation plus the object's hardness; or is there just one potential object of acquaintance, namely, the sensation?

We already have in hand one argument for the conclusion that Reid was of the view that perception on the standard schema does not yield acquaintance with the world. If he had disagreed with the Way of Ideas theorists on a point of such significance, surely he would have said so; but he does not. Are there any additional arguments for that conclusion – systematic considerations, perhaps?

First, an argument for that conclusion in the case of secondary qualities. We saw Reid to be of the view that perception of secondary qualities affords us no knowledge of what they are; if we want to know what they are, we shall have to consult science. But surely if perception afforded us acquaintance with secondary qualities, we would not be in total ignorance of their essence. If we had acquaintance with the physical basis of the tendencies in objects to produce color sensations in us, we would know, to some

---

[13] There are of course tactile illusions, as a counterpart to visual illusions. But visual illusions are not accounted for by the geometry of visibles.

extent, what that is. On the other hand, if the secondary qualities are not that basis but are the dispositions themselves, then acquaintance seems ruled out for ontological reasons. Dispositions aren't the sorts of entities with which one could have acquaintance. Reid pretty much says as much when he discusses how we come by the conception and conviction that we have mental *faculties*. "The faculty of smelling," he observes, "is something very different from the actual sensation of smelling; for the faculty may remain when we have no sensation" (IHM II, vii [110b; B 37]). Reid's doctrine is that introspection yields acquaintance with one's olfactory sensations. He says nothing of the sort for one's *faculty* for having olfactory sensations. Instead he says that the sensation of smelling "suggests to us both a faculty and a mind; and not only suggests the notion of them, but creates a belief of their existence" (ibid.).

What then about our perception of primary qualities, on the standard schema? May it be that here the world is present to us? Reid regularly speaks of tactile sensations as *signs* of external qualities; and he describes the conception and immediate belief of those external qualities, which these signs suggest, as *interpretations* of the signs. The conceptions and beliefs interpret the sensations so as to extract the information about external qualities which the sensations carry by virtue of being signs of those qualities. But if the conception of the external quality that is evoked by the sensation were acquaintance with that quality, it would surely not be right to describe the conception (and corresponding belief) as an *interpretation* of the sensation. To extract information about the external quality from the sign, and to accept it *as* information, is one thing; to enjoy acquaintance with that quality is quite a different thing.

On this view there would, in fact, be a superfluity of information. Acquaintance with something is a source of information about it. My acquaintance with my dizziness yields me information about my dizziness. But then, if awareness of primary qualities involved acquaintance with those qualities, there would be too much information. My acquaintance with the primary quality yields me information about it; but the sensory experience is also supposed to function as source of information about the primary quality. Something seems definitely wrong here. Given acquaintance with primary qualities, the sensory experience seems otiose;

given the sensory experience, acquaintance with primary qualities seems otiose.

Consider a passage already quoted in which Reid is arguing against construing the Way of Ideas theorists as holding that we do genuinely perceive the external object: "If we do really perceive the external object itself, there seems to be no necessity, no use, for an image of it" (EIP II, vii [263b]). I submit that if perception consisted in acquaintance with the object perceived, there would also be "no necessity, no use" for a *sign* of the object. If we interpret the conception involved in our perception of primary qualities as apprehension by acquaintance, Reid's standard schema becomes just as incoherent for our perception of primary qualities as for our perception of secondary qualities.

What are we then to make of the passage in which Reid says that primary qualities, "by means of certain corresponding sensations of touch, are *presented* to the mind as real external qualities" (IHM V, iv [123b; B 62]; my italics), and of the passage in which he says that "feelings of touch . . . *present* extension to the mind" (IHM V, v [124a; B 63]; my italics)? There are a good many other passages in which Reid speaks the same way. Well, notice that Reid does not say that real external qualities are "present" to the mind in tactile perception; he says that they are "presented" to the mind by sensations. From the fact that Reid thinks sensations *present* external qualities to the mind, I do not think we can reliably infer that he thinks they are thereby made *present* to the mind. "Presented" may well mean something like "represented."

More to the point is a passage in which Reid unambiguously suggests an analysis of tactile perception similar to his analysis of perception of visible figure: "why may not a material impression upon the *retina* suggest visible figure, as well as the material impression made upon the hand, when we grasp a ball, suggest real figure? In the one case, one and the same material impression suggests both colour and visible figure; and in the other case, one and the same material impression suggests hardness, heat, or cold, and real figure, all at the same time" (IHM VI, viii [146b; B 101]). In every other passage with which I am acquainted Reid uses his standard schema to analyze our tactile perception of primary qualia. What's striking about this passage is that here he tacitly rejects the standard schema and replaces it with the alternative schema that he used to analyze our perception of visible figure. On this alternative schema, perception does incorporate acquaintance with objective qualities. But on this schema, the sensations have disappeared. Thus, once again, no double source of information. And that, I suggest, was consistently Reid's view: either sensations functioning as signs, as on the standard schema, or acquaintance with objective qualities, on the alternative schema; never both.

I think Reid was right about that: Double information is theoretically incoherent. That is to say, double information is theoretically incoherent when understood as Reid would have understood it. Reid would have understood it as acquaintance with external objects plus sensations yielding the same perceptual knowledge as that acquaintance yields. It would not be incoherent to hold that perception consists of acquaintance with external objects, and that such acquaintance is rather often accompanied by sensations of one sort and another. But of course the alternative schema no more involves double information than does the standard schema. So the question remains: Should we not use the alternative schema for our analysis of the tactile perception of primary qualities?

Consider an example of the analysis offered by the standard schema. One's act of touching some hard object evokes in one a pressure sensation of a certain sort, which in turn evokes in one an apprehension of that hardness by means of the singular concept, *the hardness of the object I'm touching.* One of the basic questions to put to this analysis is the following: How does one acquire the (general) concept of *hardness,* which is a constituent of that singular concept, if acquaintance with hardnesses is not available to us human beings?

In section vi of his discussion of tactile perception in the *Inquiry* Reid poses the following question: "whether from sensation alone we can collect any notion of extension, figure, motion, and space" [125; B 65]. That is to say, whether the theory of concept origination offered by the Way of Ideas theorists is plausible for our concepts of extension, figure, motion, and space. What follows after the posing of the question is an imaginative and compelling line of argument extending for the remainder of the section and the two following. I shall have to refrain from discussing the argument, fascinating though it is. What's important for our purposes here is just the conclusion at which he arrives: "it appears, that our philosophers have imposed upon themselves, and upon us, in pretending to deduce from sensation the first origin of our notions of external existences, of space, motion, and extension, and all the primary qualities of body, that is, the qualities whereof we have the most clear and distinct conception. These qualities . . . have no resemblance to any sensation, or to any operation of our minds; and therefore they cannot be ideas either of sensation or reflection" (IHM V, vi [126b; B 67]).[14]

But if we do not form our concepts of hardness and other primary qualities by operating on our sensations with the processes of abstraction, generalization, distinction, and combination, how then, on Reid's view, do we come by such concepts? One possibility, abstractly speaking, is that Reid thought that the concept was innate in us; shortly we will have evidence that that was definitely not his view. His view was rather that we are hard wired in such a way that, upon touching a hard object, the sensation evoked calls forth in us whatever concepts may be necessary for our apprehending the object's hardness with the singular concept, *the hardness of the object I'm touching*. This would of course include the concept of *hardness*. Though the concept of hardness is not an innate concept, it is an *a priori* concept. And in general: Reid was of the view that sensations are capable of evoking concepts in us which neither themselves apply to those (or any other) sensations nor can they be composed from concepts which do apply to sensations by such processes as abstraction, distinction, generalization, and combination. Reid's view, in short, was that the mind is conceptually creative in a manner and to a degree that no empiricist would concede; his affinities on this point are to Kant, rather than to the empiricists.

Here, for example, is what he says in the course of discussing olfactory perception: "it is impossible to show how our sensations and thoughts can give us the very notion and conception either of a mind or of a faculty. The faculty of smelling is something very different from the actual sensation of smelling; for the faculty may remain when we have no sensation. And the mind is no less

---

[14] Cf. EIP III, v [347a–348a]. There's an excellent discussion of this important aspect of Reid's attack on the Way of Ideas in the article of Keith de Rose already cited: "Reid's Anti-Sensationalism and His Realism," *The Philosophical Review*, XCVIII, No. 3 (July 1989).

different from the faculty; for it continues the same individual being when that faculty is lost. Yet this sensation suggests to us both a faculty and a mind; and not only suggests the notion of them, but creates a belief of their existence" (IHM II, vii [110b; B 37]). Some thirty pages later Reid refers back to this passage, and then brings the thought directly into relation with our present topic:

The conception of a mind is neither an idea of sensation nor of reflection; for it is neither like any of our sensations, nor like any thing we are conscious of. The first conception of it, as well as the belief of it, . . . is suggested to every thinking being, we do not know how.

The notion of hardness in bodies, as well as the belief of it, are got in a similar manner; being by an original principle of our nature, annexed to that sensation which we have when we feel a hard body. And so naturally and necessarily does the sensation convey the notion and belief of hardness, that hitherto they have been confounded by the most acute inquirers into the principles of human nature. . . .

I take it for granted, that the notion of hardness, and the belief of it, is first got by means of that particular sensation, which, as far back as we can remember, does invariably suggest it; and that if we had never had such a feeling, we should never have had any notion of hardness. (IHM V, iii [122a–b; B 60–1])[15]

There is perhaps some question as to whether Reid means by "the notion of hardness" the (general) concept of *hardness* or the conceptual apprehension of some particular hardness. I think the most plausible reading of the passage as a whole is that he is using

---

[15] Cf. IHM V, ii [121a; B 57–8]: "Hardness of bodies is a thing that we conceive as distinctly, and believe as firmly, as any thing in nature. . . . First, as to the conception: shall we call it an idea of sensation, or of reflection? The last will not be affirmed; and as little can the first, unless we will call that an idea of sensation, which hath no resemblance to any sensation. So that the origin of this idea of hardness, one of the most common and most distinct we have, is not to be found in all our systems of the mind: not even in those which have so copiously endeavoured to deduce all our notions from sensations and reflection." And IHM VII [208b; B 214]: "when it is asserted, that all our notions are either ideas of sensation, or ideas of reflection, the plain English of this is, That mankind neither do, nor can think of any thing but of the operations of their own minds. Nothing can be more contrary to truth, or more contrary to the experience of mankind. I know that Locke, while he maintained this doctrine, believed the notions which we have of motion and of space, to be ideas of sensation. But why did he believe this? Because he believed those notions to be nothing else but images of our sensations. If therefore the notions of body and its qualities, of motion and space, be not images of our sensations, will it not follow that those notions are not ideas of sensation? Most certainly."

"notion" as synonymous with our "concept," and that it is his view that one's first pressure sensation evokes in one the *concept* of hardness (or of *a* hardness), along with a *conceptual apprehension* of the hardness of the object one is touching.[16]

The choice confronting a "Reidian" in his analysis of our tactile perception of primary qualities comes down then to this: We can follow Reid himself in applying his standard schema to such perception. On that analysis, we have sensations functioning as signs of the primary qualities but not acquaintance with those qualities themselves; of them we have only conceptual apprehension by means of singular concepts. And the (general) concepts of primary qualities that are constituents of those singular concepts are evoked in us by the sensations even though they don't apply to the sensations – a priori concepts, but not innate. Or we can apply the alternative schema that Reid himself used to analyze perception of visible figure. On this analysis, though there may be sensations accompanying perception of primary qualities, they do not function as signs in our perception. Rather, brain states caused in us by touching some object bring about acquaintance with the primary qualities of the object. Reid insists that we all know the essence of primary qualities. On this alternative account, that would be because we have acquaintance with primary qualities. The qualities are present to us, just as one's dizziness, say, is present to one; they belong to the intuitional contents of one's perceptions.

Which analysis is correct? I have argued that the evidence is that, with the exception of our perception of visible figure, Reid opted for the *hermeneutic of sensation* interpretation, as opposed to the *acquaintance with external objects* interpretation. Which interpretation *should* he have opted for? I must limit myself here to a few observations.

Reid not only concedes but emphasizes that it is extremely difficult, when pereiving primary qualities, to isolate those sensations which, on his analysis, are signs of those qualities: extremely difficult, for example, when perceiving something hard to isolate those pressure sensations which are a sign of the object's

---

[16] In his letter to James Gregory of Dec. 31, 1784 [64b] Reid makes clear that he uses the word "notion" both for general concepts (simple apprehensions of properties, on his analysis) and for what he calls "apprehensions of individuals."

hardness. The reason for this difficulty, so he says, is that we have
been so formed that all our attention is on the hardness. The
strategy he typically follows for helping us to note the sensation
is to invite us to keep pressing ever more firmly against some hard
object until the pressure-sensation becomes so intense as to be
painful.[17]

Several things must be observed about this line of defense. It's
an inductive argument that Reid is offering us: Since we're able
to isolate sensations in some cases of tactile perception, namely,
those in which we feel pain, it's likely that sensations are present
in all cases. Hardly a powerful line of defense! But second,
suppose we grant Reid his conclusion: sensations are always
present when tactile perception occurs. This falls far short of
establishing the *hermeneutic of signs* analysis, versus the *acquaintance with external objects* analysis. For the person who holds that
tactile perception consists of acquaintance with external objects
can happily concede that such acquaintance is typically accompanied by sensations; what he denies is that perception consists
of those sensations functioning as signs to be interpreted.

Third, not only does the above line of argument constitute, at
best, precarious support for his analysis; the account Reid gives
of why we find it so difficult, most of the time, to attend to the
sensations which function as signs, is also less than compelling.
Here's a vivid statement of his account:

Nature intended them [i.e., the sensations ingredient in perception]
only for signs; and in the whole course of life they are put to no other
use. The mind has acquired a confirmed and inveterate habit of inattention to them; for they no sooner appear than quick as lightning the
thing signified succeeds and engrosses all our regard. . . . although we
are conscious of them when they pass through the mind, yet their
passage is so quick, and so familiar, that it is absolutely unheeded; nor

[17] For example, EIP II, xvi [311a]: "Pressing my hand with force against the table, I feel
pain, and I feel the table to be hard. The pain is a sensation of the mind, and there is
nothing that resembles it in the table. . . . I touch the table gently with my hand, and I
feel it to be smooth, hard, and cold. . . . This sensation not being painful, I commonly
give no attention to it." And IHM V, ii [120a; B 56]: "If a man runs his head with violence against a pillar, I appeal to him, whether the pain he feels resembles the hardness of the stone. . . . The attention of the mind is here entirely turned toward the
painful feeling; and, to speak in the common language of mankind, he feels nothing
in the stone, but feels a violent pain in his head. It is quite otherwise when he leans his
head gently against the pillar; for then he will tell you that he feels nothing in his head,
but feels hardness in the stone. Hath he not a sensation in this case as well as in the
other? Undoubtedly he hath. . . ."

do they leave any footsteps of themselves, either in the memory or imagination. (IHM VI, iii [135b; B 82])

Let's be clear what this account comes to, on the *hermeneutic of signs* analysis of perception. Our attention is not diverted from one domain of intuitional content to another domain of intuitional content: from sensations to the objective qualities with which we are acquainted. For we have no acquaintance with objective qualities. There's only one domain of intuitional content; namely, the sensations. Our attention is diverted from the sensations, which constitute the intuitional content of perception, to the external object, of which our apprehension is only conceptual.

The analogue Reid wants us to consider is our response to speech. One's transition from the sentences a person uses to what he said with those sentences is so rapid and customary that often, after even a short interval, we don't any longer know what sentence he used; we only know what he said. And of course, what he said is not something we perceive. But I find the analogy less compelling than Reid does. If I'm told to take note of the sentences the speaker is uttering, I have no trouble doing so. Why then should it be so difficult for us to attend to our pressure sensations when we have tactile perception? After all, those pressure-sensations are, on this account, the only intuitional content present before the mind; what's added, to bring it about that perception occurs, is not some additional intuitional content but a singular concept of the external object and a belief about it. Given the fact that my grip on the object is only by way of a singular concept, why would the fact that normally my thought goes straight to the object make it difficult *ever* to attend to the sensations – since these constitute the whole of the intuitional content? If perception involved both acquaintance with sensations and acquaintance with objects, one might well expect the sort of difficulty Reid's theory requires; but on the *hermeneutic of signs* account, it involves only the former sort of acquaintance.

Should Reid have broken even more radically with the Way of Ideas than he did? I judge Reid's theory of perception to be the most cogent version we have of the view that says that perception, at its core, consists of interpreting inputs from objects. And the only articulate version with which I am acquainted, of the view that says that perception consists of acquaintance with external objects, is the so-called theory of appearing.[18] The question, then, can be put like this: Rather than developing yet one more version of the *hermeneutic of input* type of theory, should Reid have gone yet farther, scrapped that line of thought entirely, and developed a theory of appearing? Arriving at a fully reasoned answer to that question will have to await another occasion.

DO CONCEPTS PROHIBIT ACQUAINTANCE?

It is regularly said and assumed nowadays that concepts "go all the way down"; and that, accordingly, there's no such thing as reality being present to us – no such thing as our having acquaintance with reality. I enter the room and perceive what I see under the concept of a computer; someone from some tribal society in central Brazil who doesn't have the concept of a computer enters the room and perceives what he sees under the concept, say, of a mysterious gray box. So is it or is it not a computer that we both saw? Who's to say? Eskimos reputedly recognize twenty-three kinds of snow; we, no more than three. Who's to say how many there are? Neither of us has direct acquaintance with reality by reference to which we could determine who's right; to neither of us is reality present. Always concepts are in the way; our cognitive engagement with reality is always mediated by concepts. The inescapability of conceptualizing bars us from all godlike ways of knowing; concepts are the flaming swords that make us forever exiles from Eden. But if that is so, what's the point of even talking about *being right?* Best to give up thinking and talking as if there were some objective interpersonal reality accessible to us, by acquaintance or any other way, and best to give up thinking and talking as if we could somehow "get it right" or "get it wrong." Best to confine ourselves to thinking and talking about our own conceptualized construction of reality.

If this were how things are, then Reid's view, as I have expounded it, would be fundamentally flawed. For running throughout his thought is the assumption that we do, at certain points, have acquaintance with reality. We have acquaintance with our own mental states, and with properties and propositions; like-

[18] See William P. Alston, "Back to the Theory of Appearing" in *Philosophical Perspectives*, 13 (1999).

wise our perception of visible figure incorporates acquaintance with such figure. Furthermore, Reid's assumes throughout his entire discussion that the beliefs ingredient in perception and memory, and evoked by awareful consciousness and intellection, by and large *get it right*. (In Chapters VIII and IX we'll find that he has much more to say on this topic than we have heard him saying thus far.)

I submit that rather than Reid's view being untenable, the objection is a farrago of confusions and nonsequiturs. In the first place, how could one's mental life possibly be totally devoid of presentational content – totally devoid of acquaintance, of something being present to one? Let us concede, for the sake of the argument, that all presentational content is already conceptualized. Then it's that conceptualized presentational content that is present to the mind. Or will it be said that that conceptualized presentational content must in turn be conceptualized – that the original conceptualized presentational content must become the content of a new act of conceptualization? If so, then that's present to the mind. Or will it be said in turn that – and so forth, ad infinitum? Those who espouse the view presented see themselves as standing in the line of Kant. But Kant was not so mindless as to deny all acquaintance – all presence to the mind. He was indeed of the view that the entire intuitional content of the mind has the status of being inputs from noumenal reality; and he insisted that this intuitional content, to be present to the mind, must be conceptualized. But that done, then it is *present to the mind*. So the issue is not whether there's presence but what is present.

Let's dig deeper. Reid insists that the objects of consciousness do really exist: sensations, feelings, fears, qualms, and so forth. Had he read Kant on the topic of inner sense, he would have discerned a sharp conflict of conviction on this point. The objects of one's consciousness, on Reid's view, are not appearances to oneself *qua* noumenal of some noumenal reality – this latter possibly also being one's noumenal self. They are not appearances of anything at all. They are reality – by no means all of reality, but definitely reality.

As we have seen, it was Reid's view that much of what we are conscious of escapes our attention; we take no notice. It evokes no beliefs about itself; nothing about the object of consciousness gets stored in memory. I have interpreted Reid as holding that

many objects of consciousness not only do not evoke the enduring state of a belief; they do not even evoke a momentary act of
judgment. We are not sufficiently aware of them for them to do
that.[19] So consider those of which we are sufficiently aware for
them to evoke beliefs about themselves. Was it Reid's view that in
such cases we have conceptually unmediated acquaintance with
those mental states and acts?

Before answering, let's notice that Reid's understanding of the
relation of concepts to those mental states and acts is very different from Kant's understanding. For the situation, as Reid sees it,
is not that we are confronted with a manifold of intuition whose
ontological status is that this is how noumenal reality puts in its
appearance to us *qua* noumenal, and that we then organize this
manifold by the imposition of concepts. The situation is rather
that we are confronted with genuinely real entities that aren't
appearances of anything at all – mental states and acts that aren't
appearances of something else and that have their own identity
and character quite independent of our conceptual activity. Distinct mental entities are not the *product* of our conceptualizing
activity; the situation is rather that we are *acquainted* with mental
entities *under* concepts.

But what is it to be acquainted with some mental state under
the concept, say of *my dizziness*? It is to be acquainted with it *as*
my dizziness. And what, in turn, is that? I think it eminently clear
what Reid would say: To be acquainted with it as dizziness is for
one's acquaintance with it to evoke in one the belief, about it, that
it is a case of dizziness. To be acquainted with something under
the concept of *a K* is for one's acquaintance to evoke in one the
belief, about the object of the acquaintance, that it is *a K*.

Consider, then, those acts of consciousness of which one is sufficiently aware for them to evoke in one beliefs about their
objects: Our acquaintance with those acts is thereby acquaintance
under concepts. But this acquaintance under concepts does not
consist of structuring these acts conceptually, for they are already
structured; it consists, to say it again, of one's acquaintance with
those acts evoking in one *de re*/predicative beliefs about themselves, the predicative component of which is then the concept.

---

[19] Admittedly this interpretation flies in the face of passages like this: "In persons come
to years of understanding, judgment necessarily accompanies all sensation, perception
by the senses, consciousness, and memory, but not conception" (EIP VI, i [414a–b]).

From this it obviously does not follow that we are not after all acquainted with those mental acts – that they are not present to us. What follows is rather just what was said: We are acquainted with them under concepts.

A theme running through John McDowell's recent book, *Mind and World*,[20] is that the reason experience can be caught up into the "space" of beliefs and of reasons for beliefs is that experience is conceptualized. Reid would agree. The reason he would agree, however, is that he would deny that there is any "space" between being acquainted with something under some concept and having a belief about that entity; to be acquainted with something under some concept just is for one's acquaintance to evoke a *de re*/predicative belief about that entity.[21]

When it comes to those modes of perception that satisfy the standard schema, our conclusion was that Reid does not think that we have acquaintance with the entity perceived; our apprehension of the entity is rather *conceptual* apprehension. A sensation evoked by the perceived object evokes a conceptual apprehension of that object, along with a belief, about it, that it exists as an external object (or a belief which entails that). In case I do not already have the concepts requisite for that apprehension and belief, the sensation also evokes those concepts. Thus it is that we gain information about the world which outstrips the information gained from beliefs about objects of acquaintance and from what can be inferred from those.

So suppose I apprehend what I perceive with some such concept as *the computer which I see*, and suppose someone from some tribal society apprehends it with some such concept as *the mysterious gray box which I see*. What's incoherent about saying that we see the very same thing, and that our two different ways of conceptualizing it are both correct? I perceive it as a computer; he perceives it as a mysterious box. It's both of those. Where's the problem?

Notice this implication: If it is in fact a computer which I per-

---

[20] Cambridge, Mass.: Harvard University Press, 1994.

[21] Here's a slightly different way of making the same point: "There are many forms of speech in common language which show that the senses, memory and consciousness, are considered as judging faculties. We say that a man judges of colours by his eye, of sounds by his ear. We speak of the evidence of sense, the evidence of memory, the evidence of consciousness. Evidence is the ground of judgment, and when we see evidence, it is impossible not to judge" (EIP VI, i [415a]).

ceive as a computer, then I perceive it *as what it is*; and if it is in fact a mysterious gray box (*mysterious* is, of course, a person-relative concept) which my tribal comrade perceives as a mysterious box, then he perceives it *as what it is*. The conceptualizing which goes into perception does not obstruct access to reality; it *enables* access – often, anyway. Our possession of concepts makes it possible for us to perceive things as what they are. Conceptualizing, when it goes well – and often it does – is our way of detecting the properties of things, that is, the real properties that real things really have. Concepts are not barriers between us and reality – flaming swords preventing access. The object in the room has the property of being a computer; and possessing the concept of a computer incorporates grasping the property of being a computer. So when I perceive a computer as a computer, the property that I therein and thereby believe it to have is a property that it does have. Mind and world are connected by the double function of concepts: grasped and predicated by me, instantiated by the object.

In being acquainted with my state of mind as a case of dizziness, I don't structure my inner life so that contains my dizziness; I presentationally *recognize* it as having the structure and character that it does already have. Provided, of course, that it *is* a state of dizziness – which it very well might be. So too, in perceiving something as a computer I do not thereby structure my environment so as to contain a computer; I perceptually recognize the structure and character that this part of my environment already has. Provided, of course, that it is a computer – which it very well might be.

THE MYSTERY OF PERCEPTION

In concluding our discussion of Reid's analysis of perception, let me call attention to one very striking feature of the analysis which, thus far, I have allowed to go unremarked. It's not a feature that Reid himself explicitly calls to our attention.

It's natural to assume, so it seems to me, that the most fundamental distinction between presentational apprehension and all other modes is that it is by acquaintance that we gain information about reality. I know that I am feeling nauseous because the feeling is present to my consciousness; I know that it's impossible to have a spouse who has no spouse because the proposition is right before my mind's eye. Or to put the same point in a slightly different way: It's natural to suppose that all our information about the world is, at bottom, acquired by, and evidentially grounded in, acquaintance. One is tempted to add: and by inferences from beliefs about the objects of acquaintance. But inference itself, if good inference, involves acquaintance – acquaintance with logical relations.

I do not doubt that Reid succeeded in extracting some of the fundamental assumptions that shaped the Way of Ideas. But perhaps just as important as the assumptions he extracted was the unspoken assumption that perception, to be a source of information about the external world, must be analyzed as evidentially grounded in acquaintance. The suggestion of the Way of Ideas theorists was that it is grounded in acquaintance with sense data, and with those logical relations which (supposedly) justify us in drawing inferences about the external world from beliefs about sense data.

A striking feature of Reid's analysis of perception is the tacit denial of this ever-so-natural assumption. Perception does indeed give us knowledge of the external world. But the apprehensions that are ingredient in perception are not acquaintances with the external world, nor with anything else; in particular, they are not acquaintances with sensations. Though evoked by sensations, they are not apprehensions of sensations. Worse yet, the sensations evoke concepts that don't even apply to the sensations. Likewise, the beliefs ingredient in perception are not grounded in acquaintance of any sort. Though also evoked by sensations, they are not evidentially grounded on those sensations; indeed, the sensations that evoke them typically pass by so unnoticed that we form no beliefs at all about the sensations.

Similar things must be said about inductively formed beliefs, and about beliefs formed by acceptance of testimony; they too are not evidentially grounded in acquaintance. In the next chapter we'll see Reid teasing out some of the affinities between perception, induction, and acceptance of testimony.

I said that this was a feature of his analysis that Reid never explicitly calls to our attention. But he may have had some inkling of it. For he often says that he finds perception "mysterious." I think the contexts of those remarks makes it reasonable to surmise that it was, at bottom, this feature of perception that made it seem mysterious to him. Perhaps also it is, at bottom, this same feature of perception that has always made it seem, to the skeptic, so ripe for attack. Perception, once one sees it for what it is, just seems implausible!

CHAPTER VII

The Epistemology of Testimony

"The wise and beneficent Author of nature . . . intended," says Reid, "that we should be social creatures, and that we should receive the greatest and most important part of our knowledge by the information of others" (IHM VI, xxiv [196a; B 193]). That is by no means a stray, decorative comment on Reid's part. It points to an important and fascinating component of his thought; namely, his development of an epistemology of testimony.

THE SIGNIFICANCE OF REID'S DISCUSSION OF TESTIMONY

Before we set out on an exploration of Reid's account of testimony let's reflect for a moment on the significance of the fact that he gives such an account. In chapter viii of Essay I of his *Essays on the Intellectual Powers of Man*, Reid, after distinguishing between the "social" operations of our mind and the "solitary," asks: "Why have speculative men laboured so anxiously to analyze our solitary operations, and given so little attention to the social?" [245b]. I judge the situation not to have changed significantly since Reid's day.[1]

By "social operations" he understands, says Reid, "such operations as necessarily suppose an intercourse with some other intelligent being" (EIP I, viii [214b]). When a person "asks information, or receives it; when he bears testimony, or receives the testimony of another; when he asks a favour, or accepts one; when

---

[1] The response might be forthcoming that this is true, at best, for the analytic tradition, not for the continental; witness all the attention paid to interpretation within the continental tradition. I beg to differ: The contemporary continental tradition has relentlessly assumed and insisted that the thing interpreted is a text, and that texts are to be interpreted without regard to the fact that they originate as instruments of discourse and of intended communication.

he gives a command to his servant, or receives one from a superior; when he plights his faith in a promise or contract: these are acts of social intercourse between intelligent beings, and can have no place in solitude" (ibid.).

It seems obvious, says Reid, that "the Author of our being intended us to be social beings, and has, for that end, given us social intellectual powers, as well as social affections. Both are original parts of our constitution, and the exertions of both no less natural than the exertions of those powers that are solitary and selfish" (ibid.). The reason epistemologists have given so little attention to such social operations as believing on testimony cannot be that such operations do not play a significant role in our lives.

Why then? The only answer he can think of, says Reid, is that the social operations fall outside the classic logician's scheme of simple apprehension, judgment, and reasoning with which his philosophical predecessors and contemporaries operated. "To ask a question is as simple an operation as to judge or to reason; yet it is neither judgment, nor reasoning, nor simple apprehension; nor is it any composition of these. Testimony is neither simple apprehension, nor judgment, nor reasoning" (ibid.). Reid observes that Hume broke free from the traditional scheme sufficiently to offer an account of testimony; the account is reductionist, however, since Hume did not succeed in breaking free from his own implausible principles. We will see later what Reid has in mind by that charge.

Reid's account of why testimony has received so little attention from epistemologists cannot be the whole truth of the matter. For the scheme of simple apprehension, judgment, and reasoning plays no role whatsoever in contemporary philosophy; yet discussions of the epistemology of testimony are not much more common in our century than they were in Reid's.[2] Something else is going on.

---

[2] Perhaps things are changing. Significant recent discussions of testimony include the following: Robert Audi, "The Place of Testimony in the Fabric of Knowledge and Justification," *American Philosophical Quarterly* 34 (1997); Tyler Burge, "Content Preservation," *The Philosophical Review*, 102, Issue 4 (Oct. 1993); and C. A. J. Coady, *Testimony: A Philosophical Study* (Oxford: Clarendon Press, 1992). A rather different treatment, from the continental tradition, is Paul Ricoeur, "The Hermeneutics of Testimony," in Paul Ricoeur, *Essays on Biblical Interpretation*, ed. Lewis S. Mudge (Philadelphia: Fortress Press, 1980).

I suggest that an additional factor is that the great fathers of modern Western epistemology, Descartes and Locke, were, each in his own way, very much opposed to tradition and to the acceptance of things on testimony which tradition presupposes; and that the course which they set for philosophy has not been significantly altered. Descartes insisted that if *scientia* is to be properly practiced, the individual must begin by doubting everything anybody has ever told him or her, and continue that doubt for a very long time – how long, is not clear. Locke insisted that when we are required to do our best to determine the truth or falsehood of some proposition we must set believing on testimony off to the side and go "to the things themselves."

This explanation invites the further question: "Why has the course Descartes and Locke set not been altered?" To this question, I have no satisfactory answer. The image of the human being which inhabits and shapes modern epistemology in the analytic tradition is that of a solitary individual sitting mute and immobile in a chair, receiving perceptual inputs and reflecting on his own inner life. For the continental tradition replace "receiving perceptual inputs" with "reading a text." The significance of Reid's discussion of testimony is that in this discussion there's a different image at work – an image of the person as a "social being." It would be natural to supplement our discussion of Reid's account of perception with a discussion of his account of memory; the latter account fits closely with the former account in fascinating ways. But because Reid, in his discussion of testimony, breaks with the epistemological tradition at a fundamental level, I have chosen instead to look at that. My judgment is that Reid did not think through his account of testimony as carefully as he thought through his account of perception; nonetheless, it's a fascinating and provocative treatment.

NATURAL SIGNS

Just now I spoke of the close fit of Reid's account of memory to his account of perception. The fit is almost as close for his account of testimony. Reid remarks that "the objects of human knowledge are innumerable, but the channels by which it is conveyed to the mind are few. Among these, the perception of external things by our senses, and the informations that we receive upon human testimony, are not the least considerable: and so remarkable is the analogy between these two, and the analogy between the principles of the mind, which are subservient to the one, and those which are subservient to the other, [that] without further apology we shall consider them together" (IHM VI, xxiv [194b; B 190]). It's the pursuit of this analogy that shapes Reid's discussion. Recall the distinction between original and acquired perception; add a distinction between "natural language" and "artificial language." Reid's thesis will be that "between acquired perception, and artificial language, there is a great analogy; but still a greater between original perception and natural language" (IHM VI, xxiv [195a; B 190]).

What Reid will show, in the first place, is the rather close similarity of the structure of testimony, and of believing on testimony, to the structure of perception on the standard schema. The core of the analogy will be seen to lie in the role of signs in both phenomena, and of immediate, noninferential interpretation of signs. Second, what Reid will show is the close similarity of the "principles" operative in believing on testimony to those operative in perception.

Distinguish, says Reid, artificial signs from natural signs; and then, within the latter, distinguish three types (IHM V, iii [121b–122b; B 59–60]). The standard schema for perception deals with one type of natural sign. In those cases of perception that fit the schema, some sensation is a *sign* of the external quality that caused it, and our interpretation of the sign occurs immediately. A second type of natural sign comprises all the causal effects to be found in nature, outside the self, whose interpretation by us does not occur immediately. If two events are related causally, then the effect is a sign, an indicator, of its cause; it carries information about its cause.[3] For most such cases of causality, you and I do not straight off interpret the effect for the information it bears concerning its cause; what's required for interpretation is

---

[3] I take the effects to be signs of their causes; the red spots are a sign of measles. Reid perplexingly reverses the order: "What we commonly call natural *causes*, might, with more propriety, be called natural *signs*, and what we call *effects*, the *things signified*" (IHM V, iii [122a; B 59]). I can only assume that this is a slip on Reid's part; measles are not a sign of red spots. That slip should not distract us from the point of the passage, which is that natural "causes have no proper efficiency or causality, as far as we know; . . . all we can certainly affirm, is, that nature hath established a constant conjunction between them and the things called their effects."

experience, investigation, inference, theorizing. Natural science is our most systematic attempt at such interpretation. Natural science is an interpretative enterprise; the natural scientist interprets the signs of nature.[4]

The third type of natural sign is the one most relevant to our purposes here. It's like the second type in that the sign is a causal effect external to one's self; it's like the first type in that one's interpretation occurs immediately "by a natural principle, without reasoning or experience" (IHM V, iii [122a; B 60]). And where do we find examples of this third type? Examples are "the features of the face, the modulation of the voice, and the motion and attitude of the body" which are natural signs of "the thought, purposes, and dispositions of the mind" (IHM V, iii [121b; B 59]).

On the one side, "certain features of the countenance, sounds of the voice, and gestures of the body, indicate certain thoughts and dispositions of mind" (EIP VI, v [449a]). "Nature hath established a real connection" between these (IHM VI, xxiv [195a; B 190]). This much, says Reid, no one will dispute. Nor, on the other side, will anyone dispute that, often anyway, we interpret these signs immediately. Call such signs, then, "the natural language of mankind" (IHM V, iii [121b; B 59]). The workings of this natural language parallel that of the standard schema for perception: "the sign suggests the things signified and [immediately] creates the belief of it" (IHM VI, xxiv [195a; B 190]). It's on account of this natural language and our ability to interpret it that "a man in company, . . . without uttering an articulate sound, may behave himself gracefully, civilly, politely; or, on the contrary, meanly, rudely and impertinently. We see the disposition of his mind, by their natural signs in his countenance and behavior . . ." (IHM VI, xxiv [195a; B 190–1]).

The question to be considered is "whether we understand the signification of [these signs of natural language] by the constitution of our nature, by a kind of natural perception similar to the [original] perceptions of sense; or whether we gradually learn the signification of such signs from experience, as we learn that

---

[4] Cf. IHM V, iii [121b; B 59]: "The whole of genuine philosophy consists in discovering such connections, and reducing them to general rules. The great lord Verulam [i.e., Francis Bacon] had a perfect comprehension of this, when he called it *an interpretation of nature*." And IHM VI, xxiv [199a; B 198]: "All our knowledge of nature beyond our original perceptions, is got by experience, and consists in the interpretation of natural signs."

smoke is a sign of fire, or that the freezing of water is a sign of cold" (EIP VI, v [449a]). Reid has no doubt that the first of these options is the correct one.

Why so? Reid offers four reasons; let me mention three. In the first place, infants, before they have had the requisite experience, already interpret certain facial expressions and vocal modulations. "Children, almost as soon as born, may be frighted, and thrown into fits by a threatening or angry tone of voice. . . . Shall we say, that previous to experience, the most hostile countenance has as agreeable an appearance as the most gentle and benign? This surely would contradict all experience" (EIP VI, v [449a–b]).

Various adult experiences argue for the same conclusion. Dumb persons, in the use of their sign language, make themselves understood to a considerable extent even by those who do not know the language. Merchants, traveling in countries whose language they do not know, find that they "can buy and sell, and ask and refuse, and show a friendly or hostile disposition by natural signs" (EIP VI, v [450a]).[5] Actors communicate as much by tone and gesture as by words; and pantomimes communicate with no words at all.

These considerations, though weighty, are not for Reid the decisive consideration. That is this:

When we see the sign, and see the thing signified always conjoined with it, experience may be the instructor, and teach us how that sign is to be interpreted. But how shall experience instruct us when we see the sign only, when the thing signified is invisible? Now is this the case here; the thoughts and passions of the mind, as well as the mind itself, are invisible, and therefore their connection with any sensible sign cannot be first discovered by experience; there must be some earlier source of this knowledge. (EIP VI, v [449b–450a]; see also EIP VI, vi [460a])

The analogy between the workings of our natural language, on the one hand, and perception on the standard schema, on the other, are thus very close indeed. "When I grasp an ivory ball in my hand, I feel a certain sensation of touch. In the sensation, there is nothing external, nothing corporeal. The sensation is neither round nor hard. . . . But, by the constitution of my nature, the sensation carries along with it the conception and belief of a

---

[5] There are fascinating examples of this in Stephen E. Ambrose's narration of the Lewis and Clark expedition: *Undaunted Courage* (New York: Simon & Schuster, 1996).

round hard body really existing in my hand." Similarly, "when I see the features of an expressive face, I see only figure and colour variously modified. But, by the constitution of my nature, the visible object brings along with it the conception and belief of a certain passion or sentiment in the mind of the person." In short: "In the former case, a sensation of touch is the sign, and the hardness and roundness of the body I grasp, is signified by that sensation. In the latter case, the features of the person is the sign, and the passion or sentiment is signified by it" (EIP VI, v [450a]).[6]

There's much, indeed, that's provocative and suggestive in these claims; but since it is testimony delivered in artificial language that is our topic in this chapter, we must move on.

WHY DO WE BELIEVE TESTIMONY?

Let's begin by having before us Reid's own brief statement of the analogy between natural and artificial language:

In artificial language, the signs are articulate sounds, whose connection with the things signified by them is established by the will of men; and in learning our mother tongue, we discover this connection by experi-ence; but not without the aid of natural language, or of what we had before attained of artificial language. And after this connection is discovered, the sign, as in natural language, always suggests the things signified, and creates the belief of it. (IHM VI, xxiv [195a–b; B 191])

Some points of obscurity in this passage have to be illuminated before we can see what Reid is up to. Begin with this: What is it that Reid understands as "signified" by the "signs" of language? What is it that gets connected to the "articulate sounds" of lan-guage by "the will of men"? If one thinks of language along the lines of speech act theory, the answer would be that it is *illocu-tionary actions* – to use J. L. Austin's terminology – that get con-nected to articulate sounds: actions such as asserting something, issuing some command to someone, asking someone something, and so forth.

I see nothing in Reid's thought that would lead him to reject this approach to language; on the contrary, though Reid is not

---

[6] The fact that we interpret facial expressions, vocal modulations, and bodily gestures, as signs of mental life, presupposes, obviously, that we construe those expressions, modu-lations, and gestures, as the actions of a person. Reid has a brief discussion of what accounts for such belief in "other minds" at EIP VI, v [448b–449a].

developing a theory of language, and that's important to realize, he does seem to have assumed something along the general lines of speech act theory. Nonetheless, that's not the aspect of language on which he has his eye. For the connection between the words we utter and the speech acts we thereby perform is not a causal connection but something more like a "conventional" connection; in one way or another it depends on "the will of men." A *sign* for Reid, however, is always a sign or indicator of some thing by virtue of some regularity – be it a causal law or some regularity of human action.

Recall that Reid is pursuing an analogy between the natural language of humankind, and our various artificial languages.[7] Our natural language, as we saw, provides us with signs of our mental states and acts – signs, but not resemblances. Reid's thought, I suggest, is that in our use of artificial language we likewise instantiate signs, indicators, of what we believe, of what we want done, of what we want to be told, etc. It will be important to the development of his case that language can also be used, and sometimes is used, to assert what we do not believe, to command what we do not really want done, to ask what we do not really want to be told, etc. That's why I said that Reid assumes something very much like a speech act account of language. But his eye here is on the workings of testimony. And he's assuming

[7] I will have to neglect Reid's interesting additional point, mentioned in the paragraph quoted at the beginning of this section, that our acquisition of artificial language *presupposes* our use of natural language. Natural language, he says, "is scanty, compared with artificial; but without the former we could not possibly attain the latter" (IHM VI, xxiv [195b; B 191]). "When we begin to learn our mother tongue, we perceive by the help of natural language, that they who speak to us, use certain sounds to express certain things: we imitate the same sounds when we would express the same things, and find that we are understood" (IHM VI, xxiv [195b–196a; B 192]). (Reid gives a different, and, to my mind, not very plausible reason for thinking that our acquisition of artificial language presupposes our use of natural language at IHM IV, ii [117b–118a; B 51].)

I would add that natural language is not only involved in our acquisition of artificial language, but that it continues to be involved in our use of artificial language. To a considerable extent, our discernment of which illocutionary action a person is performing depends not just on our understanding of the words she is uttering but on our interpretation of her gestures, her facial expressions, and her tone of voice.

That is connected with an interesting deficiency of artificial language, as compared to natural, to which Reid points. For the most part, artificial language makes up for deficiencies in natural. However, "artificial signs signify, but they do not express; they speak to the understanding, as algebraical characters may do, but the passion, the affections, and the will, hear them not: these continue dormant and inactive, till we speak to them in the language of nature to which they are all attention and obedience" (IHM IV, ii [118b; B 53]).

that, to understand those workings, we have to have in view what might be called the "signing" function of language. Not only is it the case that the person's utterance of words counts as his asserting so-and-so; that's the aspect of language on which the speech-act theorist has his eye. It's also the case that his utterance of words, both in fact and by intention, is a sign, an indication, of one and another aspect of his mental life.[8] And as is the case for signs in general, these signs are not resemblances.

Once we attain a reflective grasp of the natural language of humankind, we can use that language to dissemble – though some of us, admittedly, prove rather incompetent at that. We put on some facial expression which, in the natural language of humankind, is a sign of one's dismay, when we are not at all dismayed. The facial expression is then not an indicator of dismay. Viewers may take it as such; the dissembler wants it to be taken as such. But since he feels no dismay, it cannot be an indicator of his dismay. That's the end of the matter. It's not the end of the matter when it comes to our use of artificial language. I can assert what I do not believe; I may in fact believe it to be false. My utterance of the words is not then a sign of my believing that, since I do not believe it. Nonetheless, it does count – this is the additional factor – as my having performed the illocutionary action of asserting that.

Up to this point I have followed Reid in speaking of *the words* – or strictly, someone's *utterance* of words – as a sign of what the person believes, wants done, and so forth. But that conceals the complexity of the situation. It's not my utterance as such of the words, "I didn't see Michelle leave the house," that's a sign of my believing that I didn't see Michelle leave the house. To suppose that it is would be to take the workings of artificial languages as more like that of natural language than it is. By way of uttering these words in a certain manner and circumstance I assert that I did not see Michelle leave the house. It's my *asserting that* which is a (rather good) sign of my believing that – on account of the inclination of human beings generally to follow the "sincerity norm" for the use of language, that is, the norm that one has a (prima facie) obligation not to assert some-

---

[8] That then is why Reid says that "By language, I understand all those signs which mankind use in order to communicate to others their thoughts and intentions, their purposes and desires" (IHM IV, ii [117b; B 51]).

thing unless one believes it. There's this regularity in human behavior.

By contrast, the relation of my utterance of the words, in that manner and circumstance, to my making the assertion, is not a causal regularity, but, rather, that my uttering counts as my asserting. There's a rule in effect that brings it about that the former counts as the latter; otherwise it wouldn't.[9] But given that the rule is in effect, and given that a language could not exist unless its rules for which utterances count as which assertions were not by and large followed, there's also a regularity here of utterance to assertion. It's because of these two regularities – of assertion to belief and of utterance to assertion – backed up in the way indicated by norms and rules, that my utterance, in a certain manner and circumstance, of the words, "I did not see Michelle leave the house," is a sign of my believing that I did not see Michelle leave the house.

One additional point must be made about Reid's brief statement of the analogy with which we opened this section. He concludes the paragraph by saying that after we have learned the language, "the sign, as in natural language, always suggests the thing signified, and creates the belief of it." Thus far I have suggested that to understand Reid we must realize that for him the thing signified is not the assertion made but rather the belief of the speaker – though once again it must be emphasized that Reid does not see himself as doing any such thing here as giving "a theory of language." The point to be made now is that the belief created in the hearer is not just the belief that the speaker has the belief – though that belief is indeed created in the hearer. What transpires in accepting testimony is that, upon believing that the speaker believes what (one believes) he asserted, one then *believes what he believes*. Obviously it's important to keep this distinction in mind – that is, the distinction between believing that the speaker believes P and believing P; yet Reid quite regularly blurs it in his account of testimony. Perhaps he allowed his pursuit of the analogy of artificial language to natural language (and to perception) to conceal from him this particular complexity. We do allow the sign, that is, the speaker's utterance and/or the

---

[9] I discuss the nature and role of these norms and rules in a great deal more detail in Chapter 5 ("What is it to speak") of my *Divine Discourse* (Cambridge: Cambridge University Press, 1995).

speaker's assertion, to lead us to a conception and immediate belief of the thing signified, that is, to a grasp of the speaker's belief and to an immediate belief of its present existence. But from there, we go on to believe what the speaker believes. The peculiarity and the mystery of believing what others tell us is primarily to be located in that last move, from believing that the speaker believes P, to believing P.

The main question that draws Reid's attention is: Why does that happen? Why is it that, upon interpreting someone as telling me that P, I immediately believe that P? As the reader will expect by now, what Reid is looking for is the principle – in his sense of "principle" – which accounts for that. Though, as we have seen, Reid thinks there is an analogy between the workings of testimony and the workings of perception on the standard schema, he devotes very little time to laying out the details of the analogy. It's the explanatory principle that he is after. We have already seen that the analogy is somewhat less close than he apparently thought it was – though perhaps it's correct to infer some doubt in his own mind from the remark that "Between acquired perception, and artificial language, there is a great analogy; but still a greater between original perception and natural language" (IHM VI, xxiv [195a; B 190]). Put the point the other way round: Between original perception and natural language there is a rather close analogy; between acquired perception and artificial language the analogy is less close. In any case, Reid devotes the great bulk of his discussion not to the analogy per se but to the nature of the principles that account for the fact that we regularly believe testimony.

The question divides into two: What accounts for the fact that the assertions people make are signs of what they believe – that my asserting P is a sign of my believing P?[10] And what accounts for the fact that hearers tend to *believe* what they take speakers to be asserting – and readers, what they take authors to be asserting? As one would expect, prominent in Reid's treatment of the latter

[10] Counterpart questions arise for all the other illocutionary acts; for example, what accounts for the fact that my commanding that P be done is a sign that I want P to be done? And in general, what accounts for the fact that our performance of some illocutionary act is a sign that its sincerity conditions have been satisfied? It is because the issue at hand is the epistemology of testimony, testimony being assertion, that I confine my discussion to assertion. Of course, that narrowing of focus also considerably simplifies formulation of the points to be made.

question will be his persistent question: Are we dealing here with "original" principles or with "acquired" ones?

Begin with the first question. Reid's thesis is that our assertions are signs of our beliefs because God has "implanted in our natures" what may be called "the principle of veracity" – that is, the "propensity to speak truth, and to use the signs of language, so as to convey our real sentiments" (IHM VI, xxiv [196a; B 193]). Of course we are, on Reid's view, free agents. So this propensity to speak truth is just that: a propensity, not a causal necessity. It can be resisted; rather often it *is* resisted. We are not dealing here with causal laws. Nonetheless, there is the propensity. "Truth . . . is the natural issue of the mind. It requires no art or training, no inducement or temptation, but only that we yield to a natural impulse. Lying, on the contrary, is doing violence to our nature; and is never practised, even by the worst men, without some temptation" (IHM VI, xxiv [196a–b; B 193]).

Thus, an asymmetry. We speak truth out of an innate disposition to do so; "speaking truth is like using our natural food, which we would do from appetite, although it answered no end" (IHM VI, xxiv [196b; B 193]). We tell lies to achieve some purpose or other; "lying is like taking physic, which is nauseous to the taste, and which no man takes but for some end which he cannot otherwise attain" (ibid.).

The objection is likely to be forthcoming that though it's true that when people lie they have some purpose in mind for doing so, the same is true for telling the truth; they may, for example, "be influenced by moral or political considerations" to tell the truth. Hence their speaking truth "is no proof of [an] original principle" of veracity (ibid.). There is no asymmetry. No matter whether a person speaks truth or falsehood, he or she does so for a purpose.

Reid does not deny that we do sometimes speak the truth to achieve some purpose. His reason for thinking that that is not the case in general, however, is twofold. In the first place,

moral or political considerations can have no influence until we arrive at years of understanding and reflection; and it is certain, from experience, that children keep to truth invariably, before they are capable of being influenced by such considerations. . . . If nature had left the mind of the speaker *in equilibrio*, without any inclination to the side of truth more than to that of falsehood; children would lie as often as they speak truth, until reason was so far ripened, as to suggest the imprudence of lying, or conscience, as to suggest its immorality. (IHM VI, xxiv [196b–197a; B 193–4])

And secondly,

when we are influenced by moral or political considerations, we must be conscious of that influence, and capable of perceiving it upon reflection. Now, when I reflect upon my actions most attentively, I am not conscious, that in speaking truth, I am influenced *on ordinary occasions* [italics added], by any motive moral or political. I find, that truth is always at the door of my lips, and goes forth spontaneously, if not held back. It requires neither good nor bad intention to bring it forth. . . . where there is no . . . temptation [to falsehood], we speak truth by instinct. (IHM VI, xxiv [196b; B 193–4])[11]

Looking ahead a bit, it has to be said that Reid's argument here does not establish all that is required to be established if the other half of his full account of testimony is to go through – the half, that is, consisting of his account of why we *believe* what people tell us. Reid's argument thus far is for the conclusion that there is in us an innate propensity to assert something only if we believe it. One might describe it with Reid's own words as the propensity "to use the signs of language, so as to convey our real sentiments." For Reid's account of the epistemology of testimony, he needs more. In the very same sentence he indicates the "more" that's needed when he describes the propensity in question as the "propensity to speak truth." These are two quite different propensities. One might have the propensity to assert only what one believes, while not having the propensity to speak truth; there might, sad to say, be a high proportion of falsehood in what one believes. If I found you to be regularly insincere in your assertions, that would lead me to place little confidence in them in the future; but likewise, if I found you to be regularly sincere but

---

[11] Though Reid doesn't actually argue that if the symmetry thesis were correct, truth-telling in particular, and sincerity of speech in general, would be much more infrequent than they are, nonetheless, that is clearly his view. Motivation to tell the truth would often be absent. Furthermore, since the existence of language, as we know it, depends on people by and large speaking sincerely, Reid regards the very existence of language as depending on the presence within us of the principle of veracity: "By this instinct, a real connection is formed between our words and our thoughts, and thereby the former become fit to be signs of the latter, which they could not otherwise be. And although this connection is broken in every instance of lying and equivocation, yet these instances being comparatively few, the authority of human testimony is only weakened by them, but not destroyed" (IHM VI, xxiv [196b; B 194]).

misguided in your assertions, that would lead me to place little confidence in them in the future. Reid's full account of testimony requires that the principle of veracity be understood not just as the disposition to assert only what one believes, but as that disposition combined with some sort of tendency to get it right. It would be better to call the explanatory principle the principle of *verisimilitude* than the principle of veracity.

What sort of tendency to get it right? Was Reid of the view, and is it an essential part of his account of testimony, that most beliefs of most people are true? If so, his account would not have much going for it. To see how he was probably thinking, it's best to move on to the other side of his account.

Corresponding to the principle of veracity, says Reid, is the *principle of credulity*; that is, the innate disposition to "confide in the veracity of others, and to believe what they tell us" (ibid.). "The wise and beneficent Author of nature, who intended that we should be social creatures, and that we should receive the greatest and most important part of our knowledge by the information of others, hath, for these purposes, implanted in our natures two principles that tally with each other" (IHM VI, xxiv [196a; B 193]).

"To believe what they tell us": I suggest that those words, and similar words sprinkled throughout the text, indicate that Reid did not intend his principle of credulity to apply to all cases of assertion. His examples indicate this as well, plus the fact that over and over he says that what he's speaking about is testimony. It's cases of someone *telling* me something that Reid invites me to reflect on – and cases of someone *telling you* something that he invites you to reflect on. Lots of cases of assertion are not like that. In writing his dialogues, Plato was making assertions; but he wasn't telling me anything, and probably wasn't telling anyone anything. Perhaps we ought to insert one additional qualifier: It is cases of someone *confidently* telling me something that Reid invites *me* to reflect on; hesitant testimony is a different matter.[12]

---

[12] There is one passage in which Reid reflects a bit on what constitutes testimony; the passage makes it very clear that he does not regard every case of assertion as a case of testimony: "Affirmation and denial is very often the expression of testimony, which is a different act of the mind, and ought to be distinguished from judgment.

"A judge asks of a witness what he knows of such a matter to which he was an eye or ear witness. He answers, by affirming or denying something. But this answer does not express his judgment; it is his testimony. Again, I ask a man his opinion in a matter

And now to return to the other side of the matter, Reid's assumption must be that when people tell others something, they by and large speak truth – that is, by and large they say what they believe and what they believe is true. This is the principle of verisimilitude that "tallies with" the principle of credulity.

Of course we often accept the say so of other persons when that say so is not a case of their *telling us* something; it's indispensable that we do so. But as we shall see, Reid is of the view that the "principle" that accounts for such belief is different from the "principle" that accounts for very much, if not most, of what we believe of what people confidently tell us. Admittedly, the concept of *someone confidently telling someone something* is not among the clearest of concepts; but it's clear enough to discern Reid's line of thought, and also clear enough, I judge, to discern the plausibility of that line of thought.

Reid's argument for the presence of a principle of credulity in us – the disposition to believe what people confidently tell us, what they testify to us – goes as follows:

If nature had left the mind of the hearer *in equilibrio*, without any inclination to the side of belief more than to that of disbelief, we should take no man's word until we had positive evidence that he spoke truth. ... It is evident, that, in the matter of testimony, the balance of human judgment is by nature inclined to the side of belief; and turns to that side of itself, when there is nothing put into the opposite scale. If it was not so, no proposition that is uttered in discourse would be believed, until it was examined and tried by reason; and most men would be unable to find reasons for believing the thousandth part of what is told them. ...

Children, on this supposition, would be absolutely incredulous; and therefore incapable of instruction: those who had little knowledge of human life, and of the manners and characters of men, would be in the next degree incredulous: and the most credulous men would be those of greatest experience, and of the deepest penetration; because, in many cases, they would be able to find good reasons for believing the testimony, which the weak and the ignorant could not discover.

In a word, if credulity were the effect of reasoning and experience, it

of science or of criticism. His answer is not testimony; it is the expression of his judgment.

"Testimony is a social act, and it is essential to it to be expressed by words or signs. A tacit testimony is a contradiction: but there is no contradiction in a tacit judgment. ...

"In testimony, a man pledges his veracity for what he affirms; so that a false testimony is a lie: but a wrong judgment is not a lie; it is only an error" (EIP VI, i [413a–b]).

must grow up and gather strength, in the same proportion as reason and experience do. But if it is the gift of nature, it will be strongest in childhood, and limited and restrained by experience; and the most superficial view of human life shows, that the last is really the case, and not the first. (IHM VI, xxiv [196b–197a; B 194–5])

Though he doesn't actually say so here, Reid's thought is that the principle of credulity is a principle of immediate belief formation.

Upon taking someone to be telling me that P, I immediately believe that P. I believe *on the basis of* her telling me that P. If someone asks me why I believe that P, meaning thereby, *what ground* do I have for believing it, my answer is that I believe it because she asserted it. The principle of credulity thus operates, in several ways, like inference – when inference is operating as a principle of belief formation. (Inference need not operate that way: One can infer Q from P without believing P, in which case the inference will not produce the belief that-Q.) Inference as a principle of belief formation starts, like credulity, from belief. And I believe the conclusion on the basis of the premises – that is, on the basis of the propositional content of the beliefs from which the process starts.

So wherein lies the difference? Well, in the case of inference as a principle of belief formation, not only must I believe the propositions that are the premises; I must believe that those premises logically support the conclusion – that they entail the conclusion, or if not that, that they at least make the conclusion significantly more probable than not. It's that combination of beliefs that evokes my belief of the conclusion. My acceptance of the conclusion on the basis of the premises is mediated by my belief that those premises logically support the conclusion. I might believe that the premises support the conclusion because somebody told me that they do; in the ideal case, however, I "see" that they do. That is to say: I'm aware of the fact that they do. What's different, as Reid sees it, about the working of the principle of credulity, is that there is no such mediating belief. I believe that she asserted that P; and *thereupon* I believe that P. My believing that P is not mediated by the additional belief, that the proposition that she asserted that P logically supports the proposition that P. What activates the principle of credulity in me is just the belief that she asserted that P – this belief of mine then producing in me the belief that P.

Reid noted that there's a strong temptation in philosophers to try to assimilate all cases of believing what people assert – including, then, cases of believing what they tell us – to believing for reasons. He has Hume especially in mind. The philosopher suggests that what *really* happens, when I believe what someone asserts on the basis of her asserting it, is that I believe on the basis of an argument whose premises are of this sort:

   (i)   she asserted that P,
  (ii)   her assertion that P is an example of a type of assertion whose examples exhibit a relatively high proportion of true assertings,
 (iii)   so probably this example of that type is true.

The thought is, of course, that (ii) is confirmed by induction.

As we saw, Reid's argument against this analysis is that it is exceedingly implausible to suppose that children who believe what's told them have gone through, or even could go through, such a process of reasoning. But suppose they could, and that to some extent they do. The relevant question would then be how we could ever acquire the evidential basis necessary, on this analysis, for believing the bulk of what we do believe. For notice that in our determination of the truth of assertions, we are never to make use of what anybody asserts unless we have confirmed that the assertion belongs to a reliable type. In fact, of course, what any one of us believes to be true depends massively on believing what others assert. My teacher of high school chemistry based his teaching almost entirely on what others had said; they, in turn, based theirs heavily on what others had said; those, on yet others; and so forth. What would my *personal* evidential basis for the reliability of this massive and intricate body of claims even look like, if it contained nothing that I believe on say so unless I had confirmed that that say so belongs to a reliable type?

The proposed analysis also remains void for vagueness until we are told how the types to be tested for reliability are to be determined. Any assertion will belong to some type or other that is reliable, and to some type or other that is unreliable. So given a particular assertion, which of the multitude of types to which it belongs is one to test for reliability?[13]

---

[13] There's an excellent defense of Reid's analysis in the article by Tyler Burge already cited, "Content Preservation."

Given these rather obvious difficulties, the question arises: Why have philosophers been tempted to analyze believing on say so as a case of reasoning? Well, when I believe P on someone's say so, my belief is produced neither by my acquaintance with the fact that P nor by evidence that I might have for P. To believe on say so is in that way to form ungrounded beliefs. It's to trust one's fellow human beings. As I suggested at the end of the preceding chapter, a good many philosophers have found it difficult to acknowledge that our constitution as human beings falls this far short of their ideal of "rational animals" – and that in the nature of the case this is how it must be. I'll have more to say about this at the end of the next chapter.

Lest the precise force of Reid's argument be misunderstood, it's important to add that he is by no means of the view that reasoning plays no role whatsoever in our believing what people assert – nor even, more particularly, in our believing what people tell us. This is what he says:

It is the intention of nature, that we should be carried in arms before we are able to walk upon our legs; and it is likewise the intention of nature, that our belief should be guided by the authority and reason of others, before it can be guided by our own reason. The weakness of the infant, and the natural affection of the mother, plainly indicate the former; and the natural credulity of youth and authority of age, as plainly indicate the latter. The infant, by proper nursing and care, acquires strength to walk without support. Reason hath likewise her infancy, when she must be carried in arms: then she leans entirely upon authority, by natural instinct, as if she was conscious of her own weakness; and without this support, she becomes vertiginous. When brought to maturity by proper culture, she begins to feel her own strength, and leans less upon the reason of others; she learns to suspect testimony in some cases, and to disbelieve it in others; and sets bounds to that authority to which she was at first entirely subject. But still, to the end of life, she finds a necessity of borrowing light from testimony, where she has none within herself, and of leaning in some degree upon the reason of others, where she is conscious of her own imbecility.

And as in many instances, Reason, even in her maturity, borrows aid from testimony; so in others she mutually gives aid to it, and strengthens its authority. For as we find good reason to reject testimony in some cases, so in others we find good reason to rely upon it with perfect security, in our most important concerns. The character, the number, and the disinterestedness of witnesses, the impossibility of collusion, and the incredibility of their concurring in their testimony without collusion, may give an irresistible strength to testimony, compared to which, its native and intrinsic authority is very inconsiderable. (IHM VI, xxiv [197a–b; B 195])

As we mature, we slowly develop a repertoire of types of testimony relevant to our interest in believing what's true and not believing what's false, with the consequence that, rather than believing pretty much what anyone tells us, we now "suspect testimony in some cases," "disbelieve it in others," and in yet others, find ourselves believing with even more firmness than otherwise we would have. Never, though, do we find ourselves in the position of no longer depending on the workings of our credulity principle.

Reid understands this process of maturation, in our believing what people tell us, as the result of the interplay of two "principles": the credulity principle and the reasoning principle. The interplay goes like this. What happens first is that now and then, after believing what someone says, we subsequently learn that it was false – or at least, come to believe that it was false. The occurrence of such learning presupposes, of course, that the proposition that we concluded to be false was believed by us with less firmness than some other proposition that we took to be in conflict with it – and also with less firmness than the proposition that that other was indeed in conflict with it. The least firmly held belief gives way. What makes it possible to learn that something one believed, on someone's telling it to one, is false, is that one's believing it because they told it is done with less than maximal firmness.

What happens secondly is that, beyond learning on a number of occasions that what one earlier believed on someone's testimony was in fact false, we also learn to spy cues to false speech – and more generally, to unreliable speech. For there are such cues. We learn that what is said by a certain sort of person speaking in a certain sort of way on a certain sort of topic in a certain sort of situation is often false; and we learn to pick out such cases from the totality of speakings – to discriminate them from the others. Likewise we learn how to pick out speakings of extremely reliable sorts. For there are those as well, along with discernible and discriminable cues to some of them. All these learnings are stored in memory in the form of beliefs.

The proclivity to believe what someone tells one remains a component of one's constitution. But now that one is an adult, that proclivity gets inhibited for certain tellings because one sorts those into types for whose unreliability one remembers having gained evidence: one has learned that people with that sort of slick manner are not to be trusted. The belief that the case before one belongs to a relevantly unreliable type inhibits the workings of the credulity principle. It is along these lines that I take Reid to be thinking.

Analogies in the field of perception come readily to mind. The road ahead certainly has the look of water standing on it; however, prior experience has produced in me the belief that this is how roads in the middle distance often look on hot summer days even when they're entirely dry. So I don't believe what "my eyes tell me." The belief produced by experience inhibits the normal workings of perception.

THE INDUCTIVE PRINCIPLE

The thesis of Reid that we have been considering is that "if we compare the general principles of our constitution, which fit us for receiving information from our fellow-creatures by language, with the general principles which fit us for acquiring the perception of things by our senses, we shall find them to be very similar in their nature and manner of operation" (IHM VI, xxiv [195b; B 192]). We have noted a good deal of the similarity; but we have not yet noted the similarity on which Reid places most emphasis.

Notice, in the first place, that "if there were not a principle of veracity in the human mind, men's words would not be signs of their thoughts: and if there were no regularity in the course of nature, no one thing could be a natural sign of another" (IHM VI, xxiv [198a; B 197]). That's one half of the analogy to be noted.

To get into a position where we can discern the other half, notice that experience plays a role at two pivotal points in the acceptance of testimony by adults. One is the role we have just been exploring. The other is a role suggested earlier, though not developed. We learn from experience which words, uttered in which manner and context, are signs of which "sentiments," to use Reid's word. Only if there is considerable regularity in this regard can we learn the language to which the words belong; indeed, only if there is considerable regularity in this regard can there even *be* the language.

But now notice, says Reid, that the observation that goes into this last sort of learning experience is observation concerning how "men *have* used such words to express such things." The point holds for learning in general: The observation that goes into learning from experience is "of the *past*, and can, of itself, give no notion or belief of what is *future*. How come we then to believe, and to rely upon it with assurance, that men who have it in their power to do otherwise, will continue to use the same words when they think the same things" (IHM VI, xxiv [196a; B 192])?

This question provides Reid with his opening. In learning by experience, there's the same principle at work as in the acquisition of acquired perceptions. "Upon this principle of our constitution, not only acquired perception, but all inductive reasoning, and all our reasoning from analogy, is grounded: and therefore, for want of another name, we shall beg leave to call it *the inductive principle*" (IHM VI, xxiv [199a; B 198]). The deepest similarity between, on the one hand, language acquisition and our acceptance of testimony, and, on the other hand, acquired perception, is that in both cases the inductive principle is at work.

It's by virtue of one disposition (i.e., "principle") that a certain tactile sensation evokes the conception and belief of a hardness, and by virtue of another, that a certain tactile sensation evokes the conception and belief of a certain real figure; likewise, it's by virtue of one disposition that a certain facial expression evokes the conception and belief of anger, and by virtue of another, that a certain facial expression evokes the conception and belief of benevolence. In short, "Our original perceptions, as well as the natural language of human features and gestures, must be resolved into particular principles of the human constitution" (IHM VI, xxiv [195b; B 191]).

By contrast, "our acquired perceptions, and the information we receive by means of artificial language, must be resolved into [the same] general principle of the human constitution. When a painter perceives that this picture is the work of Raphael, that the work of Titian, ... these different acquired perceptions are produced by the same general principles of the human mind"

(IHM VI, xxiv [195b; B 191–2]). Likewise, "when certain articulate sounds convey to my mind the knowledge of the battle of Pharsalia; and others, the knowledge of the battle of Poltowa, . . . the same general principles of the human constitution" are at work (ibid.). In all these cases it is in fact the inductive principle that is at work.

We don't yet have before us Reid's analysis of the workings of the inductive principle. That analysis will come as no surprise: "when we have found two things to have been constantly conjoined in the course of nature, the appearance of one of them is immediately followed by the conception and belief of the other" (IHM VI, xxiv [197b; B 195–6]). Corresponding to the regularities by virtue of which there are signs in nature and in human expression, the author of our nature has "implanted in human minds an original principle by which we believe and expect the continuance of the course of nature, and the continuance of those connections which we have observed in time past. It is by this general principle of our nature, that when two things have been found connected in time past, the appearance of the one produces the belief of the other" (IHM VI, xxiv [198a–b; B 197]).

Hume already discerned, says Reid, that "our belief of the continuance of nature's law is not derived from reason" (IHM VI, xxiv [199a; B 198]).[14] He went astray, however, in his conviction that it is nonetheless not an original principle of our constitution but to be accounted for in terms of "his favourite hypothesis, That belief is nothing but a certain degree of vivacity in the idea of the thing believed" (IHM VI, xxiv [198b; B 197]). I will refrain from quoting the wickedly hilarious passage in which Reid attacks this hypothesis (IHM VI, xxiv [198b–199a; B 197–8])!

---

[14] Reid observes that "if we believe that there is a wise and good Author of nature, we may see a good reason, why he should continue the same laws of nature, and the same connections of things, for a long time; because, if he did otherwise, we could learn nothing from what is past, and all our experience would be of no use to us. But though this consideration, when we come to the use of reason, may confirm our belief of the continuance of the present course of nature, it is certain that it did not give rise to this belief; for children and idiots have this belief as soon as they know that fire will burn them. It must therefore be the effect of instinct, not of reason" (EIP VI, i [413a–b]).

CHAPTER VIII

Reid's Way with the Skeptic

Two stock characters constantly put in their appearance in Reid's writing: the madman and the skeptic. I shall introduce the madman in the next chapter; for now, it's the skeptic – though the madman will put in a brief appearance as well.

Skeptics come in many types. Reid has his eye on just one – a type that haunts Western philosophy from the seventeenth century onward. Whether it's quite right to call him a skeptic is a good question. Apart from his dissent on certain epistemological issues, he doesn't actually doubt more than the rest of us.

REID'S SKEPTIC

Who is Reid's skeptic? Recall Reid's standard schema for perception: The perceived object evokes in the perceiver a sensation that is a sign of itself; this sensation then evokes a conception of the object and an immediate belief about it, that it exists as something external (or a belief which entails that). In perceiving the sun, the sun evokes in me a sensation that is a sign of itself; and that sensation evokes in me an apprehension of the sun and the immediate belief, about it, that it exists as something in my environment. It's to that immediately formed belief, and the apprehension that it presupposes, that Reid's skeptic directs his attention. What he has on his mind is the fact that sometimes what's immediately evoked by sensory experience, though *taken* by the perceiver as an apprehension of, and belief about, some external object, is not that, since there's no object that stands in the requisite relation to the sensation for the latter to have been the right sort of sign of it. Call what's evoked a "purported apprehension" and a "purported belief."

He's also a skeptic concerning memory; and his skepticism

is focused on the counterpart phenomenon. In remembering something, an apprehension of the remembered event, and an immediate belief about it, that it did once happen, are formed in one. It's that immediately formed belief, and the apprehension that it presupposes, that draws the skeptic's attention: he has on his mind the fact that sometimes what gets formed is only a *purported* apprehension of a prior event and a *purported* belief about it.

What is it that Reid's skeptic wants to say about those purported apprehensions and believings? "The skeptic asks me," says Reid, "Why do you believe the existence of the external object which you perceive?" adding that "There is nothing so shameful in a philosopher as to be deceived and deluded; and therefore you ought to resolve firmly to withhold assent, and to throw off all this belief of external objects, which may be all delusion" (IHM VI, xx [183b; B 169]). The thought occurs to the skeptic that possibly all those occurrences that purport to be perceptually formed believings about external objects, and memorially formed believings about prior events, are never anything of the sort – since the requisite objects and prior events are missing. Accordingly he enjoins the philosopher to throw off all such purported believings until he, the philosopher, has established that there is an external world and that perception is a reliable mode of access thereto, and that events did take place in the past and that memory is a reliable mode of access to them.

Why does the skeptic enjoin that? Reid's skeptic is addressing the philosophers of the world, issuing to them an injunction. Why the injunction? Because the skeptic has in mind a certain understanding of the philosopher's role in culture – a certain understanding of the high calling of the philosopher. He's simply applying that understanding to the case in hand.

What is that understanding? Speaking of his skeptic, Reid says this: "That our thoughts, our sensations, and every thing of which we are conscious, hath a real existence, is admitted in this system as a first principle; but everything else must be made evident by the light of reason. Reason must rear the whole fabric of knowledge upon this single principle of consciousness" (IHM VII [206b; B 210]). All the necessary clues are there in that passage. Reid's skeptic is a *foundationalist of the classically modern sort.* Let me explain.

FOUNDATIONALISM

To describe a position as "foundationalist" without further explanation is to plunge into a swamp of verbal vagueness. The range of positions called "foundationalism" has been expanding by leaps and bounds in recent years, so much so that the expansion is well on the way to the point where the shared property will be little more than *being an epistemological position of which the speaker disapproves.* To be called a "foundationalist" in the contemporary academy is like being called a "reactionary" in general society. One is not so much described as accused. To the accusation, everyone in his or her right mind pleads innocent; no one responds: "Yes, that's what I am; and so what?"

The term "foundationalism" was first used, to the best of my knowledge, some twenty-five years ago in the writings of epistemologists working within the analytic tradition of philosophy; there it had, and continues to have, a rather precise meaning. The term's other uses can all be traced, genetically, to extension by analogy from its meaning there. That original meaning is the one with which I will be working.

The most important preliminary point to get and keep in mind is that there is no one position which is *foundationalism*; there's only an extended family of positions that are foundationalist in character. There are foundational-*isms*. Furthermore, the members of this clan differ from each other along a number of different dimensions. It will be sufficient for our purposes here to point to just a few.

Deep in human life, so deep that a life would not be human without them, are such states and activities as judging that, believing that, hoping that, wishing that, accepting that, fearing that, regretting that, and so forth – what are regularly called *propositional attitudes* by philosophers. In their incorporation of propositional content, the states and activities I have mentioned are similar to intending that, trying to bring it about that, and so on; they differ in that the latter go beyond taking up of an "attitude" toward a proposition, to trying or planning to change the world in such a way as to bring it about that some proposition is made true or false.

All of us assume that these propositional attitudes of ours have a variety of different merits and demerits; we all evaluate them in various ways, our own and those of others. A judgment or belief, for example, may be justified, warranted, entitled, reliably formed, satisfactory for good science, and so forth. Some of the terms I have just used are from ordinary discourse; others are "terms of art" taken from the discourse of philosophers. They are alike in that, in one way or another, the concept of each incorporates a reference to truth. They pick out *truth-relevant* merits in judgments and beliefs, with the mode of relevance different from case to case. There are other merits and demerits in our propositional attitudes whose concepts do not incorporate a reference to truth; for example, the merit of making one happy and the demerit of making one unhappy.

At the core of every foundationalism is a thesis as to the conditions under which some particular truth-relevant merit attaches to propositional attitudes – as to the conditions under which some judgment or belief, say, is warranted, or entitled, or justified, or whatever. A particular foundationalism might limit the scope of its criterion to judgments and beliefs of a certain type; alternatively, it might intend the criterion it proposes to hold for all judgments and beliefs, or all hopes or acceptances. The members of the foundationalist clan differ from each other in that (among other things) they focus on different merits and demerits; what nonetheless unites all of them into the clan is their shared focus on conditions for the presence of truth-relevant merits in propositional attitudes. There are, of course, other epistemological "isms" that also focus on conditions for the presence of truth-relevant merits in propositional attitudes. What not only unites foundationalisms but sets them off from their nonfoundationalist competitors is a certain pattern in the criterion offered.

Which truth-relevant merit does Reid's skeptic have his eye on? And let me henceforth, to make things easier, speak only of judgments and beliefs. Though the passage quoted is less clear than many others on this particular matter, the clue is there in the words "everything else *must* [my italics] be made evident." Reid's skeptic has his eye on *entitlement* – on what one is permitted to believe and on what one is not permitted to believe – on what one may believe and on what one must not believe. The "one" in question is any one who is a philosopher. Reid's skeptic is not addressing Everyman but every philosopher.

What is the shared pattern among foundationalist criteria for truth-relevant beliefs? Every foundationalist makes use of the distinction between *mediate* and *immediate* judgments and beliefs. Start with the former. We form one judgment on the basis of others in the judgment that those others evidentially support it; for example, we infer it from them. And we form and hold one belief on the basis of others in the belief that those others evidentially support it. Those are *mediately* formed judgments, and *mediately* formed and held beliefs. The idea behind calling them that is that their formation or possession is mediated by other judgments and beliefs. A judgment and belief not formed or held on the basis of others, and in the judgment or belief that those others provide evidential support for it, is *immediate.*[1] In the nature of the case, there have to be immediate judgments and beliefs. For though the judgment B on the basis of which I form this present judgment A may itself have been formed on the basis of another judgment C, there has to be an end to this sequence somewhere, or it couldn't get going. In the mental workings of all of us there must be some "mechanism" of judgment formation other than that of forming one judgment on the basis of another which one judges to provide evidential support for it, and some "mechanism" of belief formation and maintenance other than that of forming or holding one belief on the basis of another which one believes to provide evidential support for it.

This distinction, between mediate and immediate judgments and beliefs, is used by all foundationalisms in the following way: The theorist first specifies the conditions under which an immediate judgment or belief possesses the merit in question; then, for mediate judgments and beliefs, he singles out a certain support relationship, such that a mediate judgment or belief possesses the merit in question only if it stands in that relationship to immediate judgments or beliefs that possess it. The core idea is that the merit in question gets transferred by that support relationship

---

[1] Given the analysis of testimony offered in the preceding chapter, the terminology of "mediate" and "immediate," which has become traditional for these purposes, is not entirely felicitous. When a belief is formed in me immediately by my believing what I believe someone to be telling me, it would be entirely natural to describe the former belief as "mediated" by the latter; in the typology offered above, however, it falls under immediate beliefs – because the formation occurs without believing that *the proposition that he said P* provides evidential support for the proposition *P*.

from judgments and beliefs that possess it originally to judgments and beliefs that then possess it derivatively, these latter being the mediate ones.[2]

So much for foundationalism in general. Now, for *classical* foundationalism. Ever since Plato, a certain picture of the ideally formed belief has inhabited Western philosophy. The picture presupposes what has already been prominent in our discussion; namely, that fundamental in the life of the mind is acquaintance. More specifically, the picture presupposes that there are facts among the entities with which one has acquaintance: I introspect *that I am feeling rather dizzy*, I intellect *that the proposition green is a color, is necessarily true*, and so forth. The picture of the ideally formed belief then is this: One's acquaintance with some fact, coupled, if necessary, with one's awareness of that acquaintance, produces in one a belief whose propositional content corresponds to the fact with which one is acquainted. My acquaintance with the fact that I am feeling rather dizzy produces in me the belief that I am feeling rather dizzy. The content of my belief is, as it were, read directly off the fact with which I have acquaintance. How could such a belief possibly be mistaken? It must be the case that it is certain.

That's one type of ideally formed belief, the first grade, as it were: the belief formed by one's acquaintance with a fact to which the propositional content of the belief corresponds. There is a second type: the belief formed by one's acquaintance with the fact that the belief is logically supported by other facts with which one is acquainted – by one's acquaintance with the fact that it is logically grounded on facts with which one is acquainted. The logical support may take the form of entailment, in which case the certainty of one's belief concerning the premises, coupled with the certainty of one's belief concerning the entailment, are transmitted to one's belief of the conclusion: It too is certain for one. Or the logical support may take the form of probability less than

---

[2] Suppose that a person holds that some proposition possesses the merit in question only if it both stands in the support relation to immediate beliefs that possess the merit, and *also* stands in some sort of coherence relation to other beliefs. Such a person counts as a foundationalist with respect to those beliefs, by the above criterion. A *pure* foundationalist, concerning certain beliefs, would be one who holds that standing in that support relation is not only necessary to, but sufficient for, those beliefs to possess the merit in question.

maximal, in which case certainty is not transmitted to one's belief concerning the conclusion.

The fact that one's belief in this last sort of case is not certain makes beliefs thus formed significantly different from the other two – so much so that by no means all philosophers in the tradition would have regarded them as ideally formed. They should, in any case, be regarded as the lowest grade of ideally formed beliefs. But they are like the others in this regard: They are entirely formed by *acquaintance*, specifically, by acquaintance with the premises and acquaintance with the logical support that those premises provide to the conclusion. Furthermore, it should be noted that our second type of belief is already less than the "ideal" – already a second grade of ideal belief. For one may be acquainted with the facts constituting the premises in an argument, and acquainted with the fact that those premises deductively support the conclusion, without being acquainted with that fact which constitutes the conclusion. Deductive arguments, even though grounded in acquaintance, already typically carry us beyond acquaintance; probabilistic arguments carry us beyond certainty as well.

To be a *classical foundationalist* with respect to some particular truth-relevant merit, is to hold that a condition of some judgment or belief possessing that merit is that it be an ideally formed belief.

It is clear from the foregoing discussion that there is controversy as to the scope of the facts with which we human beings are acquainted. It's at this point that that special version of classical foundationalism that is *classically modern* foundationalism enters the picture. The classically modern foundationalist is a classic foundationalist who embraces the position of the Way of Ideas on the scope of the facts accessible to human acquaintance. The only source of acquaintance with facts is inner awareness, with *reason* understood as a special case thereof: reason yields acquaintance with the logical properties of states of mind and of their logical interconnections.

Reid's skeptic, to say it again, is a classically modern foundationalist with respect to entitlement – at least with respect to the philosopher's entitlement to his or her beliefs. He's a classically modern foundationalist reminding Reid of his obligations as a philosopher. Until now Reid has merely described how things go – or seem to go. The skeptic insists that at the point under consideration Reid has an obligation as philosopher to go beyond description. His obligation as philosopher is to (try to) do the best to find out whether those purported apprehensions and believings are what they purport to be; he is obligated as philosopher to assemble a satisfactory body of evidence on the matter. That done, he is then obligated to believe or disbelieve in accord with the demands of classically modern foundationalism. The skeptic, to repeat Reid's description, assumes as "a first principle," that "our thoughts, our sensations, and every thing of which we are conscious, hath a real existence," while insisting that "everything else must be made evident by the light of reason. Reason must rear the whole fabric of knowledge upon this single principle of consciousness."

Reid's skeptic is even a bit more severe in his demands on the philosopher than this. The calling of the philosopher is not to conduct the inquiry and then to believe or disbelieve in accord with the evidence. Rather, while conducting the inquiry he is to throw off belief. If the result of his inquiry is positive, then he's entitled to rejoin the vulgar and once again let the natural processes of belief formation do their work; but if the result is negative or indecisive, then he's obligated to continue in his doxastic abstinence. He would be acting in a manner unworthy of his high calling as philosopher if he did not.

REID'S STRATEGY – AND HIS SYMPATHY

Though Reid's response to the skeptic has several distinct components, those components are all, at bottom, different facets of just one strategy. Rather than trying to follow the skeptic's injunction, Reid argues that the injunction itself is seriously and irreparably flawed in several ways.

Reid thinks it most unlikely that the injunction to provide the arguments will ever be met. He observes that Descartes, Malebranche, and Locke all accepted the injunction as appropriate – indeed, issued it to themselves – and accordingly "employed their genius and skill, to prove the existence of a material world; [but] with very bad success."

Poor untaught mortals believe undoubtedly, that there is a sun, moon, and stars; an earth, which we inhabit; country, friends, and relations, which we enjoy; land, houses and moveables, which we possess. But philosophers, pitying the credulity of the vulgar, resolve to have no faith but what is founded upon reason. They apply to philosophy to furnish them with reasons for the belief of those things, which all mankind have believed without being able to give any reason for it. And surely one would expect, that, in matters of such importance, the proof would not be difficult: but it is the most difficult thing in the world. For these three great men, with the best good will, have not been able, from all the treasures of philosophy, to draw one argument, that is fit to convince a man that can reason, of the existence of any one thing without him. (IHM I, iii [100b–101a; B 18])

The fact that Descartes, Malebranche, and Locke failed to prove the existence of an external world and the reliability of perception as a mode of access thereto has not deterred a multitude of later philosophers from making the attempt; a comprehensive survey of such attempts, and a penetrating analysis of how they all fail, can be found in William P. Alston's *The Reliability of Sense Perception*.[3] Reid himself, as I mentioned, saw no prospect of success and accordingly never put his hand to the attempt.

This is not to say that Reid had no sympathy with the skeptic. He did, and we cannot understand the upshot of his discussion unless we see that he did. Though Reid will be arguing that the injunction of the skeptic must be rejected as fatally flawed, he nonetheless thinks that the skeptic has put his finger on a feature of our constitution which shows that we human beings fall short of a certain ideal. We are so constituted as to fall short of that ideal. It is this peculiar "falling short" that is the burr under the saddle of Western philosophy which the philosopher is restlessly trying to remove.

It is no doubt the perfection of a rational being to have no belief but what is grounded on intuitive [i.e., introspective] evidence, or on just reasoning; but man, I apprehend, is not such a being; nor is it the intention of nature that he should be such a being, in every [i.e., any] period of his existence. . . . [Our belief] is regulated by certain principles, which are parts of our constitution. . . . [W]hat name we give to them is of small moment; but they are certainly different from the faculty of reason. (EIP II, xxi [332b–333a])

We human beings would be more admirable than we are if our beliefs were all rationally grounded, or if the philosopher could

---

[3] Ithaca, New York: Cornell University Press, 1993.

bring it about that they were all rationally grounded. We are not of that kind. This theme of antirationalism is played over and over in Reid. He sounds like a man of our own time! I'll be coming back to the point later.

WE COULDN'T DO IT IF WE TRIED

Let us now consider the various facets of Reid's undercutting of the skeptic's injunction, moving through them in the direction from the less toward the more provocative – though in my judgment even the least provocative facets constitute decisive reasons for rejecting the skeptic's injunction as misguided. As will become clear, Reid's rhetorical skill reaches its apogee in his discussion of skepticism!

Begin with a consideration that culminates in a point characteristic of Hume. Descartes, Malebranche, and Locke failed to construct sound proofs, of the sort desired, for the existence of an external world and the reality of past events, and for the reliability of perception and memory as modes of access thereto. Does it follow that these three great philosophers and their cohorts were obligated to not believe the evidence of their senses and their memory? There's also the question of whether they were obligated to not do so even while attempting the proofs. But let that pass. Does their failure imply that *after* the attempt they were culpable if they continued believing – as of course they did?

There are some complicated issues here that we could dig in to. What if they were ignorant of their failure but their ignorance itself was not culpable – would that make them innocent in their continuing to believe? Best to sidestep all those issues, because there is a decisive reason for concluding that at no time – neither before their endeavor nor during nor after – did they have an obligation to throw off those purported believings. That reason is that they could not have done so if they had tried. And no matter whether a person himself thinks that some goal is attainable, if it's not, then he's not culpable for not having achieved it. It's true that in some circumstances he might still be culpable for not having tried. But what the skeptic says to the philosopher is that he ought to throw off such believings, not just that he ought *to try* to throw them off. And it would be very odd of the skeptic if he insisted that the philosopher ought to try to throw off those purported believings while himself believing that the philosopher could never succeed in the attempt. Thus it turns out that the skeptic's injunction is based on a false assumption. "It is not in my power," says Reid, to throw off this "belief of external objects, which may be all delusion."

why, then, should I make a vain attempt? . . . My belief is carried along by perception, as irresistibly as my body by the earth. And the greatest sceptic will find himself to be in the same condition. He may struggle hard to disbelieve the information of his senses, as a man does to swim against a torrent; but, ah! it is in vain. It is in vain that he strains every nerve, and wrestles with nature, and with every object that strikes upon his senses. For after all, when his strength is spent in the fruitless attempt, he will be carried down the torrent with the common herd of believers. (IHM VI, xx [183b–184a; B 169])

As an extra fillip, Reid adds that even if it were possible to restrain the process of formation of believings while reliability is being determined, and to continue doing so should the results prove negative, it would be most imprudent to do so. (Of course the person himself, while determining reliability, couldn't even actively consider issues of prudence – which again makes it questionable whether, all things considered, there really is any obligation on the part of philosophers to do what the skeptic insists they should do.) What would be

the consequence? I resolve not to believe my senses. I break my nose against a post that comes in my way; I step into a kennel; and, after twenty such wise and rational actions, I am taken up and clapped into a mad-house. . . . If a man pretends to be a skeptic with regard to the informations of sense, and yet prudently keeps out of harm's way as other men do, he must excuse my suspicion, that he either acts the hypocrite, or imposes upon himself. For if the scale of his belief were so evenly poised, as to lean no more to one side than to the contrary, it is impossible that his actions could be directed by any rules of common prudence. (IHM VI, xx [184a; B 170])

To understand how Reid is thinking here, we must realize that he's not talking about "paper doubts" but about *real* doubts concerning external objects: Recognizing that there appears to be a post before me but not believing that there really is, acknowledging that there appears to be a kennel of dogs over there but not believing that there really is, and so forth.[4] Really doubting, in that way.[5] Reid recognizes that the normal connection between sensory input and perceptual belief may in some cases become so seriously disordered that, to use one of his examples, a man believes his body is made of glass – or to cite a contemporary example from Oliver Sachs, that a man mistakes his wife for a hat. But if a person – a philosopher, say – really began to refrain from believing what the skeptic says philosophers ought to refrain from believing, we wouldn't regard this as a noble achievement on his part, nor would we offer him arguments for the reliability of sense perception; we'd try to get treatment for him:

Des Cartes finding nothing established in this part of philosophy, in order to lay the foundation of it deep, resolved not to believe his own existence till he should be able to give a good reason for it. He was, perhaps, the first that took up such a resolution; but if he could indeed have effected his purpose, and really become diffident of his existence, his case would have been deplorable, and without any remedy from reason or philosophy. A man that disbelieves his own existence, is surely as unfit to be reasoned with, as a man that believes he is made of glass. There may be disorders in the human frame that may produce such extravagancies; but they will never be cured by reasoning. Des Cartes indeed would make us believe that he got out of this delirium by this logical argument, *Cogito, ergo sum*. But it is evident he was in his senses

---

[4] "It is one thing to profess a doctrine of this kind, another seriously to believe it, and to be governed by it in the conduct of life. It is evident, that a man who did not believe his senses, could not keep out of harm's way an hour of his life; yet in all the history of philosophy, we never read of any skeptic that ever stepped into fire or water because he did not believe his senses, or that showed, in the conduct of life, less trust in his senses than other men have. This gives us just ground to apprehend, that philosophy was never able to conquer that natural belief which men have in their senses" (EIP II, v [259b]).

[5] We have to move carefully here if we are to understand Reid's point. John Hare has forcefully reminded me that a number of religious perspectives and philosophical positions are such that one speaks correctly if one says that their adherents doubt the existence of an external world. Reid did not have such positions in his purview; but there's nothing in his thought that would lead him to deny what I just said about them. The inability that he has in mind, when he claims that normal adult human beings are incapable of doubting the existence of an external world, is an inability that he would also attribute to those adherents. Some people doubt that life exists on any planet other than ours. *That* activity, which those people perform with respect to life on other planets, namely, doubting its existence – Reid thinks that nobody does and nobody can perform that activity for everything external. Everybody does it for some such things; nobody does it for all. The Buddhist, the Parmenidean, the Eckhartian, all step out of the way of horses. If, in the relevant sense of "doubt" and "exist," they doubted (didn't believe) that horses or any other such thing exist, they wouldn't do that. So consider the inability that Reid has in view: Having that inability is compatible with believing that the so-called external world doesn't exist but is only appearance or illusion.

all the time, and never seriously doubted of his existence. For he takes it for granted in his argument . . . (IHM I, iii [100a; B 16]).

THE SKEPTIC'S INJUNCTION IS ARBITRARILY DISCRIMINATORY

Suppose Reid's skeptic concedes the force of this point; but rather than leaving the field, issues a revised, somewhat weaker, injunction to the philosopher. Let it be conceded that no one, not even the philosopher, is under obligation to throw off those purported *de re* beliefs, because it can't be done. It nonetheless remains the obligation of Reid and his ilk to go beyond description and determine whether there is an external world and a past, and whether perception and memory give us reliable access to that.

What we've had from Reid so far is statements like this: "If . . . we attend to that act of our mind which we call the perception of an external object of sense, we shall find in it these three things. *First,* some conception or notion of the object perceived. *Secondly,* a strong and irresistible conviction and belief of its present existence. And, *thirdly,* that this conviction and belief are immediate, and not the effect of reasoning" (EIP II, v [258a]). And statements like this: "Memory is always accompanied with the belief of that which we remember, as perception is accompanied with the belief of that which we perceive, and consciousness with the belief of that whereof we are conscious" (EIP III, i [340a]). Purely descriptive statements. It's the obligation of the philosopher, in his role as philosopher, to go beyond description and ask the question: By what right? Of course it's true that in normal life we trust our senses, trust our memory, and so forth. But by what right? *Quid juris?* Are they reliable? Is our trust rationally grounded? If the results of the inquiry come in positive, then it will be the further obligation of the philosopher to present to the rest of us his reasons for concluding that there is an external world and a past, and his reasons for concluding that perception and memory give us reliable access to those. Henceforth we can then all live our lives in the confidence that our practices are rationally grounded. If the results come in negative or indecisive – well, then the philosopher will have to give us instructions for meditating on the "whimsicality" of our human condition, to use Hume's word: Though we cannot help believing, we have no good reason for supposing that what we believe is true. One way or the other, that's the contribution which the philosopher can make to culture, to *Bildung*. It's the contribution he is called to make.

The point Reid will now develop is that even this weakened injunction is fatally flawed. Let's be sure, says Reid, that we see what's being asked of us and what's presupposed by that. We're asked to run a credit check on perception and memory as producers of belief. We're asked to do so because perceptual and memorial beliefs rather often prove false, or prove not even to be beliefs about what they purport to be about, namely, external objects and prior events. And even if this weren't true for any of them, it is, so far as we can see, logically possible that it would be true for many of them – indeed, for all of them – while our sensory experience continued on its merry way. After all, it's not immediately evident that perception and memory are reliable producers of belief – nor, admittedly, that they are not. That's why it's the calling of the philosopher to do his best to find out, one way or the other.

And what is the philosopher allowed to use as evidence in running the credit check? He's allowed to use the deliverances of consciousness and of reason – only those. For remember: Reid's skeptic is a foundationalist of the classically modern sort. The philosopher is to run a credit check on perception and memory; as evidence, he is to use the deliverances of consciousness and reason.[6]

This endeavor might turn up results that are interesting in one way or another, or it might not. But notice, says Reid to the skeptic, that you are allowing the philosopher to use the deliverances of consciousness and of reason without requiring of him that he first run a credit check on those. Which implies, if you think it is the reliability of perception and memory that will be determined one way or the other, that you are assuming the reliability of consciousness and of reason. But what difference is there, between perception and memory on the one hand, and consciousness and reason on the other, that would authorize this radical difference in treatment for this purpose?

For one thing, they all come from the same shop. Nowadays

---

[6] This is the position that Reid ascribes to Descartes, and describes as "Cartesian"; see EIP VI, vii [468a]; see also IHM I, iii [100a; B 16], IHM VII [204b–205a; B 208], and IHM VII [206b; B 210–11].

many would say that shop was evolution; Reid thought the shop was divine creation by fiat:

The skeptic asks me, Why do you believe the existence of the external object which you perceive? This belief, sir, is none of my manufacture; it came from the mint of nature; it bears her image and superscription; and, if it is not right, the fault is not mine: I even took it upon trust, and without suspicion. Reason, says the skeptic, is the only judge of truth, and you ought to throw off every opinion and every belief that is not grounded on reason. Why, sir, should I believe the faculty of reason more than that of perception; they came both out of the same shop, and were made by the same artist; and if he puts one piece of false ware into my hands, what should hinder him from putting another. (IHM VI, xx [183b; B 168–9])

More important is the fact that in regard to the reasons cited by the skeptic for his claim that the philosopher has an obligation to run a credit check on perception and memory, there is no relevant difference between perception and memory, on the one hand, and reason and consciousness, on the other. Perceptual beliefs and memorial beliefs are indeed sometimes false; but so too are rational beliefs and introspective beliefs.

One source of error in the formation of beliefs is haste. We allow our beliefs to be formed on the basis of a quick glance at the car, at the argument, or whatever. The skeptic acknowledges that this source of error invades rational beliefs as much as perceptual beliefs. He's talking about the cases in which due care has been taken – the cases in which one has attended carefully to the the intuitional content of one's experience. His assumption is that, *for such cases*, there's a reason to run a credit check on perception and memory that doesn't hold for reason and introspection.

It's worth distinguishing two sources of going wrong even when one pays close attention to the intuitional content of one's perceptual experience. There may be something deceptive about that intuitional content; or there may be some breakdown in the move from awareness of that content to the belief. The classic skeptics have emphasized the former, to the virtual ignoring of the latter. Here's an example of the latter: It may both be, and seem to me to be, a piece of marble that I am looking at. But if I have been led to believe, falsely, that it is instead a piece of "marbleized" wood, I won't come out believing that it is a piece of marble but that it is an extraordinarily skillful example of marbleizing.

As to deceptiveness in intuitional content, there are, in turn, two ways in which that can come about; call them, *the way of appearance* and *the way of hallucination*. Rather often, how things appear to us in perceptual experience is different from how they really are. The object looks as a green thing would look; in reality it's blue. It sounds as a sound that is rising in pitch would sound; in reality it's steady in pitch but approaching us. And so forth. That's the way of appearance. And as to the way of hallucination, we need only remind ourselves of a point made earlier: Now and then we have experiences that mimic perception but aren't that; rather than perceiving, we are hallucinating, merely imaging, or whatever.

With these points in mind, Reid invites us to look at reason and introspection. Start with reason. It may be that a proposition not only is, but appears to me to be, a necessary truth; but if some intimidatingly brilliant logician friend has succeeded in persuading me that he, or some other logician, has proved that it cannot be true, my consideration of the proposition won't yield the belief that it is necessarily true. Instead it will yield the belief that though it certainly appears necessarily true, it must not be. That's a case of slip-up between intuitional content and belief. But the intuitional content can also be deceiving – which, of course, is what one's logician friend capitalizes on. It happens all the time that some proposition appears to a person as a proposition that is necessarily true would appear, when it's not; or that an argument appears to a person as an argument that is valid would appear, when it's not. It's only when we go beyond how the proposition or argument presents itself to us on that occasion, and explore its connections with other propositions and arguments, that we discover the truth of the matter. What's especially disturbing is that sometimes the members of a set of propositions all retain the "glow" of necessary truth even when we rightly come to realize that they can't all be true, let alone necessarily true: witness Russell's Paradox.

This already undercuts the skeptic's injunction; if reason cannot be trusted, then the project of assembling evidence pro and con the reliability of memory and perception can't even get off the ground. But Reid turns the screws tighter by arguing that the situation is no better for introspection. Our mental life no more wears its reality on its face, and only its reality, than does the external world; as a result, our introspective beliefs are filled with error and confusion. This claim runs throughout Reid's philosophy. It's extremely difficult, often impossible, to describe accurately the sensory content in perception; we are propelled by constitution and habit to move immediately from the sensation to the apprehension of, and belief about, the perceived entity.

Speaking of Descartes, Reid says that

> what appeared to him, first of all, certain and evident, was, that he thought – that he doubted – that he deliberated. In a word, the operations of his own mind, of which he was conscious, must be real, and no delusion; and, though all his other faculties should deceive him, his consciousness could not. This, therefore, he looked upon as the first of all truths . . . ; and he resolved to build all knowledge upon it, without seeking after any more first principles. . . . every other truth, therefore, and particularly the existence of the objects of sense, was to be deduced by a train of strict argumentation from what he knew by consciousness. (IHM VII [205a; B 208])

It was sheer illusion on Descartes' part to suppose that incorrigibility was to be found in his introspective beliefs. Before Descartes, it was the conviction of most Western thinkers that the heart is even more deceitful than the world is deceptive. A theme running throughout Reid's entire polemic with the Way of Ideas is that philosophy makes things even worse: The ontological and epistemological assumptions of philosophers lead them into saying downright silly things about the mind – witness Hume's suggestion that believing something differs from imagining something in that the "idea" one entertains in the former case is more vivid than the "idea" one entertains in the latter case!

In short, skepticism, in the difference of treatment it extends to perception and memory on the one hand, and to reason and inner awareness (introspection) on the other, is arbitrarily discriminatory. The arbitrariness of the discrimination undermines the injunction.

> there is no more reason to account our senses fallacious, than our reason, our memory, or any other faculty of judging which nature has given us. They are all limited and imperfect; but wisely suited to the present condition of man. We are liable to error and wrong judgment in the use of them all; but as little in the informations of sense as in the

deductions of reasoning. And the errors we fall into with regard to objects of sense are not corrected by reason, but by more accurate attention to the informations we may receive by our senses themselves. (EIP II, xxii [239a])

That last point is worth developing. How do we know that our perceptual beliefs are sometimes false? Usually it's perception that tells us – which presupposes the trustworthiness of perception. We looked again, or looked from closer up, or measured, or felt as well as looked, and thus discovered our mistake. In Reid's words, if I had not given "implicit belief to the informations of nature by my senses, . . . I should not even have been able to acquire that logic which suggests these sceptical doubts with regard to my senses" (IHM VI, xx [184a–b; B 170]). Of course reason sometimes tells us, concerning a pair of perceptual beliefs, that they cannot both be true – since they are contradictory. But it's usually not just reason that tells us which of the pair is correct but additional perceptions, or "more accurate attention to the informations" we have already received from perception. Shortly the point will be developed further, in our discussion of the track-record argument.

Let me break into my exposition of Reid to raise a question about one of the things he says about the fallibility of consciousness. Reid appears to have held not just that even carefully formed introspective beliefs are sometimes false. He appears to have held that if the skeptic is going to insist that the philosopher determine whether there is an external world, with perception as a reliable mode of access to that, and determine whether events occurred in the past, with memory as a reliable mode of access to them, then, on pain of arbitrary discrimination, he must also determine whether there are mental phenomena, with consciousness as a reliable mode of access to those. In a discussion of Hume, Reid says, for example, that

I affirm, that the belief of the existence of impressions and ideas, is as little supported by reason, as that of the existence of minds and bodies. No man ever did or could offer any reason for this belief. Des Cartes took it for granted, that he thought, and had sensations and ideas; so have all his followers done. . . . what is there in impressions and ideas so formidable, that [Hume's] all-conquering philosophy, after triumphing over every other existence, should pay homage to them? . . . A thorough and consistent sceptic will never . . . yield this point. . . . [O]f the semi-sceptics, I should beg to know, why they believe the existence of their impressions and ideas. (IHM V, vii [129b–130a; B 71])

Of course Reid didn't believe that there are any entities that satisfy Hume's *concepts* of ideas and impressions. But that appears not to be his main point here. He's just asking why Descartes and Hume didn't undertake to prove the existence of their thoughts.

Why should they have done that? Reid asks, "can any man prove that his consciousness may not deceive him?" (IHM I, iii [100a; B 17]). Deceive him, apparently, with respect to the very existence of acts of thought and states of mind – sensations, doubts, deliberations, and so forth. But how could there be that sort of deception? What might Reid have had in mind?

It can seem to one that a mental act is a case of perceiving some external object when it is not. It's something else; hallucination, perhaps. In such a case, one can obviously not hold any *de re* belief about that which one perceived, since there isn't any such thing about which to hold a belief – even though one definitely believed that there was. So too, it can seem to one that a mental act is a case of remembering some event from one's past, when it is not. It is something else; fantasizing, perhaps. In such a case too, one cannot hold any *de re* belief about what which one remembered, since there isn't any such thing – though one may well think that there is. But is there really any analogue to this in the case of introspection? How could it seem to one that a mental act is a case of being introspectively aware of some mental phenomena when it's not that, when it's something else instead? What else could it possibly be?

In the chapter entitled "Explication of Words," at the beginning of his *Essays on the Intellectual Powers*, Reid says that "*Consciousness* is a word used by philosophers, to signify that immediate knowledge which we have of our present thoughts and purposes, and, in general, of all the present operations of our minds" [222b]. Earlier in the chapter he had said that "By the *operations* of the mind, we understand every mode of thinking of which we are conscious" [221a]. He cites as examples: thinking, remembering, believing, reasoning, willing, desiring, apprehending, seeing, and hearing.

We are being led around in a very small circle here. Still, maybe some clues have been dropped on the way as to what Reid had in mind. Introspection is the faculty whereby one is aware, among other things, of one's rememberings, one's seeings, one's hearings, and so forth. But it can seem to one that one is aware of one of those when one is not; rememberings, seeings, and hearings are more, after all, than just a momentary experiential "feel." And so are willings and desirings: We have all learned from Freud that it can seem to one that one is aware of some desire or intention when, as it turns out, there was no such desire or intention to be aware of. Self-deception. Intentions and desires are no more to be identified with a momentary experiential "feel" than are rememberings and perceivings. Maybe, indeed, such a "feel" isn't even a necessary component of these.

Might this be what Reid had in mind? If so, he has fallen into confusion. It can seem to one that one is aware of being angry over some slight when one is not; it's not anger but something else. Nonetheless, it's still the case that there is some mental state of which one is aware; it's just that one has miscategorized it, applied the wrong concept. In the case of perception, one can believe that one is perceiving a so-and-so when instead one is perceiving something of a different sort, and one can also believe, about one of one's mental acts, that it is a case of perceiving, when it's not a case of perceiving but an activity of some other sort. Likewise in the case of recollection: one can miscategorize what one is recollecting; and one can believe, about some mental act, that it is a case of recollecting, when it's not a case of recollecting but an activity of some other sort. But in the case of introspection, though one can believe that one is aware of a so-and-so when instead it is something of a different sort that one is aware of; one cannot believe, about some act of mind, that it's a case of awareness of an act or state of mind, when in fact it's an activity of some other sort.

Or perhaps Reid would deny this. Perhaps he had a truly radical point in mind. He says, in one place, that "we cannot give a reason why we believe even our sensations to be real, and not fallacious; why we believe what we are conscious of" (EIP VI, vi [455a]). This suggests that perhaps Reid had in mind the Kantian sort of claim, that sensations are nothing more than how reality puts in its appearance to us.

No matter. Whether or not introspection can lead us astray in believing that we have acquaintance with something when we do not, it can and does lead us astray at many points; the beliefs it evokes in us are often false, just as the beliefs that perception and recollection evoke in us are often false. The reason the skeptic offers for his conclusion that perception and memory must undergo a credit check before we can accept the believings and purported believings produced thereby, is a reason that applies just as much to reason and introspection. It would be arbitrarily discriminatory to excuse reason and introspection from undergoing a credit check while insisting that perception and memory undergo one – at the hands of reason and introspection!

Two points in conclusion of this part of Reid's argument. Some skeptics have discerned, with more or less clarity, the force of the sort of considerations that Reid brings against the assumption that introspection is an infallible belief-forming faculty; accordingly, they have attempted to single out a class of mental entities that, when present to the mind, are both *fully present* and *unmistakable* in their presented qualities. Emotions, for example, are never fully present; there's more to an emotion than just a certain feel. But suppose certain mental phenomena are such that there is nothing more to them than what is present to the mind on a certain occasion; they are nothing but a Reidian "feel." Reid thought that sensations were that sort of entity. He also thought, however, that because sensations are so regularly interpreted by us as signs of external objects, it is in general extremely difficult to form accurate beliefs about them – or indeed, *any* beliefs about them. They are not unmistakable in their presented qualities. For the sake of the argument suppose, however, that there is a certain class of mental items so luminous that, if one has a belief about them at all, that belief is correct. Perhaps afterimages fill the bill. Surely our beliefs about such entities, formed in us by our awareness of them, are infallible! Surely that special use of introspection, which consists of introspection of these entities, does not need a credit check run on it!

Maybe not – though take the belief that it is such an entity that is the object of one's present acquaintance: Is that belief infallible? In any case, the concession won't do the skeptic any good. For if he is to develop and appraise evidence, gathered from such deliverances of introspection, concerning the reliability of perception and memory, he has to be able to appraise the logical force of arguments. Their *real* force. But as we saw, and as we all

knew anyway, the attempt to discern the logical force of arguments is also an endeavor fraught with error. Should the skeptic
think to circumvent this difficulty by reporting the *apparent* force
– on the supposition that the apparent force of an argument is
something that is fully present to him and unmistakable in its presented qualities – he would then have abandoned reason for introspection. To report on how good or bad a body of evidence
concerning the reliability of perception and memory *seems* to one
to be, is not to appraise that evidence.

Second, an implication of the foregoing is that the notion of
certainty, of which I made use when expounding the traditional
notion of the ideally formed belief, is fundamentally useless for
the purposes of the skeptic. A belief was considered to be *certain*,
I said, if the cause of its formation in one was one's awareness
of the fact to which the propositional content of the belief
corresponded. It's true that such a belief cannot be mistaken. But
the concept is of no use to the skeptic because we can be mistaken in our judgments as to which of our beliefs satisfy the
concept and which do not. The skeptic may enjoin the philosopher to determine the reliability of perception and memory by
arguments whose premises and validity are certain for him; but if
the philosopher accepts the injunction, we can be assured that
he, a fallible human being, will be making mistakes in his judgments of certitude. The pursuit of certainty is the pursuit of a will
o' the wisp.

THE SKEPTIC PLUNGES INTO ABSURDITY

Suppose now that the skeptic recognizes the force of Reid's
charge of arbitrary discrimination against perception and
memory and that, in response, he once again revises his injunction to the philosopher. This time he says that it's the calling of
the philosopher to determine the reliability of *all* our fundamental modes of belief-formation. Since reason and introspection
might go as radically wrong, or almost as radically wrong, as perception and memory, it is the high calling of the philosopher to
check out their overall reliability as well. If his results prove positive, he is then called to display for the rest of us the grounding
that he has uncovered for reason and introspection, along with
that which he has uncovered for perception and memory. If his

results prove negative – well, then the "whimsicality" of our human condition will be even more obvious.

If this is the skeptic's response, says Reid, he will have liberated himself from arbitrary discrimination at the cost of plunging himself into mindless absurdity. For now we're left with neither evidence nor inference – with neither premises nor arguments. You can't run a credit check on anybody if you're running a credit check on everybody.

If a sceptic should build his scepticism upon this foundation, says Reid, that all our reasoning and judging powers are fallacious in their nature, or should resolve at least to withhold assent until it be proved that they are not, it would be impossible by argument to beat him out of this stronghold; and he must even be left to enjoy his scepticism. (EIP VI, v [447b])

I dare say the intuitive reaction of almost all of us – if not indeed all – is to accept this as a devastating reply on Reid's part. There's no way the skeptic can now escape twisting in the wind. He's either arbitrarily discriminatory in what he enjoins on the philosopher or absurdly mindless. Give him his pick of rope!

But maybe we ought to take some time for second thoughts. Reid asks at a certain point why Descartes did "not prove the existence of his thought?" Earlier I quoted a fragment of Reid's response. Let's now have his full response before us: "Consciousness, it may be said, vouches that. And who is voucher for consciousness? Can any man prove that his consciousness may not deceive him? No man can; nor can we give a better reason for trusting to it, than that every man, while his mind is sound, is determined, by the constitution of his nature, to give implicit belief to it, and to laugh at or pity the man who doubts its testimony" (IHM I, iii [100a; B 17]).

Suppose a Cartesian replies that he has a better reason for trusting the deliverances of reason and introspection than that; namely, the excellence of their track record.[7] True, they are not infallible.[8] Nonetheless, if one placed before one's mind's eye a

---

[7] In what follows, I am heavily indebted to the excellent discussion of these matters by William P. Alston, "Epistemic Circularity," in his *Epistemic Justification: Essays in the Theory of Knowledge* (Ithaca, New York, Cornell University Press, 1989). The reader should consult Alston's essay for a much more extensive discussion of the issues than I will be offering.

[8] With perhaps the "thin" exception, noted above, for introspection of a certain type of mental entity.

representative and ample sample of judgments of reason, took note of which of those were true and which not, and then calculated the relative frequency of true judgments within the totality, it's obvious that the proportion would be high. So too for introspective judgments. So, yes, reason and introspection are generally reliable. Their track record is evidence for that. Of course reason plays an indispensable role in the very activity of discerning which of its deliverances are true and which not, as does consciousness in the counterpart discernment. Reason and introspection are in good measure self-evaluating, and hence self-correcting, faculties. (It would be worthwhile to try to understand how that can be.)

Now I dare say that if anyone actually offered such a track-record argument for the reliability of reason or introspection, it would strike us all like Baron von Münchhausen trying to lift himself off the ground by tugging on his own bootstraps. And let it not be overlooked that if this is a legitimate line of argument for reason and introspection, it will also be a legitimate line of argument for perception and memory. Furthermore, it's not obvious that the results would be much worse for perception and memory. Thus, whatever the merits of the track-record style of argument, it's of no use to the skeptic; were he to allow it for reason and introspection, and disallow it for perception and memory, he would be guilty, once again, of arbitrary discrimination. But still, is a track-record argument of this sort a bad argument? If so, why exactly?

Notice the following two features of the argument. First, it's not a circular argument. An argument is circular when the conclusion occurs among the premises. The track-record argument for the reliability of reason is not like that. It does not include, among its premises, its conclusion; namely, that reason is reliable. Its premises are instead all of the following form: Belief ∂ was formed in me by reason, and I now discern (by the use of reason and perhaps other faculties) that ∂ is true; belief β was formed in me by reason, and I now discern (by the use of reason and perhaps other faculties) that β is true, and so forth.

To get at the second feature, let me introduce a piece of terminology. Let us say that a belief possesses the merit of being *warranted* for the person holding it if it was produced by a reliable faculty working properly in an environment for which that faculty was designed, provided the faculty was designed for arriving at truth.[9] And now let us suppose that one's reason is in fact a reliable faculty, designed for arriving at truth, and that the judgments of truth and falsehood concerning the items on one's sample from reason's track record were formed in a situation in which one's reason was working properly in an environment for which it was designed. Then one will be warranted in one's judgments of truth and falsehood concerning the items on one's sample from reason's track record. And if one's sample from that track record is indeed representative and ample, then the conclusion at which one arrives inductively, that reason is overall reliable, will also be something that one is warranted in believing (assuming that, when one draws the inference, one's reason is working properly in a situation for which it was designed). It doesn't make any difference whether or not one has previously entertained the proposition that reason is reliable – and if one has, whether or not one believed it.

It was for no more than illustrative purposes that I singled out warrant.[10] The counterpart points hold for a number of other doxastic merits: The judgments concerning the truth and falsehood of items on the sample from the track record will have the merit in question no matter what the person believes, if anything, about the reliability of her reason; and that merit will get transferred, by inductive inference, to the conclusion that her reason is over all reliable.

So once again, what if anything is wrong with such an argument? Isn't Reid just mistaken when he says that no better reason can be given for trusting introspection, or reason, than that "every man, while his mind is sound, is determined, by the constitution of his nature, to give implicit belief to it, and to laugh at or pity the man who doubts its testimony"? Isn't the track-record argument a much better reason than that?

Well, notice this about the track-record argument. In determining the proportion of items that are true, in the sample of the track record that one assembles, one takes for granted the

---

[9] I am, of course, borrowing the concept from Alvin Plantinga. See his *Warrant and Proper Function* (Oxford: Oxford University Press, 1993).

[10] Alston conducts his discussion in terms of *justification*. I have avoided using that concept because I don't grasp it – or more precisely, because I think the word "justification" is used in contemporary epistemological literature to express a bewildering array of different concepts.

reliability of one's reason when making that determination. It's not that, while making the determination, one actively believes the proposition, *my reason is now functioning reliably*, and that this proposition then functions, in one way or another, as a premise of the argument. It's rather that, in one's actions of determining the proportion of truth, one takes the reliability of one's reason for granted.[11] As Alston puts it: One assumes it "in practice"; one "practically" assumes it.[12] (In the next chapter, I will have more to say about this phenomenon of *taking for granted*.) In offering or accepting a track-record argument for the reliability of reason, one takes for granted reason's reliability. And so, likewise, for such arguments offered or accepted for the reliability of perception, memory, and introspection.

Whether or not one is willing to embrace such arguments for the reliability of one's fundamental faculties depends entirely, then, on whether one is willing to take their reliability for granted. But we all do, and can't help doing so, says Reid. That was the point of his comment about being determined by "the constitution of [one's] nature." When we see the track-record argument for what it is, then we see that, so far from being a different and better reason than the ineluctability reason, the argument highlights the fundamental point that Reid was making about our human constitution. We all take for granted, in the living of our lives, "that the natural faculties, by which we distinguish truth from error, are not fallacious. If any man should demand a proof of this, it is impossible to satisfy him. For suppose it should be mathematically demonstrated, this would signify nothing in this

---

[11] Perhaps Reid saw this point when he made the following comment: "If a man's honesty were called in question, it would be ridiculous to refer it to the man's own word, whether he be honest or not. The same absurdity there is in attempting to prove, by any kind of reasoning, probable or demonstrative, that our reason is not fallacious, since the very point in question is, whether reasoning may be trusted" (EIP VI, v [447b]).

[12] Speaking about the reliability of sense perception, he elaborates the point as follows: "If one wholeheartedly denied or doubted [the reliability of perception], he could not, rationally, be convinced by the argument, if he kept his wits about him. Being disposed not to accept the reliability of sense perception, he would not accept the premises. Again, one need not have explicitly accepted [the reliability of perception] in order to be able, rationally, to accept or use this argument. But a person who truly rejects [the reliability of perception] does not accept it even practically, and hence cannot accept the premises. What all this comes down to is that in using or taking this [track-record] argument to establish [the reliability of perception], one is already, implicitly or explicitly, taking [the proposition that perception is reliable] to be true. In this way we might say that the argument 'presupposes' the truth of the conclusion, although the conclusion does not itself appear among the premises" (p. 328).

case; because, to judge of a demonstration, a man must trust his faculties, and take for granted the very thing in question. . . . [I]f our faculties be fallacious, why may they not deceive us in this reasoning as well as in others? And if they are to be trusted in this instance without a voucher, why not in others? Every kind of reasoning for the veracity of our faculties, amounts to no more than taking their own testimony for their veracity." Which in any case is what we all do and "must do implicitly, until God give us new faculties to sit in judgment upon the old . . ." (EIP VI, v [447a–b]). Whereupon we'll have to trust the new faculties in the same way we did the old. Even if our basic faculties are reliable, in the nature of the case we can't prove their reliability without taking for granted their reliability.

Of course we make mistakes, and we know that we do. But coming to believe that something one believed is false presupposes trusting one's faculties; and coming to believe, more generally, that one of one's belief-forming faculties is not reliable in such-and-such conditions presupposes trusting one's faculties. We have no choice but to treat our belief-forming faculties as innocent until proved guilty. Proving them guilty will never come to anything more than proving them guilty on a particular occasion or type of occasion. And we'll have to take them at their own word that they were guilty then. We cannot squirm out of our doxastic skin. "If we are deceived in [our constitution], we are deceived by him that made us, and there is no remedy" (IHM V, vii [130b; B 72]). But as a matter of fact we all take for granted that we are not thus deceived.

Reid observed that the person who believes that it is God who has endowed us with our faculties can and will on that account regard them, whatever their deficiencies, as fundamentally reliable. "Common sense and reason have both one author; that almighty Author, in all whose other works we observe a consistency, uniformity, and beauty which charm, and delight the understanding: there must therefore be some order and consistency in the human faculties, as well as in other parts of his workmanship" (IHM V, vii [127a; B 68]). And speaking specifically of perception, Reid says that "now I yield to the direction of my senses, not from instinct only, but from confidence and trust in a faithful and beneficent monitor, grounded upon the experience of his paternal care and goodness" (IHM VI, xx [184b; B 170]).

So when all is said and done, the person who believes in a good, wise, and powerful God does, thereby, have a belief from which he can appropriately infer the overall reliability of his basic native faculties.

But such a person will not single out introspection and reason for preferential treatment. And accepting God's goodness as a reason for trusting in one's faculties presupposes trusting in, if nothing else, one's faculty of reason. To which Reid adds that we all trust our faculties long before, and whether or not, we have this theistic reason for doing so. "[A] man would believe his senses though he had no notion of a Deity. He who is persuaded that he is the workmanship of God, and that it is a part of his constitution to believe his senses, may think that a good reason to confirm his belief. But he had the belief before he could give this or any other reason for it" (EIP II, xx [329b]). "The wise Author of our nature intended, that a great and necessary part of our knowledge should be derived from experience, before we are capable of reasoning, and he hath provided means perfectly adequate to this intention" (IHM VI, xiv [198a; B 196]).

THE UPSHOT

In closing, let me return to the theme of Reid's antirationalism. In a passage I quoted in my opening chapter, Reid observes that evidence comes in various kinds: "the evidence of sense, the evidence of memory, the evidence of consciousness, the evidence of testimony, the evidence of axioms, the evidence of reasoning" (EIP II, xx [328a]). He then goes on to make this very interesting point:

When I compare the different kinds of evidence above mentioned, I confess, after all, that the evidence of reasoning, and that of some necessary and self-evident truths, seems to be the least mysterious, and the most perfectly comprehended; and therefore I do not think it strange that philosophers should have endeavoured to reduce all kinds of evidence to these.

When I see a proposition to be self-evident and necessary, and that the subject is plainly included in the predicate, there seems to be nothing more that I can desire, in order to understand why I believe it. And when I see a consequence that necessarily follows from one or more self-evident propositions, I want nothing more with regard to my belief of that consequence. The light of truth so fills my mind in these cases, that I can neither conceive, nor desire any thing more satisfying. (EIP II, xx [330a])

When he reflects on perceptual and memorial beliefs, he feels dissatisfied, says Reid. They compel his belief no less than does awareness of an axiom. But when he as a philosopher reflects on these beliefs so as to trace them to their origins, he's not able to "resolve" the process "into necessary and self-evident axioms, or conclusions that are necessarily consequent upon them." He is forced to conclude that in perception and memory, he, along with humanity in general, lacks "that evidence which [he] can best comprehend, and which gives perfect satisfaction to an inquisitive mind . . ." (ibid.). Yet it would be "ridiculous to doubt, and I find it is not in my power" (ibid.).

To a philosopher, this is humiliating. "By his reason, he can discover certain abstract and necessary relations of things. . . ." But "his knowledge of what really exists, or did exist, comes by another channel, which is open to those who cannot reason. He is led to it in the dark, and knows not how he came by it" (ibid.).

When we have dug down to the deepest stratum of our human understanding, what confronts us is mystery. Deep impenetrable mystery: We do not understand. When Locke talked about *not understanding*, as he often did, it was usually the world about us that he had in mind as not understood. What Reid emphasized, over and over, was the mystery within.

But we find more than mystery when we dig down to the deepest stratum. We find trust. Practical trust. We trust our senses, trust our memory, trust our introspection, trust our reason, trust our intellection. We trust where there are no grounds for trust except grounds infected by practical circularity – trust where we know nothing at all about the explanatory workings. "We are born under a necessity of trusting to our reasoning and judging powers; and a real belief of their being fallacious cannot be maintained for any considerable time by the greatest skeptic, because it is doing violence to our constitution. It is like a man's walking upon his hands, a feat that some men upon occasion can exhibit; but no man ever made a long journey in this manner. Cease to admire his dexterity, and he will, like other men, betake himself to his legs" (EIP VI, v [448a]).

One can imagine two very different pieties evoked by this

account of our human condition. The Nietzschean piety of railing against that darkness which is the mystery at the core of our existence.[13] And a Christian (Jewish, Muslim) piety that rests content with that trust which it is our nature to exhibit in the face of the mystery. That latter, as we shall see in more detail in our final chapter, was Reid's piety. "I rest contented, and quietly suffer myself to be carried along . . ." (IHM VI, xx [183b–184a; B 169]).

It's no wonder that philosophers have tried either to ground perceptual and memorial beliefs in reason or to throw them off. Reason "is the faculty wherein they assume a superiority to the unlearned. The informations of sense are common to the philosopher and to the most illiterate: they put all men upon a level, and therefore are apt to be undervalued" by philosophers (EIP II, xxii [339a]). "But the wise and the humble will receive [even the knowledge they cannot account for] as the gift of Heaven, and endeavour to make the best use of it" (EIP II, xx [330b]).

---

[13] Though there is a great deal of railing against the darkness in Nietzsche, it was probably not his final position. That final position is astonishingly close to Reid's. Two passages, called to my attention by Gordon C. F. Bearn, can be cited to put the point nicely. First a passage from *The Birth of Tragedy* (1872) which, in Nietzschean manner, echoes Reid's insistence on the limits of reason:

> But science, spurred by its powerful illusion [that by using the thread of causality it might be able to penetrate the deepest abysses of being] speeds irresistibly toward its limits where its optimism, concealed in the essence of logic, suffers shipwreck. For the periphery of the circle of science has an indefinite number of points; and while there is no telling how this circle could ever be surveyed completely, noble and gifted men, nevertheless reach, ere half their time and inevitably, such boundary points on the periphery from which one gazes into what defies illumination. When they see to their horror how logic coils up at these boundaries and finally bites its own tail – suddenly the new form of insight breaks through, *tragic insight* which, merely to be endured needs art as a protector and remedy (para. 15, Kaufmann tr.).

And then a passage which echoes, again in Nietzschean manner, Reid's "piety":

> A step further in convalescence: and the free spirit again draws near to life – slowly, to be sure, almost reluctantly, almost mistrustfully. It again grows warmer around him, yellower, as it were; feeling and feeling for others acquire depth, warm breezes of all kinds blow across him. It seems to him as if his eyes are only now open to what is near [*das Nahe*]. He is astonished and sits silent: where *had* he been? These near, nearest things: how changed they seem! what bloom and magic they have acquired! . . . How he loves to sit sadly still, to spin out patience, to lie in the sun! Who understands as he does the happiness that comes in winter, the spots of sunlight on the wall! They are the most grateful animals in the world, also the most modest, these convalescents and lizards again half turned towards life: – there are some among them who allow no day to pass without hanging a little song of praise on the hem of its departing robe (from para. 5 of Nietzsche's new preface to the first volume of the two volume [1886] republication of *Human, All Too Human*).

CHAPTER IX

Common Sense

Reid's philosophy became known far and wide as "Common Sense Philosophy." That was its great misfortune. Which philosopher – except for Reid himself and a handful of his followers – wishes to be known among his fellow philosophers as a philosopher of common sense? Recall Kant's caustic comments in the Introduction to his *Prolegomena to Any Future Metaphysics*:

It is indeed a great gift of God to possess . . . plain common sense. But this common sense must be shown in action by well-considered and reasonable thoughts and words, not by appealing to it as an oracle when no rational justification for one's position can be advanced. To appeal to common sense when insight and science fail, and no sooner – this is one of the subtle discoveries of modern times, by means of which the most superficial ranter can safely enter the lists with the most thorough thinker and hold his own. But as long as a particle of insight remains, no one would think of having recourse to this subterfuge. Seen clearly, it is but an appeal to the opinion of the multitude, of whose applause the philosopher is ashamed, while the popular charlatan glories and boasts in it.

It was not by some accident of history that Reid's philosophy came to be known as "Common Sense Philosophy." What Reid himself called "common sense" had central place in his philosophy. Or rather, his followers at the time regarded it as having central place; whether Reid himself so regarded it is much less clear. Important, Yes. Central? Not so clear.

Most of Reid's reflections and polemics, in his *Inquiry into the Human Mind* and in his *Essays on the Intellectual Powers*, revolve around a fundamental feature of our human constitution: the impact on the self of objects and events is processed by us in such a way that contingently true beliefs get formed immediately about entities quite other than the self and its states and activities. In the preceding chapter we found Reid saying that he found himself less than happy with this aspect of our human intellectual constitution. He has the sense that he understands why, when he has the proposition *All bachelors are unmarried* clearly in mind, that he believes, about it, that it is necessarily true. Though he doesn't say so, one guesses that he also has the sense that he understands why he believes things about his sensations when he's fully aware of them. But he doesn't have any such sense of understanding why contingent propositions about things quite other than the self and its states and activities are believed by him immediately – especially when it is a perceptual belief. Upon having a certain tactile sensation he immediately believes that his body is in contact with a hard object. That's mysterious, in a way in which believing that it is a necessary truth, about the proposition *All bachelors are unmarried* when one has it in mind, is not mysterious. All he knows is that this is how it goes.

It's this unease, this dissatisfaction, on which the skeptic preys – more precisely, on which the Reidian skeptic preys. For skepticism is protean. The skeptic who preoccupied Reid was a foundationalist of the classically modern sort who tried to lay on the philosopher the obligation to use the deliverances of reason and of introspection to assess the reliability of all other belief-forming faculties. To fail to devote oneself to this task of critique is to defect from the high calling of the philosopher to live the life of reason; it is to live as the herd lives.

We followed Reid in his argument that the philosopher has no such obligation. It's entirely acceptable that the philosopher join with the vulgar in taking for granted the fundamental reliability of his intellectual faculties, in part because he has no option but to do so; the philosopher has no obligation to establish a tribunal with reason and introspection as judges. He may do so if he wishes, as a matter of curiosity; he may try grounding everything in reason and introspection. But not only do the prospects of succeeding at that project look singularly unpromising; success at the project would leave reason and introspection ungrounded. So what's gained? Until such time as God gives us new faculties whose output we can use to assess the reliability of our present ones, we'll just have to take for granted the fundamental reliability of our present ones. And if and when God does grant us super faculties, we'll have to take *their* reliability for granted!

We have all been taught to think of Hegel as the first to speak of the "spirit of modern philosophy." So it comes as a surprise to find Reid saying that this "may be considered as the spirit of modern philosophy, to allow of no first principles of contingent truths but this one, that the thoughts and operations of our own minds, of which we are conscious, are self-evidently real and true; but that every thing else that is contingent is to be proved by argument" (EIP VI, vii [464a]).

What Reid is saying here goes a bit beyond what we discussed in the last chapter and what I just summarized. It's the *critical* task of the philosopher, says the Reidian skeptic, to assess the degree to which our intellectual constitution puts us in touch with reality, using reason and consciousness as the source of credit information. But no one suggested that the critical task of appraising our intellectual constitution constitutes the entirety of the philosophical task; and to know the critical task of the philosopher is not, so far forth, to know the proper basis and touchstone for *constructive* philosophy. For example, if it should prove to be the case that though we cannot establish the reliability of perception and memory by appealing only to reason and introspection, we nonetheless cannot slough them off for life in the everyday, it doesn't follow that the philosopher, given his high calling, is entitled to use the ungrounded output of perception and memory for constructive philosophy. Perhaps it's the calling of the philosopher to impose on himself a certain self-limitation when engaged in philosophy that is lifted when he engages in life in the everyday. What Reid is saying in the passage quoted is that it is the spirit of modern philosophy to allow no other contingent propositions in constructive philosophy than those which are immediate deliverances of consciousness or established on the basis of those by reason.

It will come as no surprise to learn that Reid's rejection of the Way of Ideas, and his articulation of an alternative picture of our human constitution, led him to a profound rethinking of this received picture of the philosopher. His famous – or infamous – doctrine of Common Sense constituted the core of that rethinking. It's not in his substantive philosophy, but in his *meta*philosophy – in his philosophy of philosophy – that Reid's doctrine of Common Sense has its home.

Reid's doctrine of Common Sense represents the convergence

of a number of lines in his thought; thus one can approach it from other angles than that which I just sketched out. A theme that emerged in our discussion in the preceding chapter, of Reid's way with the skeptic, was the theme of *taking for granted*, or *taking on trust*. We all do take for granted, and in the nature of the case must take for granted, the fundamental reliability of our basic belief-forming faculties. "Who is voucher for consciousness?" asks Reid in a passage we quoted earlier. "Can any man prove that his consciousness may not deceive him? No man can: nor can we give a better reason for *trusting* to it, than that every man, while his mind is sound, is determined by the constitution of his nature, to give *implicit belief* to it, and to laugh at, or pity, the man who doubts its testimony. And is not every man, in his wits, as much determined to take his existence upon *trust* as his consciousness" (IHM I, iii [100a; B 17]; italics added). One can think of Reid's doctrine of Common Sense as taking this theme of *taking on trust*, or *taking for granted*, and running with it!

WHAT IS COMMON SENSE?

In the preceding chapter we followed Reid in his reflections on the relation of the philosopher to that intellectual constitution which the philosopher shares with human beings in general. The topic now before us is not so much our human intellectual constitution, as our human intellectual condition. Common Sense constitutes a certain component of the actual output of our human intellectual constitution. We want to arrive at an understanding of what Reid sees as the proper relation of philosophy to that part of our intellectual condition. Let's begin the journey by trying to get a grip on what component that is – a grip on what Reid takes Common Sense to be.

It has to be conceded that Reid's discussion of Common Sense is confusing. And not just confusing but confused: It both confuses us and reveals confusion in Reid. I judge it to be, in fact, the most confused part of Reid's thought. Ironic that it should also be the most famous! Nonetheless, I think that in spite of the confusion it is possible to discern the points Reid was trying to make. That is what I will be trying to do: discern the points he was trying to make. I won't so much exegete Reid for the purpose of laying out what he says as try to think his thoughts better than he himself succceeded in thinking them. At the end of my discussion I will offer a speculation as to why Reid's own attempts to get clear on the points he was trying to make proved so fumbling.

It will be asked: Why bother with a philosopher who can't get clear on some of his most fundamental points? My response is that so it was with almost all the great philosophers of the modern period. One witnesses in them a struggle, desperate at times, to break free from received ways of thinking and bring into the light of day the radically new ideas they were straining to give birth to.

One point of confusion need not detain us long. In "common language," says Reid, "sense always implies judgment. A man of sense is a man of judgment. Good sense is good judgment. Nonsense is what is evidently contrary to right judgment. Common Sense is that degree of judgment which is common to men with whom we can converse and transact business" (EIP VI, ii [421b]). In short, "sense, in its most common, and therefore its most proper meaning, signifies *judgment*, though philosophers often use it in another meaning. From this it is natural to think, that common sense should mean common judgment; and so it really does" (EIP VI, ii [423a]).

What does Reid mean by "judgment"? Does he mean the faculty of judging, or the judgments rendered? Does Common Sense consist of belief-forming faculties that we all share in common, with a particular principle of Common Sense being one of those shared faculties? Or does Common Sense consist of propositions judged or believed by human beings in common, with a particular principle of Common Sense being some item in that totality of shared beliefs? Or – here's yet a third possibility – does Common Sense consist of those shared faculties that produce beliefs we all share in common?

From the passages quoted it's not clear. And in general, though Reid usually meant to pick out certain propositions believed in common with his phrase, "principles of Common Sense," quite clearly he sometimes meant to pick out certain belief-forming faculties shared in common. One wishes he had been more consistent. Usually, though, it won't make any difference; when it does, the context will usually resolve the ambiguity. On the ground that Reid usually means, by "principles of Common Sense," shared beliefs or judgments – that is, propositions believed or judged in common – let me work with that interpretation.

Reid is also confused and confusing over which beliefs those are; this is a more serious matter. My conclusion will be that two quite different lines of thought were in conflict in his mind: He thinks of the principles of Common Sense both as *shared first principles*, and as *things we all take for granted*. Let's begin with the former line of thought.

In Chapter II of Essay VI of the *Intellectual Powers*, a chapter titled "Of Common Sense," Reid offers his official definition of "Common Sense: "We ascribe to reason two offices, or two degrees. The first is to judge of things self-evident; the second to draw conclusions that are not self-evident from those that are. The first of these is the province, and the sole province of common sense; and therefore it coincides with reason in its [i.e., common sense's] whole extent, and is only another name for one branch or one degree of reason" (EIP VI, ii [425b]).

The passage is eccentric in that whereas Reid usually means by "reason" that capacity whereby we discern and come to believe the necessity of propositions and the validity of arguments, here he treats Common Sense as a "branch" of reason. In the paragraph immediately following, the rationale for this eccentric usage becomes clear. Reid thinks that ordinary people don't do much reasoning – not much *good* reasoning, anyway. But he doesn't want to call them "unreasonable" or "irrational" on that account. So, having said that self-evident beliefs are a manifestation of reason as well as those inferred from such, he says that "It is this degree [of reason] that entitles them to the denomination of reasonable creatures" (ibid.).

The difficult problem of interpretation is what Reid means by "self-evident." The contrast drawn between things self-evident and things not self-evident but inferred from those that are leads one to wonder whether the distinction Reid has in mind is that between beliefs formed by inference and beliefs not so formed. The answer is that this is certainly part of what Reid means, but not the whole. "Things self-evident" are beliefs not formed by inference; but not all such beliefs are "things self-evident."

What must be added to a belief not formed by inference to make it "a thing self-evident"? After devoting Chapter III of Essay VI to other matters, Reid returns to the topic of Common Sense in Chapter IV. He leads off by contrasting beliefs formed by inference with *intuitive* judgments – rather than with *self-evident* judgments: "One of the most important distinctions of our judgments is, that some of them are intuitive, others grounded on argument" (EIP VI, iv [434a]). But at once he forestalls the thought that this is a different approach by explaining this distinction with the concept of evidence. Judgment, he says, "is carried along necessarily by the evidence, real or seeming, which appears to us at the time." He then observes that in some cases the proposition "has the light of truth in itself," whereas in other cases it has to borrow its evidence from another. The former are of course the *self-evident*. Then he offers the traditional definition of "self-evident": "no sooner understood than they are believed. The judgment follows the apprehension of them necessarily . . . ; the proposition is not deduced or inferred from another; it has the light of truth in itself, and has no occasion to borrow it from another" (ibid.). He concludes by observing that the propositional contents of intuitive judgments "are called *first principles, principles of common sense, common notions, self-evident truths*" (ibid.).

Provisionally then, what we have is this: Principles of common sense are to be found among those propositions which (a), are not believed on the basis of inference, and (b), are self-evidently true.

But this is perplexing. For Reid holds that contingent propositions are to be found among the principles of Common Sense. Now of course lots of contingent propositions that we believe are not believed on the basis of inference; no problem there. The question is whether any of those contingent propositions also satisfy that traditional concept of the self-evident? It was traditionally assumed that the concept of *a self-evidently true proposition* applies only to necessary truths. Was Reid of a different view?

Consider the following passage, in which Reid develops his thought on the matter of evidence just a bit. "It is demonstrable," he says, "and was long ago demonstrated by Aristotle, that every proposition to which we give a rational assent, must either have its evidence in itself, or derive it from some antecedent proposition. And the same thing may be said of the antecedent proposition. As, therefore, we cannot go back to antecedent propositions without end, the evidence must at last rest upon propositions, one or more, which have their evidence in themselves, that is, upon first principles" (EIP VI, viii [466b]).

This does nothing to dissolve our perplexity; it reinforces it. Reid allows just two options. Those propositions believed on the basis of inference, for which our assent is rational, derive their evidence from some antecedent proposition. Those propositions for which our assent is rational but not believed on the basis of inference, have their evidence in themselves. But this seems just not correct; there's a third option. Suppose that, with everything working properly, the perceptual belief is formed in me that there's something green before me. Does that contingent proposition have "its evidence in itself"? Certainly it doesn't satisfy the traditional concept of a self-evident truth: "no sooner understood than believed." In fact its evidence consists of what Reid, in other places, calls "the evidence of sense." The evidence for it is the sensory experience one is having.[1]

Be all that as it may, however; I think we can safely settle on a modification of the interpretation formulated provisionally above: Principles of Common Sense are to be found among those beliefs not held on the basis of inference *for which the person has evidence* – evidence which *justifies* him in holding the belief. Reid notes that disputes will arise as to whether a certain proposition is or is not a principle of Common Sense. Such disputes are not to be settled simply by determining whether or not the proposition in question is held on the basis of inference; we must find out, in addition, whether it really came with good evidence or only seemed to do so. Nonpropositional evidence, of course, for otherwise it wouldn't be held immediately. Principles of Common Sense are to be found among beliefs held immediately and justifiedly.

Reid adds that if one knows anything at all by inference, one must have such beliefs; and that the scientist looks to base his scientific reasoning on such beliefs:

all knowledge got by reasoning must be built upon first principles.
This is as certain as that every house must have a foundation. . . .
When we examine . . . the evidence of any proposition, either we find it self-evident, or it rests upon one or more propositions that support it.

---

[1] The counterpart point holds for the evidence of consciousness: "The operations of our minds are attended with *consciousness*; and this consciousness is the evidence, the only evidence, which we have or can have of their existence. . . . Every man finds himself under a necessity of believing what consciousness testifies, and every thing that hath this testimony is to be taken as a first principle" (EIP I, ii [231b]).

The same thing may be said of the propositions that support it; and of those that support them, as far back as we can go. But we cannot go back in this track to infinity. Where then must this analysis stop? It is evident that it must stop only when we come to propositions, which support all that are built upon them, but are themselves supported by none, that is, to self-evident propositions. (EIP VI, iv [435a–b])

The conclusion I settled on was that principles of Common Sense are to be found among those beliefs that are held noninferentially and justifiedly. But Reid says something stronger than that in the passages quoted. He says that the principles of Common Sense are *identical* with beliefs held noninferentially and justifiedly. That can't be right, for an obvious reason. Whereas principles of Common Sense are *common*, lots of such beliefs aren't common at all; they're entirely personal. The noninferential belief I have when writing this sentence, for which I have excellent evidence, that my left leg is now bent at the knee – no one else believes that. Surely the principles of Common Sense have to be a certain subset of immediate and justifiedly held beliefs; they are those of such beliefs which are shared by all.

One guesses that if Reid had managed to articulate this line of thought precisely and consistently, it would have been the view I just stated: principles of Common Sense are a subset of first principles, namely, those held in common. And not infrequently Reid does call a belief that is held noninferentially and justifiedly, but not in common, a first principle, without calling it a principle of Common Sense, or a *first* principle of Common Sense. For example: "Every man finds himself under a necessity of believing what consciousness testifies, and every thing that hath this testimony is to be taken as a first principle" (EIP I, ii [231b]).

That's one line of thought which one sees working in Reid's mind: Principles of Common Sense are shared first principles. Now for the other, according to which principles of Common Sense are those things we all must take for granted in our life in the everyday. In a passage in the Inquiry Reid says this:

If there are certain principles, as I think there are, which the constitution of our nature leads us to believe, and which we are under a necessity to take for granted in the common concerns of life, without being able to give a reason for them; these are what we call the principles of common sense; and what is manifestly contrary to them, is what we call absurd. (IHM II, vi [108b; B 33])

Obviously the concept of something taken for granted in one's activities is different from the concept of a justifiedly held immediate belief. It would be interesting, though for Reid's purposes ultimately not all that significant, if whatever satisfied the one concept also satisfied the other and vice versa. The best way to see that that is most definitely not the case is to look at a few of the examples that Reid himself offers of principles of Common Sense. Let me cite the first, the third, and the fifth from the list that he gives in his chapter on "The First Principles of Contingent Truths" (Essay VI, chapter v):

(1) That everything of which one is conscious exists.
(3) That those things did really happen which one distinctly remembers.
(5) That those things do really exist which one distinctly perceives by one's senses, and are what one perceives them to be.

A word first about how to understand these principles, since it will seem to almost all of us that they are not contingently but necessarily true: Necessarily it is the case that if one is conscious of something, then it exists; if one remembers something, then it did really happen; if one perceives something, then it does really exist. Recall our discussion in Chapter V of Reid's analysis of hallucinatory experiences. We there explicated Reid's claim that though perception occurs in hallucinatory experiences, there exists no object that one perceives. Reid's statement of these principles makes clear that he favors a parallel analysis for deceptive memory and for deceptive consciousness. (Whether or not there actually is any such thing as deceptive consciousness, Reid's thought is that there could be.)

On the line of thought we are presently considering, these principles, and all the others that Reid cites as examples of first principles of contingent truths and of first principles of necessary truths, are to be interpreted as if they had the preface: "We all must take for granted in our lives in the everyday. . . ." An additional understanding is that the "all" here is to be understood as short for: "all normal adults." The third in Reid's listing is thus to be understood as follows: "All those of us who are normal adults must take for granted in our lives in the everyday that those things did really happen which one distinctly remembers." Quite obviously the statement of the principle, if it is to be true, needs more qualifiers than the "distinctly" that Reid attaches; most of us learn to distrust even distinct memories of certain sorts. I judge that it would prove extremely difficult, if not impossible, to insert all the necessary qualifiers. Why that is so, and why it doesn't really make any difference to Reid's point, will become clear almost immediately.

My topic in this present section is what Reid understood by "principles of Common Sense." My thesis has been that in his writings one finds two very different understandings: Principles of Common Sense are shared first principles, and principles of Common Sense are what we all do and must take for granted in our lives in the everyday. What remains to be shown is that they don't mesh.

Presumably it is the case that everything that all those of us who are normal adults believe immediately and justifiedly is also taken for granted by all of us in the living of our lives in the everyday; elementary propositions of logic and mathematics would be examples. But the converse is definitely not true. For one thing, most people surely don't actually *believe* those propositions that all those of us who are normal adults must take for granted in our living of life in the everyday. Most people haven't even so much as entertained them, let alone believed them. And that's because what we all take for granted concerning the reliability of memory, say, is full of subtle qualifications built up by tacit rather than explicit learning, and consequently extremely difficult to extract and formulate with full precision. One doesn't have to believe something to take it for granted. Taking a proposition for granted is a different propositional attitude – if one wants to call it that – from believing it; and one can do the former, with respect to a certain proposition, without doing the latter. Second, if anybody has managed to extract one of these propositions taken for granted by all of us, and then to believe it, surely he will not have believed it immediately. The belief will have emerged from a lengthy process of reflection. And third, many of the things we take for granted do not function as beliefs on the basis of which we believe other things; they are not "principles, upon which I build all my reasoning" (IHM V, vii

[130a; B 72]). They are background and substratum for our beliefs, not basis.[2]

In a passage that occurs in his discussion of the principle that "the natural faculties, by which we distinguish truth from error, are not fallacious," Reid acknowledges the first two of these points:

> We may here take notice of a property of the principle under consideration, that seems to be common to it with many other first principles, and which can hardly be found in any principle that is built solely upon reasoning; and that is, that in most men it produces its effect without ever being attended to, or made an object of thought. No man ever thinks of this principle, unless when he considers the grounds of skepticism; yet it invariably governs his opinions. When a man in the common course of life gives credit to the testimony of his senses, his memory, or his reason, he does not put the question to himself, whether these faculties may deceive him; yet the trust he reposes in them supposes an inward conviction, that, in that instance at least, they do not deceive him.
>
> It is another property of this and of many first principles, that they force assent in particular instances, more powerfully than when they are turned into a general proposition. . . . Many have, in general, maintained that the senses are fallacious, yet there never was found a man so skeptical as not to trust his senses in particular instances, when his safety required it; and it may be observed of those who have professed skepticism, that their skepticism lies in generals, while in particulars they are no less dogmatical than others. (EIP VI, v [448a–b])

We could drop the matter at this point: two quite different lines of thought in Reid concerning principles of Common Sense. But let's see if we can take the discussion a step farther. Suppose we go beyond Reid's actual words and try to discern what he was trying to articulate; then should either of these lines of thought have priority over the other? Is one of the two to be taken as determinative?

---

[2] Here's a passage in which Reid takes note of an additional difference: "It may . . . be observed, that the first principles of natural philosophy are of a quite different nature from mathematical axioms. They have not the same kind of evidence, nor are they necessary truths, as mathematical axioms are. They are such as these: that similar effects proceed from the same or similar causes: that we ought to admit of no other causes of natural effects, but such as are true, and sufficient to account for the effects. These are principles, which, though they have not the same kind of evidence that mathematical axioms have, yet have such evidence, that every man of common understanding readily assents to them, and finds it absolutely necessary to conduct his actions and opinions by them, in the ordinary affairs of life" (EIP I, ii [231a]).

I would say that the scale tips decisively toward taking the latter line of thought as determinative. What we all take for granted in the living of our lives in the everyday will include things that we all believe noninferentially and justifiedly – elementary mathematical and logical propositions. But it goes well beyond that. And as we shall see, it was Reid's view that the philosopher is to be guided by what we all take for granted in general, not just by that subset thereof that consists of what we all believe noninferentially and justifiedly. If we treat the taking-for-granted line of thought as determinative, then all shared first principles get included among principles of Common Sense; whereas if we take the first-principle line as determinative, then a great deal of what's taken for granted in common gets excluded. I judge that to be a good reason for treating the taken-for-granted line of thought as determinative in our interpretation of what Reid was trying to articulate.

There's another question that begs for attention: Why are there these two independent and not entirely compatible lines of thought in Reid? Why didn't he see what we see? I'll offer a speculation; but let's first get more of his thought in hand.

CHARACTERISTICS OF WHAT WE ALL TAKE FOR GRANTED

Let's have before us once again the passage I quoted in which Reid gives expression to the taken-for-granted line of thought. There are many others; but this is perhaps the best brief statement of most of the elements of Reid's view:

> If there are certain principles, as I think there are, which the constitution of our nature leads us to believe, and which we are under a necessity to take for granted in the common concerns of life, without being able to give a reason for them; these are what we call the principles of common sense; and what is manifestly contrary to them, is what we call absurd.

In addition to the basic theme of things taken "for granted in the common concerns of life," four points are worth singling out for attention in this passage.

One important feature of principles of Common Sense is that

we are not "able to give a reason for" these things.[3] What Reid emphasizes rather more often than that we are incapable of giving reasons, is that we don't in fact hold them *for* reasons:

> Suppose a man's house to be broke open, his money and jewels taken away: such things have happened times innumerable without any apparent cause; and were he only to reason from experience in such a case, how must he behave? He must put in one scale the instances wherein a cause was found of such an event, and in the other scale, the instances wherein no cause was found, and the preponderant scale must determine, whether it be most probable that there was a cause of this event, or that there was none. Would any man of common understanding have recourse to such an expedient to direct his judgment?
>
> Suppose a man to be found dead on the highway, his skull fractured, his body pierced with deadly wounds, his watch and money carried off. The coroner's jury sits upon the body, and the question is put, What was the cause of this man's death . . . ? Let us suppose an adept in Mr. Hume's philosophy to make one of the jury, and that he insists upon the previous question, whether there was any cause of the event; or whether it happened without cause?
>
> Surely, upon Mr. Hume's principles, a great deal might be said upon this point. . . . But we may venture to say, that, if Mr. Hume had been of such a jury, he would have laid aside his philosophical principles, and acted according to the dictates of common prudence. (EIP VI, vi [457a–b])

A second feature of principles of Common Sense is that "what is manifestly contrary to them, is what we call absurd." Not false, but absurd. Should a sane person embrace such absurdity by singling out one or another principle of Common Sense and profess to doubt it, perhaps even to profess that he no longer accepts it, reasoning with him will more than likely prove ineffective, since his professed doubt or disbelief will likely outweigh any contrary considerations one might adduce. More appropriate, and probably more effective, is the response of gentle ridicule:

> We may observe, that opinions that contradict first principles are distinguished from other errors by this; that they are not only false, but absurd: and, to discountenance absurdity, nature has given us a particular emotion, to wit, that of ridicule, which seems intended for this very

---

[3] Sometimes Reid will speak more cautiously, thus: "As there are words common to philosophers and to the vulgar, which need no explication; so there are principles common to both, which need no proof, and which do not admit of direct proof" (EIP I, ii [230a]).

purpose of putting out of countenance what is absurd, either in opinion or practice.

This weapon, when properly applied, cuts with as keen an edge as argument. Nature has furnished us with the first to expose absurdity; as with the last to refute error. (EIP VI, iv [438a])

Recall our discussion, in the preceding chapter, of Reid's way with the skeptic: Part of Reid's way, though certainly not the whole of it, was to practice what he here preaches; namely, submit the skeptic to ridicule!

And what if we come across a person whom we judge actually to doubt certain principles of Common Sense – not just to profess to doubt, but actually to doubt? All "men that have a common understanding . . . consider [such] a man as lunatic, or destitute of common sense" (EIP I, ii [230b]).[4] We don't reason with such a person; but we also don't subject him to ridicule. We get treatment. If "any man were found of so strange a turn as not to believe his own eyes; to put no trust in his senses, nor have the least regard to their testimony; would any man think it worth while to reason gravely with such a person, and, by argument, to convince him of his error? Surely no wise man would" (EIP I, ii [230b]). He would instead be "clapped into a mad-house" (IHM VI, xx [184a; B 170]).

Professing to doubt certain principles of Common Sense versus actually doubting: the difference is important, obviously, as is manifested by our different handling of the two cases, ridicule versus treatment. Just as striking, though, is the similarity: genuine lunacy versus professed lunacy. "When a man suffers himself to be reasoned out of the principles of common sense, by metaphysical arguments, we may call this *metaphysical lunacy*; which differs from the other species of the distemper in this, that it is not continued, but intermittent: it is apt to seize the patient in solitary and speculative moments; but when he enters into society, Common Sense recovers her authority (IHM VII [209b; B 215–6]).

A third, related, feature of principles of Common Sense is that we "are under a necessity to take" these things for granted. We cannot avoid taking them for granted; in that way they are for us

---

[4] "A remarkable deviation from [the principles of Common Sense], arising from a disorder in the constitution, is what we call *lunacy*, as when a man believes that he is made of glass" (IHM VII[209b; B 215]).

indubitable. We may think we doubt them, say we doubt them; but our behavior indicates otherwise. "Those who reject [some principle of Common Sense] in speculation, find themselves under a necessity of being governed by it in their practice" (EIP VI, v [447a]). A skeptic "may struggle hard to disbelieve the information of his senses, as a man does to swim against a torrent; but ah! it is in vain. . . . For after all, when his strength is spent in the fruitless attempt, he will be carried down the torrent with the common herd of believers" (IHM VI, xx [184a; B 169]). A qualification must be attached: All this is true for *normal* adults. As noted just above, persons suffering from some severe mental disorder do sometimes genuinely doubt some principle of Common Sense.

Before moving on to the last point to be singled out for attention in the passage quoted, let me cite a feature that Reid happens not to mention in this passage. It came to our attention earlier; it's worth having it here before us along with the other features. "In most men [a principle of Common Sense] produces its effect without ever being attended to, or made an object of thought" (EIP VI, v [448a]). The principles have to be extracted from practice; and that's a fallible enterprise. For one thing, the "precise limits . . . which divide common judgment from what is beyond it on the one hand, and from what falls short of it on the other, may be difficult to determine . . ." (EIP VI, ii [423a]). But more generally, "it is not impossible, that what is only a vulgar prejudice may be mistaken for a first principle. Nor is it impossible, that what is really a first principle, may, by the enchantment of words, have such a mist thrown about it, as to hide its evidence, and to make a man of candour doubt of it" (EIP I, ii [231a]). Accordingly, Reid presents a rather lengthy discussion of "rules of thumb" for identifying principles of Common Sense (EIP VI, iv [437b ff.]). What he nowhere mentions is what seems to me the most important source of mistakes in identification of principles of Common Sense: The subtlety of our practices makes it extraordinarily difficult to identity and formulate with full accuracy what we all take for granted in those practices.

The last point to be singled out for attention in the passage before us is of a different order from the preceding ones. What we have noted thus far is the features that Reid ascribes to principles of Common Sense. This last point doesn't single out an additional feature but expresses Reid's view as to why we all take for granted, in our lives in the everyday, what we do there take for granted; namely, "the constitution of our nature leads us to" do so.

AN ILLUMINATING DETOUR: WITTGENSTEIN

To have simultaneously before one's mind's eye Reid's discussion on Common Sense, Kant's discussion of the a priori, and Wittgenstein's discussion of our shared world picture, is to see at a glance that the attention of all three is on the same phenomenon; namely, that for any normal adult's system of beliefs there is a substratum, a background, a framework – pick your metaphor – which doesn't come and go, which makes the system as a whole and the life based upon it possible, and which is common to all normal adult human beings. Each of the three identifies this phenomenon differently, and thus offers a different description – my characterization has been as neutral as possible. The account one of these offers, of the phenomenon he has identified, differs significantly from the account the others offer, of the phenomenon they have identified. Each draws different conclusions. But the multitude of differences does not conceal the striking similarity.

I judge the similarities between Reid and Wittgenstein on this matter to be closer, much closer, than those between Reid and Kant. On other matters the affinities are different. In earlier chapters we saw that the notion of *our human constitution* is fundamental in Reid; on that issue, Reid's affiliation is with Kant rather than Wittgenstein – though with important differences. Kant's interest lay in what is essential to being a finite knower and agent; what he constructed is a vast anthropological essentialism. Reid believed that in analyzing the workings of the human self we are over and over confronted with fundamental inexplicable contingency.

Wittgenstein's *On Certainty* consists of a series of brief notes that he made late in life, 676 of them in the present numbering. The phenomenon on which he has his eye is exactly the same as that on which Reid had his eye in his doctrine of Common Sense; namely, the things all those of us who are normal adults must take for granted in the living of our lives in the everyday. Wittgenstein's word for this complex is "our shared world picture." Furthermore, the features Wittgenstein ascribes to our shared world picture are, astonishingly, exactly those that we have just seen Reid ascribing to the principles of Common Sense. The account Wittgenstein gives of these features is quite different from the account Reid offers, however; Wittgenstein does not ascribe them to "the constitution of our nature."

Before concluding our account of Reid's doctrine of Common Sense, I propose turning to Wittgenstein's treatment of our shared world picture. I think this turn will prove illuminating – illuminating of Reid's account, I mean. For one thing, Wittgenstein develops more fully than Reid ever does the theme of *taking for granted.* And secondly, having before us Wittgenstein's alternative explanation will highlight the significance of Reid's explanation. The sad history of misinterpretation of Reid's doctrine of Common Sense leads me to want to say that it was impossible to understand what Reid was trying to say until *On Certainty* was published! The reason Reid has been so widely misinterpreted on this score, and his thought so trivialized, is that most of Reid's interpreters did not have *On Certainty* available to them![5]

Interspersed though they were throughout many other notes that Wittgenstein was writing at the same time, the notes comprising *On Certainty* hang together. Superficially they hang together as comments Wittgenstein made on some articles by G. E. Moore in which Moore cited certain items of knowledge on his part as a refutation of skepticism: his knowledge that he had two hands, his knowledge that he had never been far from the surface of the earth, his knowledge that the world had existed for some time before he was born, and so forth. Wittgenstein's philosophico-linguistic ear told him that there was something odd about citing these as examples of knowledge; his jottings were an attempt to identify the source of that sense of oddness. What makes the jottings hang together more profoundly is the emergence of two large themes that are both developed in their own right and made to interact with each other. Wittgenstein never quite loses sight of Moore's odd examples. But those two themes

---

[5] In the opening chapter of Peter Strawson's *Skepticism and Naturalism: Some Varieties* (New York: Columbia University Press, 1985), there's an interesting comparison between the same aspect of Wittgenstein's thought on which I will be focusing and some themes in Hume.

and their interplay prove far more interesting in their own right than whether or not they can be used to explain the oddness of Moore's examples.

We would be faithful to Wittgenstein's own style if we let those themes emerge slowly from a careful selection and arrangement of passages and leisurely rumination thereon. But in each case I shall adopt the opposite, more brisk, approach, of first stating the theme and then looking at some of the confirming passages.

Consider such actions as offering reasons, searching for evidence, raising doubts, asking questions, running tests. One theme to which Wittgenstein returns over and over is that to perform any of these, we must take things for granted.

345. If I ask someone "what colour do you see at the moment?", in order, that is, to learn what colour is there at the moment, I cannot at the same time question whether the person I ask understands English, whether he wants to take me in, whether my own memory is not leaving me in the lurch as to the names of colours, and so on.

337. One cannot make experiments if there are not some things that one does not doubt. But that does not mean that one takes certain presuppositions on trust. When I write a letter and post it, I take it for granted that it will arrive – I expect this.

If I make an experiment I do not doubt the existence of the apparatus before my eyes. I have plenty of doubts, but not *that*.

All that seems pretty obvious – once it's pointed out. The question that grips Wittgenstein's attention is whether our taking such and such for granted is always a purely local phenomenon. Is it the case that anything which I take for granted on one occasion is such that on some other occasion I – or we – do not take it for granted? Or are there are some things that I always take for granted and never question – and all my contemporaries as well? Wittgenstein is persuaded of the latter.

210. ... Much seems to be fixed, and it is removed from the traffic. It is so to speak shunted onto an unused siding.

211. Now it gives our way of looking at things, and our researches, their form. Perhaps it was once disputed. But perhaps, for unthinkable ages, it has belonged to the *scaffolding* of our thoughts. (Every human being has parents.)

105. All testing, all confirmation and disconfirmation of a hypothesis takes place already within a system. And this system is not a more or less

arbitrary and doubtful point of departure for all our arguments: no, it belongs to the essence of what we call an argument. The system is not so much the point of departure, as the elements in which arguments have their life.

232. . . . Our not doubting them all is simply our manner of judging, and therefore of acting.

It would be worth asking who exactly is the "our" here; but rather than tarrying over that, note that what Wittgenstein is exploring is not the presuppositions of propositions but the conditions of acting, especially of those actions that we perform with language. "No one ever taught me that my hands don't disappear when I am not paying attention to them. Nor can I be said to presuppose the truth of this proposition in my assertions etc., (as if they rested on it . . .)" (153). A condition of our performing actions, and especially such actions as judging and reasoning, is that we must take certain things for granted. Giving grounds must "come to an end sometime." To which Wittgenstein adds portentously: "But the end is not an ungrounded presupposition: it is an ungrounded way of acting" (110).

Ungrounded, for example, in anything that we might have "seen to be true": the things we ultimately take for granted in judging, and so forth, are not things we have "seen to be true":

204. . . . the end is not certain propositions' striking us immediately as true, i.e. it is not a kind of *seeing* on our part; it is our *acting*, which lies at the bottom of the language-game.

Ungrounded also in experience. Might it not be the case, someone asks, that those things we all always take for granted in making judgments are things we've learned from experience? Isn't it perhaps.

130. . . . experience that teaches us to judge like this, that is to say, that it is correct to judge like this? But how does experience *teach* us, then? *We* may derive it from experience, but experience does not direct us to derive anything from experience. If it is the *ground* of our judging like this, and not just the cause, still we do not have a ground for seeing this in turn as a ground.

131. No, experience is not the ground for our game of judging. Nor is its outstanding success.

In short, action ungrounded in either rational intuition or experience: "it is not based on grounds. It is not reasonable (or unreasonable). It is there – like our life" (559).

That's one theme, running throughout *On Certainty*. All of us, in all our acting, take things for granted; and some of these may well be things we all always take for granted. Now for the second theme – never, in Wittgenstein's discussion, sharply distinguished from the first.

Consider the totality of a person's beliefs at a given time – not the totality of *judgments* she is making at that time but the totality of *beliefs* she holds at that time. Such a totality is not just a collection. It's structured, organized; it's a system. It's structured in various dimensions, one such dimension being this: A given person's beliefs differ from each other with respect to their depth of ingression, of entrenchment, in the totality of that person's beliefs. That is to say, they differ from each other with respect to how many other beliefs one would find oneself giving up were one to conclude that one had been wrong about that one – how many others one would find oneself giving up in order to restore equilibrium. There's a depth-of-ingression continuum in each person's system of beliefs, with beliefs from the system strung all along that continuum.

A belief's degree of ingression within a given person's belief system is determined by a certain relation which that belief bears to other beliefs of that person. Thus it's different from the degree of firmness with which one holds the belief. But it's also different from the mediate/immediate distinction. For though that too pertains to the relationship a belief bears, or fails to bear, to other beliefs of the person, the relationship is different from the relationship determining depth of ingression. It would be interesting to explore the interconnections among these various dimensions of a person's belief system; is it true, for example, that the more deeply ingressed a belief, the more firmly held? But what's important for our purposes here is not the interconnections but just the fact that degree of ingression is distinct from all those other features of beliefs and relationships among beliefs. That's what we must keep in mind.

Wittgenstein argues that, when it comes to depth of ingression, "there is no sharp boundary between methodological propositions and propositions within a method" (318).

96. It might be imagined that some propositions, of the form of empirical propositions, were hardened and functioned as channels for such empirical propositions as were not hardened but fluid; and that this relation altered with time, in that fluid propositions hardened, and hard ones became fluid.

97. The mythology may change back into a state of flux, the river-bed of thoughts may shift. But I distinguish between the movement of the waters on the river-bed and the shift of the bed itself; though there is not a sharp division of the one from the other.

98. But if someone were to say "So logic too is an empirical science" he would be wrong. Yet this is right: the same proposition may get treated at one time as something to test by experience, at another as a rule of testing.

99. And the bank of that river consists partly of hard rock, subject to no alteration or only to an imperceptible one, partly of sand, which now in one place now in another gets washed away, or deposited.

319. But wouldn't one have to say then, that there is no sharp boundary between propositions of logic and empirical propositions? The lack of sharpness is that of the boundary between *rule* and empirical proposition.

Almost all of Wittgenstein's examples of deeply ingressed beliefs fall into one or the other of two sorts. Some are deeply ingressed in the belief systems of all of us – the "us" being all sane contemporary adults. It's a deeply ingressed belief of all of us that objects don't just disappear – this in spite of the fact that it has been the experience of all of us that some objects did just disappear so far as we were ever able to tell. One can perhaps imagine human beings who did not hold this belief; as a matter of fact, *we* all do. And giving it up would require a massive alteration of beliefs on our part. Here is the example in Wittgenstein's own words:

134. After putting a book in a drawer, I assume it is there, unless. . . . "Experience always proves me right. There is no well attested case of a book's (simply) disappearing." It has *often* happened that a book has never turned up again, although we thought we knew for certain where it was. – But experience does really teach that a book, say, does not vanish away. (E.g. gradually evaporate). But is it this experience with books etc. that leads us to assume that such a book has not vanished away? Well, suppose we were to find that under particular novel circumstances books did vanish away. – Shouldn't we alter our assumption? Can one give the lie to the effect of experience on our system of assumption?

135. But do we not simply follow the principle that what has always happened will happen again (or something like it)? What does it mean to follow this principle? Do we really introduce it into our reasoning? Or is it merely the *natural law* which our inferring apparently follows? This latter it may be. It is not an item in our consideration.

Wittgenstein sometimes calls the totality of deeply ingressed beliefs such as these, *our world picture*. They are framework beliefs shared by all of us.

Other examples that Wittgenstein offers of deeply ingressed beliefs are of quite a different sort. With his eye on his own belief system he cites, as deeply ingressed beliefs, "I am called Ludwig Wittgenstein" and "I have two hands." Obviously these do not belong to our shared picture of the world. One might call them, Wittgenstein's *personal framework* – in contrast to our picture of the world which consists of our *human framework*.

628. When we say "Certain propositions must be excluded from doubt", it sounds as if I ought to put these propositions – for example, that I am called L.W. – into a logic-book. For if it belongs to the description of a language-game, it belongs to logic. But that I am called L.W. does not belong to any such description. The language-game that operates with people's names can certainly exist even if I am mistaken about my name – but it does presuppose that it is nonsensical to say that the majority of people are mistaken about their names.

Most of the time Wittgenstein takes no note of the distinction I have just drawn between personal frameworks and our shared world picture; he moves smoothly back and forth among examples. Naturally there will be belief frameworks falling in between the two. Wittgenstein happens to give very few examples of such in *On Certainty*; judging from other writings of his, it seems likely that that's where he placed religious beliefs – in between. Beliefs that truly function as religious beliefs will be deeply ingressed; but that deep ingression will be neither peculiar to some single person nor common to all.

One more point must be added before we can move on from this second theme to the interaction of the two themes. It is, in fact, the most important point concerning this second theme. Wittgenstein argues that if something is very deeply ingressed in one's belief system, then it is exempt from doubt, and hence certain. Begin with the fact that we can't just up and doubt things.

"One doubts on specific grounds" (458). If I'm to doubt P, something has to make me dubious of P. We doubt for reasons – the reasons being things we believe. "[S]omewhere I must begin with not-doubting" (150).

115. If you tried to doubt everything you would not get as far as doubting anything. The game of doubting itself presupposes certainty.

Why does it presuppose certainty, and not merely belief? *Objective* certainty is what is at issue here. Subjective certainty is maximal confidence, "complete conviction, the total absence of doubt" (194). What's relevant here is not that sort of certainty but the sort of certainty that a belief enjoys when it's indubitable – that is to say, when one could not doubt it. Our maximally ingressed beliefs are indubitable in that way.

Why is that? Because, being deeply ingressed, they don't come by themselves; if I were to doubt one of my deeply ingressed beliefs, I would have to doubt masses of other beliefs as well. And that's just too difficult.

234. I believe that I have forebears, and that every human being has them. I believe that there are various cities, and, quite generally, in the main facts of geography and history. I believe that the earth is a body on whose surface we move and that it no more suddenly disappears or the like than any other solid body: this table, this house, this tree, etc. If I wanted to doubt the existence of the earth long before my birth, I should have to doubt all sorts of things that stand fast for me.

"What I hold fast to," when it comes to some deeply ingressed belief of mine, "is not *one* proposition but a nest of propositions" (225). "I cannot depart from this judgment without toppling all other judgments with it" (419). And that's just too hard to do!

141. When we first begin to *believe* anything, what we believe is not a single proposition, it is a whole system of propositions. (Light dawns gradually over the whole.)

143. I am told, for example, that someone climbed this mountain many years ago. Do I always enquire into the reliability of the teller of this story, and whether the mountain did exist years ago? A child learns there are reliable and unreliable informants much later than it learns facts which are told it. It doesn't learn *at all* that that mountain has existed for a long time: that is, the question whether it is so doesn't arise at all. It swallows this consequence down, so to speak, together with *what* it learns.

144. The child learns to believe a host of things. I.e. it learns to act according to these beliefs. Bit by bit there forms a system of what is believed, and in that system some things stand unshakeably fast and some are more or less liable to shift. What stands fast does so, not because it is intrinsically obvious or convincing; it is rather held fast by what lies around it.

This is not to say that such propositions are "infallible" – couldn't be false. We can imagine many if not all of them as false. The belief that I have a brain is deeply ingressed in my belief system; but logically speaking, it might be false.

4. . . . Grounds for *doubt* are lacking! Everything speaks in its favour, nothing against it. Nevertheless it is imaginable that my skull should turn out empty when it was operated on (cf. 425).

So too, it's possible that someone would cease believing that the earth existed for some time before he was born, that he has two hands, when he does and always did, and so forth. But if we actually came across such a person, we would not conclude that he was in doubt about those things, or that he had made a few mistakes. We would judge him insane, or profoundly confused. "The reasonable man does *not have* certain doubts" (220).[6]

71. If my friend were to imagine one day that he had been living for a long time past in such and such a place, etc. etc., I should not call this a *mistake*, but rather a mental disturbance, perhaps a transient one.

257. If someone said to me that he doubted whether he had a body I should take him to be a half-wit. But I shouldn't know what it would mean to try to convince him that he had one. And if I had said something, and that had removed his doubt, I should not know how or why.

That's how we would react if we took the person to be speaking seriously. To the adolescent or the philosopher who simply wants "to make objections to the propositions that are beyond doubt" we "might simply say 'O, rubbish!' [Ach, Unsinn!] . . . That is, not reply to him but admonish him" (495).

Those, then, are the two themes: The first theme is that in asking questions, raising doubts, judging on evidence, and so on, we do and must take things for granted – with the possibility that

---

[6] Which is not to say that our criteria for rationality might not alter a bit over the years (336); nor that someone might not be reared in an isolated situation in which he was told very strange things – as, for example, that the earth has existed only since his birth (92; 262–4).

some of the things we take for granted, we all always take for granted, though perhaps *humanity* did not always do so. The second is the theme that our beliefs vary with respect to depth of ingression, with the possibility that some beliefs are not only shared by all of us who are contemporaries but are deeply ingressed in the belief systems of all (normal adult) human beings.

And now for the point of interplay between the two themes. Recall that the things we all take for granted are ungrounded. It would be natural for those steeped in the philosophical tradition to assume that they are on that account shaky, precarious. Wittgenstein insists, to the contrary, that the things we all always take for granted in our everyday activities are typically immune from doubt, and hence certain. They are that because they are so deeply ingressed that doubt cannot get at them. Typically Wittgenstein doesn't so much argue as assume that what we all take for granted in inquiry, and so forth, is also so deeply ingressed as to be immune from doubt.

88. . . . *all enquiry on our part* is set so as to exempt certain propositions from doubt, if they are ever formulated. They lie apart from the route travelled by enquiry.

308. We are interested in the fact that about certain empirical propositions no doubt can exist if making judgments is to be possible at all.

341. The *questions* that we raise and our *doubts* depend on the fact that some propositions are exempt from doubt, are as it were like hinges on which those turn.

To these may be added a passage cited earlier:

337. One cannot make experiments if there are not some things that one does not doubt. But that does not mean that one takes certain pre-suppositions on trust. When I write a letter and post it, I take it for granted that it will arrive – I expect this.

If I make an experiment I do not doubt the existence of the appara-tus before my eyes. I have plenty of doubts, but not *that*.

In conclusion, here, once again, is the first theme. We learn to perform such activities as judging, doubting, and giving reasons. In learning to perform those activities we learn what is taken for granted in them, without ever being explicitly taught. "No one ever taught me that my hands don't disappear when I am not paying attention to them" (153). That's our shared world picture: the taken-for-granted background of our learning and teaching and all such activities, absorbed by us in and with our learning, communicated by us in and with our teaching. "I have a world picture. Is it true or false? Above all it is the substratum of all my enquiring and asserting" (162). "I did not get my picture of the world by satisfying myself of its correctness; nor do I have it because I am satisfied of its correctness. No: it is the inherited background against which I distinguish between true and false" (94).[7]

That's the first theme. What the second theme adds is that the bulk of what we all take for granted is not shaky and precarious – this in spite of being "ungrounded." It is in fact certain. I dare say that if the question were put to him, Wittgenstein would concede that there just might be some things that you and I always take for granted that are not so deeply ingressed in our belief systems as to be immune to doubt. Examples might be certain things that we take for granted by virtue of being members of the modern Western world. But those would be minor exceptions to the rule: The propositions we all take for granted, as we offer reasons, ask questions, search for evidence, and so forth, are so deeply ingressed in our beliefs systems that they are *certain* for us. Doubt cannot get at them there. Too many other beliefs stand guard. Our world picture, what we all take for granted in our lives in the everyday, is unshakeable for us.

BACK TO REID, WITH WITTGENSTEIN IN MIND

It would be pointless to belabor the striking similarities between Reid's doctrine of the principles of Common Sense and Wittgenstein's account of our shared world picture. Let me state them briefly: We're not able to give reasons in defense of the things we all take for granted in our lives in the everyday; to express disagreement with things thus taken for granted is absurd; we can't avoid taking them for granted – can't doubt them; it's difficult to identify and accurately formulate them; and we're seldom explicitly taught them. That last is a point I did not make

---

[7] Cf. 152: "I do not explicitly learn the propositions that stand fast for me. I can *discover* them subsequently."

in my exposition of Reid; but it is a point he mentions: "Men need not be taught them," he says (EIP I, ii [230b]).

Where Reid and Wittgenstein differ is in the account they offer of these features of our shared world picture. Reid thinks the reason we all take for granted the things we do is that "the constitution of our nature leads us to believe" them; this also explains why we don't have to be, and usually are not, taught them, and why we cannot avoid taking them for granted, and in that way, cannot doubt them. The reason it's difficult to identify and accurately formulate them is that, since their role in our lives is that of being taken for granted in our common concerns, there's no need for them to be up front in our consciousness. Last, the reason "such common principles seldom admit of direct proof" (ibid.) is that, being self-evident, they "do not admit of proof. When men attempt to deduce such self-evident principles from others more evident, they always fall into inconclusive reasoning" (EIP I, ii [231a]).[8] This last point is, of course, a mark of Reid's alternative understanding of the principles of Common Sense intruding itself into his understanding of them as things we all take for granted.

Wittgenstein agrees with Reid on why it's difficult to identify and accurately formulate the contents of our shared world picture. With everything else in Reid's account he disagrees. We don't take them for granted because "the constitution of our nature leads us to believe" them; we take them for granted because *in* performing the activities of life in the everyday *one does* take them for granted; the nature of the activities is such that in performing them one takes these things for granted. We couldn't perform these activities without taking these things for granted. That also explains why we are seldom taught them directly: We learn to perform activities; and *in* learning that, we learn to take these things for granted. And that's why we can't give reasons for them. The activity of giving reasons is one of the activities in which we take them for granted. As to why we can't doubt them, that's because they are so deeply ingressed that doubt can rarely gain access to them.

---

[8] Reid goes on to say that "the consequence of this has been, that others, such as Berkeley and Hume, finding the arguments brought to prove such first principles to be weak and inconclusive, have been tempted first to doubt of them, and afterward to deny them."

It's a fascinating disagreement. On the one hand, a person of the Enlightenment who believes firmly in a shared human nature; on the other hand, a person of the twentieth century who tries as long as possible to make do without appealing to a shared human nature.

Who's right? Well, notice in the first place that there's nothing in Reid's thought that would prevent him from agreeing with Wittgenstein's point that our activities in the everyday are such that *in* performing those activities, one takes for granted the elements of our shared world picture – just as *in* running a mile, one runs a half-mile. One couldn't do the former without doing the latter. It's not just that one *does* take these things for granted in performing those activities; one couldn't *but* do so because the activity requires doing so. And second, there's nothing in Reid's thought that would prevent him from also agreeing that the things we all take for granted are so deeply ingressed in our belief systems that giving them up would require also giving up so many other beliefs that only upon going mad could such a conversion occur. These are not points that Reid does make; there's nothing, however, to prevent him from accepting them.

The question, then, is whether this is the end of the matter, as Wittgenstein assumes. It seems to me it's not; and that Reid, accordingly, has the better of the argument. An application of Wittgenstein's general point would be that in our everyday activities of gathering evidence, offering arguments, and so forth, we all take for granted the reliability of our perceptual faculties – the fifth of Reid's First Principles of Contingent Truths. It's true that what we actually take for granted in this regard is much more finely articulated than that; but we can let that pass. Now suppose that Reid's account of perception is correct in its main outlines: We are so constituted that, upon having sensations of certain sorts, we form beliefs about the external objects causing these sensations. Then there's something more to be said than that *in* and *with* our performance of our everyday activities, we take for granted the general reliability of sense perception. Our hard wiring leaves us with no alternative in this regard. Even if one could somehow cease performing all those activities to which Wittgenstein points, while nonetheless continuing to perceive – absorbed in a meditative revery, let's say – one would still be taking for granted the general reliability of one's perceptual faculties. It's a form of taking-for-granted that one cannot do anything about – short of systematically blocking the transition from sensations caused by external objects to beliefs, about those objects, that they exist as external. In particular cases, that transition can be blocked, as I noted in an earlier chapter. A belief to the effect that the sensory experience one is having cannot on this occasion be trusted may block it. But that is, and must be, the exception. So it's not just the things we do that give us no choice but to accept our shared world picture; it's also our constitution. We are so constituted as to take for granted the reliability of our belief-forming faculties.

WHY DID REID FIND IT DIFFICULT TO GET CLEAR ON PRINCIPLES OF COMMON SENSE?

Evidently Reid found it it difficult to unravel from each other his two lines of thought about Common Sense – difficult to think consistently of the principles of Common Sense as things we all do and must take for granted in our lives in the everyday and not to think of them also as shared first principles. Why was that? One can only speculate.

My suggestion is that the culprit was his assumption – which Wittgenstein shared – that things we take for granted are things believed. Once he made this assumption, then the choice faced him: Are they formed by inference, or by some process of immediate belief formation? Given these options, the latter is obviously the choice to make. Hence Reid says that they are immediate, and intuitive. They are such as "all men of common understanding know, or such, at least, as they give a ready assent to as soon as they are proposed and understood" (EIP I, ii [230b]). But this remark is peculiar in two ways. Reid concedes that we don't, in general, give ready assent to principles of Common Sense "as soon as they are proposed and understood." And second: how can it be that we were all along believing these propositions, by virtue of taking them for granted, if they had not even been proposed to, and understood by, us?

Having said that these principles are believed immediately, the next question is whether we are justified in believing them? To this, the right answer seems yes.[9] But if so, what is their evidence? A belief that is formed on the basis of inference and justifiedly held has its evidence outside itself; but so too does an immediately formed perceptual belief; its evidence is what Reid calls "the evidence of sense." For principles of Common Sense, there doesn't seem to be anything comparable to the evidence of sense for perceptual beliefs; nothing outside themselves that constitutes evidence for them. They must, then, bear their evidence within themselves; they must be self-evident. And so it is that Reid jams together in two brief sentences his two lines of thought about principles of Common Sense: A person who has "come to years of understanding . . . must have formed various opinions and principles, by which he conducts himself in the affairs of life. Of these principles, some are common to all men, being evident in themselves, and so necessary in the conduct of life, that a man cannot live and act according to the rules of common prudence without them" (EIP I, ii [230a–b]).

But this is all confused. We are so constituted that, upon having certain sensations, we immediately believe certain things about the external object causing those sensations; this is one of our indigenous belief-forming mechanisms. In the course of experience those innate workings get corrected a bit; but the corrections depend in turn on those workings. In that way we are so constituted as to take for granted that our perceptual capacities are fundamentally reliable. But if our taking that for granted consists in turn of believing immediately that proposition about the fundamental reliability of our perceptual capacities, then there must be some process of immediate belief formation that accounts for that belief. Reid of course never tells us what that might be. And indeed, what could it be? But suppose there were such a process; call it P. Then by virtue of our constitution we would be taking for granted that the metaprocess P was reliable. But if our taking for granted that P was reliable consisted in turn of believing immediately that P was reliable, then there would

---

[9] That this is the right answer is less obvious, however, than Reid apparently takes it to be. Of course, it all depends on what one means by "justified." A probing discussion of the issues is to be found in Ernest Sosa, "P. F. Strawson's Epistemologial Naturalism" in Lewis Edwin Hahn, ed., *The Philosophy of P. F. Strawson: The Library of Living Philosophers*, Vol. 26 (Chicago: Open Court Publishing, 1998).

have to be yet another process of immediate belief formation, a meta-metaprocess – call it P* – that produced that belief. And so forth, ad infinitum.

I submit that the mistake lies in regarding *taking something for granted* as a special case of *believing some proposition*. Whatever it may be – and here I won't try to say – it's not that.

Reid says – over and over – that the principles of Common Sense are principles that our constitution leads us to believe. If his analysis of perception, memory, consciousness, and so forth is correct, then he's right about that – right about it for some of the principles, anyway. But he's not right about it in the way in which he thinks he is. What he means is that the principles of Common Sense are the output of one or another of those indigenous belief-forming processes that yield their output immediately. What's right instead is this: If the normal human adult is so constituted that, in paradigmatic situations, a sensation evoked by some external object in turn immediately evokes a belief, about that object, that it exists as something external, then it will be the case that normal human adults take for granted, to put it very roughly, the reliability of their perceptual capacities. The pattern exhibited by the working of our constitution has this phenomenon of *taking-for-granted* as its inevitable corollary.

THE DEPENDENCE OF PHILOSOPHY ON COMMON SENSE

We are now, at last, in a position to speak to the topic with which I began this chapter: the relation of the philosopher to Common Sense. The philosopher is related to the principles of Common Sense in the same way everyone else is – and in the same way the philosopher is when not doing philosophy. He does, and must, take them for granted – in his posing of questions, in his raising of doubts, in his offering of reasons. They are, and must be, the background of his reflections – not the premises from which he draws his conclusions but the ever-present substratum of his philosophical activity. One could put it like this: "though common sense and my external senses demand my assent to their dictates upon their own authority, . . . philosophy is not entitled to this privilege" (EIP II, xiv [302b–303a]).

Reid shares with Wittgenstein the conviction that the principles of Common Sense are not infallible; it's possible that something false should function as such a principle. Reid doesn't even think that we should dismiss out of hand the philosopher who says he has discovered a reason for thinking that some element of our world picture is false.[10] Thus he does not ascribe to each of the principles of Common Sense quite the indubitability that Wittgenstein apparently does. But he immediately adds that "When we come to be instructed by philosophers, we must bring the old light of common sense along with us, and by it judge of the new light that the philosopher communicates to us. But when we are required to put out the old light altogether, that we may follow the new, we have reason to be on our guard" (EIP I, i [224a–b]). In short, the *burden of proof* is on the person who would oppose some element of Common Sense. Among other things, Reid's doctrine of Common Sense is a doctrine concerning burden of proof. And I judge that philosophers do in fact regard the burden of proof in philosophical discourse as lying exactly where Reid's view implies that it lies. The burden lies not on the philosopher who holds that there are external objects, but on the one who holds that there are not. Seen in this light, Reid's disagreement with his fellow philosophers lies in their thinking that they have successfully borne the burden of proof, whereas Reid thinks they clearly have not.

Philosophy is like all other human endeavors in that it "has no other root but the principles of common sense; it grows out of them, and draws its nourishment from them: severed from this root, its honours wither, its sap is dried up, it dies and rots" (IHM I, iv [101b; B 19]). Rather often philosophers profess to reject the "principles which irresistibly govern the belief and conduct of all mankind in the common concerns of life" (IHM I, v [102b; B

---

[10] "We do not pretend, that those things that are laid down as first principles may not be examined, and that we ought not to have our ears open to what may be pleaded against their being admitted as such" (EIP I, ii [234a]). See also EIP I, i [224a].

Repeatedly Reid concludes, from his own analysis of arguments against some principle of Common Sense, that the arguments have been instructive. Always, though, what he claims to have learned is some useful points of analysis rather than the falsity of some principle of Common Sense. Thus he says, in the course of a discussion of Hume, that "I beg therefore, once for all, that no offence may be taken at charging this or other metaphysical notions with absurdity, or with being contrary to the common sense of mankind. No disparagement is meant to the understandings of the authors or maintainers of such opinions. . . . [T]he reasoning that leads to them, often gives new light to the subject, and shows real genius and deep penetration in the author, and the premises do more than atone for the conclusion" (IHM II, vi [108a; B 33]).

21]). But it turns out that to these principles "the philosopher himself must yield, after he imagines he hath confuted them." For "Such principles are older, and of more authority, than philosophy: she rests upon them as her basis, not they upon her. If she could overturn them, she must be buried in their ruins; but all the engines of philosophical subtilty are too weak for this purpose; and the attempt is no less ridiculous, than if a mechanic should contrive an *axis in peritrochio* to remove the earth out of its place" (ibid.).

Genuinely to doubt our shared world picture is to be mad, insane. Much of philosophy wears the *semblance* of madness: The ordinary person, hearing the opinions of certain philosophers, "can conceive no otherwise of [such opinions], than as a kind of metaphysical lunacy; and concludes, that too much learning is apt to make men mad; and that the man who seriously entertains [these beliefs], though in other respects he may be a very good man, as a man may be who believes that he is made of glass; yet surely he hath a soft place in his understanding, and hath been hurt by much thinking" (IHM V, vii [127a; B 68]).

But it's only pretence: Philosophers are not mad; they do not really doubt our world picture. In "all the history of philosophy, we never read of any skeptic that ever stepped into fire or water because he did not believe his senses . . ." (EIP II, v [259b]). So the appropriate response to the philosopher is the same as the appropriate response to any sane person who professes to doubt fundamental elements of our world picture: not argument but ridicule. "Ach Unsinn!"

Extraordinarily prominent in Reid's style is wit. The wit is not an adornment on his thought; it is his thought itself, holding up for ridicule philosophy's departure from Common Sense. I close with an example:

Descartes, Malebranche, and Locke, as they made much use of ideas, treated them handsomely, and provided them in decent accommodation; lodging them either in the pineal gland, or in the pure intellect, or even in the Divine Mind. They moreover clothed them with a commission, and made them representatives of things, which gave them some dignity and character. But the Treatise of Human Nature, though no less indebted to them, seems to have made but a bad return, by bestowing upon them this independent existence; since thereby they are turned out of house and home, and set adrift in the world, without friend or connection, without a rag to cover their nakedness; and who knows but the whole system of ideas may perish by the indiscreet zeal of their friends to exalt them?

However this may be, it is certainly a most amazing discovery that thought and ideas may be without any thinking being: a discovery big with consequences which cannot easily be traced by those deluded mortals who think and reason in the common track. We were always apt to imagine, that thought supposed a thinker, and love a lover, and treason a traitor; but this, it seems, was all a mistake; and it is found out, that there may be treason without a traitor, and love without a lover, laws without a legislator, and punishment without a sufferer, succession without time, and motion without any thing moved, or space in which it may move: or if, in these cases, ideas are the lover, the sufferer, the traitor, it were to be wished that the author of this discovery had farther condescended to acquaint us, whether ideas can converse together, and be under obligations of duty of gratitude to each other; whether they can make promises, and enter into leagues and covenants, and fulfil or break them, and be punished for the breach? If one set of ideas makes a covenant, another breaks it, and the third is punished for it, there is reason to think that justice is no natural virtue in this system. (IHM II, vi [109b; B 35])

CHAPTER X

In Conclusion: Living Wisely in the Darkness

TWO THOMASES: AQUINAS AND REID

Having opened his *Summa contra gentiles* with some reflections on "the office of the wise man," and having remarked that "among all human pursuits, the pursuit of wisdom is more perfect, more noble, more useful, and more full of joy" than any other (I,2,2), Thomas Aquinas, in a passage unusual in his work for its use of the first person singular pronoun, goes on to declare that "in the name of the divine Mercy, I have the confidence to embark upon the work of a wise man, even though this may surpass my powers" (I,2,2).[1] That work, he says, is the work "of making known . . . the truth that the Catholic faith professes, and of setting aside the errors that are opposed to it" (I,2,2). What follows these introductory comments is four rather lengthy books in which Aquinas articulates Christian theology in the manner of a *scientia*, polemicizing along the way against alternative positions.

Why does Aquinas think that articulating Christian theology in scientific fashion, and polemicizing against alternatives, is a way of exercising the office of a wise person? After citing Aristotle to authorize his adherence to common usage, Aquinas remarks that "the usage of the multitude . . . has commonly held that they are to be called wise who order things rightly and govern them well." He supports his view on this point of usage by appealing to Aristotle on this matter as well, remarking that "among other things that men have conceived about the wise man, the Philosopher includes the notion that "it belongs to the wise man to order" (I,1,1).

---

[1] I am quoting from the translation by Anton C. Pegis, issued by the University of Notre Dame Press (Notre Dame, Ind.) in 1975.

With this concept of the wise person in hand, Aquinas proceeds to highlight some structural features of the practical arts and their relation to each other. "The rule of government and order for all things directed to an end must be taken from that end," he says. "For, since the end of each thing is its good, a thing is then best disposed when it is fittingly ordered to its end." Accordingly, a condition of being a wise person within some practical art is knowing the end, the goal, the *telos*, of that practice. Now most artisans are of course concerned "with the ends of certain particular things, they do not reach to the universal end of all things. They are therefore said to be wise with respect to this or that thing" (I,1,1). It is to be noted, however, that the various practices to be found in human society do not constitute a mere assemblage; many are related to each other as subordinate to superordinate. One "functions as the governor and the ruler of another because it controls its end. Thus, the art of medicine rules and orders the art of the [pharmacist] because health, with which medicine is concerned, is the end of all the medications prepared by the art of the [pharmacist]" (I,1,1). Suppose, then, that there is an ultimate human *telos*; suppose even that there is a *telos* of the universe and all that dwells therein. "The name of the absolutely wise man . . . is reserved for him whose consideration is directed to the end of the universe, which is also the origin of the universe" (I,1,1). Aquinas's idea – presupposed rather than expressed – is that the person who possesses knowledge of the ultimate end of all things in general, and of all practices in particular, will be of important if not indispensable aid to all those who, in their ordering and governing activities, deal with more limited ends.

When Aquinas declared that he would be so bold as to exercise the office of the wise person, it was of the office of the *absolutely* wise person that he was thinking. He would reflect on the end of all things – which is God. Thus it is that what follows these introductory comments is a theological treatise. Of course, anyone who has read beyond the first book of the *Summa contra gentiles* knows that Aquinas speaks not just of God but of created things as well. That's because theology is not just about God; it's also about the cosmos and all things to be found therein – insofar as they are related to God.

Correspondingly, it was not medical wisdom, political wisdom, engineering wisdom, and so forth, that Aquinas had in mind when he said that "the pursuit of wisdom is more perfect, more noble, more useful, and more full of joy" than any other human activity. It was *absolute* wisdom. It is the pursuit of absolute wisdom that is more perfect than any other activity, "because, in so far as a man gives himself to the pursuit of [absolute] wisdom, so far does he even now have some share in true beatitude." It is the pursuit of absolute wisdom that is also more noble, "because through this pursuit man especially approaches to a likeness to God." Likewise, it is the pursuit of absolute wisdom that is more *useful,* "because through wisdom we arrive at the kingdom of immortality." And it is the pursuit of absolute wisdom that is more full of joy, because our true beatitude lies in the knowledgeable contemplation of God.

Thomas's explication here is so brisk and low key that it is only later, when we reflect on the entire line of argument, that it occurs to us that something strange has happened. Thomas opened his discussion by saying that the wise person is the one who orders things rightly and governs them well. He went on to observe that, given the hierarchical structure of reality and of the practical arts, ordering rightly and governing well requires that someone reflect on the end of all things, namely, God. It requires the practice of theology. But then, even though theology is a speculative enterprise, rather than a practical one concerned with ordering and governing, Aquinas proceeds to say that the practice of theology is the office of the absolutely wise person. He does not say, as the argument would require him to say, that theology is *indispensable* for wisdom in the various arts – indispensable for being a wise gardener, for being a wise lawyer, for being a wise teacher, and so forth. He says that theology itself, as such, *constitutes* the attainment of wisdom.

Correspondingly, when he explains in what way theology is the most perfect, the most noble, the most useful, and the most joyous of all human activities, he does not say that it possesses these qualities because, in revealing to us the true end, not only of our practices of ordering and governing but of all things whatsoever, it enables us to order rightly and govern well in the totality of our practices. He does not say that it enables us to be wise. He says instead that theology has those traits *just by virtue* of revealing to us the end of all things. Knowledgeable contemplation of God *just is* the most perfect, the most noble, the most useful, the most joyous, of all human activities. It does not enable wisdom; it is wisdom – absolute supreme wisdom. Our practical activities of ordering and governing have fallen from view, along with wisdom in those activities; the contemplative activity of knowing God now occupies the entire field of wisdom. Aquinas by no means regarded the *vita activa* as unimportant. However, what comes to the surface in these nonsequiturs at the beginning of the *Summa contra gentiles* is his deep conviction, often explicitly expressed in his writings, that the *vita contemplativa* is superior – provided, of course, that the object of contemplation is God.

Now turn to the Introduction to Thomas Reid's *Essays on the Active Powers*. Reid begins, as did Aquinas, with remarks on wisdom. "It is evidently the intention of our Maker," he says,

> that man should be an active, and not merely a speculative being. For this purpose, certain active powers have been given him, limited indeed in many respects, but suited to his rank and place in the creation.
>
> Our business is to manage these powers, by proposing to ourselves the best ends, planning the most proper system of conduct that is in our power, and executing it with industry and zeal. This is true wisdom; this is the very intention of our being [511a].

"Proposing to ourselves the best ends," "planning the most proper system of conduct that is in our power," "executing it with industry and zeal." This is what constitutes true wisdom. In their understanding of wisdom, there is no difference of substance whatsoever between these two Thomases – Aquinas and Reid. Where they differ is that whereas Aquinas, contradicting his own definition of wisdom, claims the theoretical enterprise of theology to be the supreme wisdom, Reid makes no counterpart claim concerning the philosophy which follows in *Essays on the Active Powers* – nor, indeed, concerning that to be found in any of his other books. Reid does not regard himself, in the *Essays*, as engaged in the office of a wise person.

Just a paragraph after the passage cited, Reid reflects on the relation of knowledge to that "true wisdom" which consists in right ordering and well governing: "Knowledge derives its value from this, that it enlarges our power, and directs us in the application of it. For in the right employment of our active power consists all the honour, dignity and worth of a man; and, in the abuse and perversion of it, all vice, corruption and depravity" [511b].

To catch the import of what Reid is saying here, we must recall his distinction between our *active* powers, and our *speculative* or *intellectual* powers. "As all languages distinguish action from speculation," he says, "the same distinction is applied to the powers by which they are produced. The powers of seeing, hearing, remembering, distinguishing, judging, reasoning, are speculative powers; the power of executing any work of art or labour is active power" (EAP I, i [515a]). What Reid means to be claiming, then, in the passage cited, is that it is not in the right employment of our intellectual powers but in the right employment of our active powers that all the honor, dignity, and worth of a human being consists.

Someone could concede this point, that the honor, dignity, and worth of a human being consists in the right employment of his or her active powers – and incidentally, I think it appropriate to hear similarities to Kant in these words – and yet insist that just by the exercise of our intellectual powers, wholly apart from the utility of the results, we often achieve something of great worth to human beings. Though a brilliant scholar may be a scoundrel, scholarship as such is nonetheless of worth to human beings.

I don't interpret Reid as wanting to deny this flat out. What he would insist on, however, is that knowledge derives its greatest value from the fact that it enlarges our power – he means our *active* power – and directs us in the application of it. "A just knowledge of our powers, whether intellectual or active, is so far of real importance to us, as it aids us in the exercise of them. And every man must acknowledge, that to act properly, is much more valuable than to think justly or reason acutely" (EAP, Intro. [511b]).

Reid no more denied all worth to the contemplative or intellectual life than Aquinas did to the active life. Yet between these two Thomases there is an unmistakable inversion of priorities. Two fundamentally different mentalities. Or better called, perhaps, *pieties: epistemological pieties*. In both of these Thomases the mentality in question was caught up into their understanding of the relation of God to the world, and of how we human beings

ought to interact with God. Two fundamentally different epistemological pieties.

DARKNESS

Between Reid and Aquinas, vast alterations had taken place in
European culture. There was the "turn toward the world" that
occurred around the time of the Renaissance, manifested
throughout European life: in the art of the late middle ages and
Renaissance, in the voyages of discovery, in the affirmation by the
Reformers of the worth of everyday life. There was the emergence
of the conviction, eloquently expressed already by Bacon, that
knowledge is for power, not contemplation. There was the spread
of skepticism as to whether natural theology could come anywhere near discovering as much about God as Aquinas thought –
and whether the scriptures came anywhere near revealing as
much about God as the Reformers thought. All of these cultural
currents influenced Reid. All of them help to explain why Reidian
epistemological piety is different from Thomistic.

Yet there's something else going on in Reid, something in
addition: something peculiar to Reid, something more interesting than the influence of those large cultural currents – more
interesting to a philosopher, anyway. Let's see what that is.

"As there is no principle," says Reid,

> that appears to be more universally acknowledged by mankind, from the
> first dawn of reason, than, that every change we observe in nature must
> have a cause, so this is no sooner perceived, than there arises in the
> human mind, a strong desire to know the causes of those changes that
> fall within our observation. *Felix qui potuit rerum cognoscere causas,* is the
> voice of nature in all men. Nor is there any thing that more early dis-
> tinguishes the rational from the brute creation, than this avidity to know
> the causes of things, of which I see no sign in brute animals. (EAP I, ii
> [516a–b])

As we saw in an earlier chapter, it is this "avidity to know the causes
of things" that motivates philosophy in particular, and the theoretical enterprise in general. "The vulgar are [often] satisfied with
knowing the fact, and give themselves no trouble about the cause
of it: but a philosopher is impatient to know how this event is produced, to account for it, or assign its cause. This avidity to know
the causes of things is the parent of all philosophy true and false.

Men of speculation place a great part of their happiness in such knowledge (EIP II, vi [260b]).[2]

As we also saw earlier, however, Reid held that we have no reason to suppose that within nature there is any causal agency *to be* discovered. Behind it all there's God, indeed. But no one has ever discovered any agency *within* nature; there are reasons for doubting that anyone ever will. Accordingly, with respect to the fundamental goal of the intellectual endeavor we are left frustrated: "With regard to the operations of nature, it is sufficient for us to know, that, whatever the agents may be, whatever the manner of their operation, or the extent of their power, they depend upon the First Cause and are under his control; and this indeed is all that we know; beyond this we are left in darkness" (EAP I, v [523b]).

"Left in darkness." What lies at the bottom of Reidian epistemological piety is acknowledging the darkness – or the "mystery," as Reid sometimes calls it. That which we as intellectuals most want to know, namely, the true efficient causes of things, is almost entirely hidden from us. If certain things other than God are the agents of what transpires in nature and accounts for our own mind and body, we know not what those are. If God alone is the cause, we know only *that* God is the cause, not *how*. The unwavering theme of the Preface to *Essays on the Intellectual Powers of Man* is the extent of what we do not and cannot know – the extent of that of which "we are perfectly ignorant" [217a].

Darkness is not a theme one normally associates with a figure from the Enlightenment. We associate the Enlightenment with the theme of *light* – naturally enough! But once we break free from the preconceptions we bring to our interpretation of Reid, it becomes evident that darkness is one of the most pervasive themes in his writings. We live in darkness – deep impenetrable darkness – with respect to what would most satisfy the desires of our intellectual nature. Our avidity to know the true causes of things cannot be satisfied.

Reid is not the only Enlightenment philosopher in whom one finds this theme of darkness. One finds it in Locke as well. Locke located the darkness at a different point, however, from where

---

[2] Cf. EIP VI, vi [456a]: "what has philosophy been employed in, since men first began to philosophize, but in the investigation of the causes of things?"

Reid located it; it is our inability to know the essences of substances that is the major cause of the darkness on which Locke had his eye. Furthermore, Locke was persuaded that the darkness need not abide. Reason, being "the candle of the Lord," can be used to cast light into the darkness, dispelling the darkness into twilight. Reason, for Reid, has no such power.[3]

The darkness that catches Reid's eye is more widespread than thus far indicated. We do not know the efficient causes of things in nature; that's the point made thus far. We know that we ourselves, in the exercise of our active powers, are efficient causes; we know that God must be an efficient cause. That's all we know about efficient causality. Yet it would be a serious mistake to conclude that natural science offers no satisfaction to our innate avidity to know the causes of things. Natural science discovers natural causal laws – these being regularities in the workings of whatever be the efficient causes at work in nature. More interesting for those of intellectual temperament, natural science discovers that often it can explain a given law by reference to other laws. Reid's example is that the law of falling bodies has been explained by reference to the laws of inertia and gravity. We now understand why the law of falling bodies holds. Of course we don't at present have an explanation, in turn, of the laws of inertia and gravity. We might someday; but if so, then we won't have an explanation of whatever laws we use to explain the laws of inertia and gravity. In the nature of the case, the pursuit of nomological explanations ultimately brings us to laws that can only be explained by the efficient causality of some agent.

Supposing that all the phenomena that fall within the reach of our senses, were accounted for from the general laws of nature, justly deduced from experience; that is, supposing natural philosophy brought to its utmost perfection, it does not discover the efficient cause of any one phenomenon in nature.

The laws of nature are the rules according to which the effects are produced; but there must be a cause which operates according to these rules. . . .

Natural philosophers, by great attention to the course of nature, have discovered many of her laws, and have very happily applied them to account for many phenomena; but they have never discovered the

---

[3] On Locke, see my "John Locke's Epistemological Piety: Reason is the Candle of the Lord," *Faith and Philosophy*, 11, No. 4 (Oct. 1994): 572–91).

efficient cause of any one phenomenon; nor do those who have distinct notions of the principles of the science, make any such pretense.

Upon the theatre of nature we see innumerable effects, which require an agent endowed with active power; but the agent is behind the scene. Whether it be the Supreme Cause alone, or a subordinate cause or causes; and if subordinate causes be employed by the Almighty, what their nature, their number, and their different offices may be are things hid, for wise reasons without doubt, from the human eye.

It is only in human actions, that may be imputed for praise or blame, that it is necessary for us to know who is the agent; and in this, nature has given us all the light that is necessary for our conduct. (EAP I, vi [527a–b])

It remains the case, nonetheless, that the discovery by natural science of nomological explanations is an important achievement; it gives considerable satisfaction to our avidity to know the causes of things.

What must now be brought into the picture, however, is a theme that has run throughout our discussion in the preceding chapters: The philosopher's attempt to offer nomological explanations of the workings of the human mind is constantly frustrated, and is almost certain to be frustrated forever. We perceive those workings well enough to discern certain laws of nature. Though we have not yet attained a precise formulation of those laws, Reid thought there could be no doubt that perception, for example, does occur in accord with laws of nature and that we have a good grasp of the basic form of those laws. Yet at the points where we would most like explanation, we have none. We have no explanation of why brain events evoke the sensations that they do evoke, nor any of why sensations evoke the apprehensions and beliefs of external objects that they evoke.[4] Worse yet, we have no explanation of why brain events evoke any sensations at all, nor of why sensations evoke any apprehensions and beliefs of external objects. "The perception of external objects is one main link of that mysterious chain, which connects the material world with the intellectual. . . . many things in this operation [are] unaccountable; sufficient to convince us, that we know but little of our own frame; and that a perfect comprehension of our mental powers, and of the manner of their operation,

---

[4] "There is a deep and dark gulf between [impressions upon the body and sensations of the mind], which our understanding cannot pass" (IHM VI, xxi [187a; B 176]).

is beyond the reach of our understanding" (EIP II, i [245b]).[5] The philosopher can "discover certain abstract and necessary relations of things"; but as to his knowledge of what really exists, "he is led to it in the dark, and knows not how he came by it" (EIP II, xx [330a]).

Some will interpret this shortfall of knowledge as marking out an area in which science has more discoveries to make. Reid demurs. Nomological explanations appeal to the natures, the constitutions, of things. Nomological explanations at this point would have to discover something about the nature of the brain, and about the nature of the mind, such that those together account for the fact that brain events evoke the sensations they do. It appears to Reid, however, that the constitution of brain and mind are such that, constitution remaining the same, the laws of operation might very well be different from what they are. Pressure on the skin might produce visual sensations, and so forth. If Reid is right about this, then no nomological explanation of the fundamental functions of the mind, and of its relation to the brain, is possible.

So darkness here too; and this darkness is likewise impenetrable. When we have discovered the laws in accord with which perception occurs, we find ourselves incapable of moving beyond those discoveries to offer nomological explanations of these workings. In fact it seems likely that there are no such explanations to be discovered. The laws we do have in hand are not to be explained, other than that they are the rules in accord with which the efficient agents operating in nature do their work. This brings us back to the earlier point: We don't know what those agents are, nor how they do their work, other than that the ultimate agent is God.

[W]hatever be the nature of those impressions upon the organs, nerves, and brain, we perceive nothing without them. Experience informs that it is so; but we cannot give a reason why it is so. In the constitution of man, perception, by fixed laws of nature, is connected with those impressions; but we can discover no necessary connection. The Supreme Being has been fit to limit our power of perception; so that we perceive not without such impressions; and this is all we know of the matter. (EIP II, ii [248a])

---

[5] How our conception and belief of external objects is produced "is hid in impenetrable darkness" (EIP II, xx [326b]).

Reid's polemic against his philosophical predecessors, especially those who espoused the Way of Ideas, is wide-ranging, touching many points. Among all those points of dispute, the deepest
was this: Reid's predecessors claimed to have explained a great
deal of the workings of the human mind. Reid's rejoinder was
that if one scrutinized their claims, one saw that nothing had
been explained. That did not surprise him. Human reason lacks
the power to explain the fundamental workings of the human
mind.

Reid was, in that way, one of the great antirationalists of the
philosophical tradition; Hume, by comparison, was one of the
great rationalists. The transition from sensation, to conception
and belief of external object, is neither a transition effected by
reason, nor a transition for which we can offer a rational explanation. On both points, powers had been ascribed to reason
which Reid was convinced it lacked.

So darkness and mystery. *Double* darkness, when it comes to
the workings of the mind: Not only do we have no agency
explanations, we also have no nomological explanations.
Abiding double darkness. Explanations of the laws have not been
discovered because almost certainly there aren't any to be discovered; and efficient-causality explanations of the workings of
nature are beyond the reach of our intellectual powers. In the
passage quoted above, from *Essays on the Active Powers*, I, vi
[527a–b], Reid used the image of a theater to state his point:
"Upon the theatre of nature we see innumerable effects, which
require an agent endowed with active power; but the agent is
behind the scene."[6]

REID'S EPISTEMOLOGICAL PIETY

The epistemological piety appropriate to this picture of reality
and our place therein will incorporate a blend of humility and
active gratitude, says Reid. Humility because we are unable to
dispel the darkness – and also because though we, unlike the

---

[6] Earlier, in Chapter vi of IHM, we found him using the same image to make a point about
perception. The point was different, however: not that the agency operative in nature is
hidden from us, but that in perception, "the impression made by the object upon the
organ, either by immediate contact, or by some intervening medium, as well as the
impression made upon the nerves and brain, is performed behind the scenes," and the
perceiver "sees nothing of it" (VI, xxi [187b; B 177]).

rocks and rills, do genuinely have active power; nonetheless our "power, in its existence, in its extent, and in its exertions, is entirely dependent upon God, and upon the laws of nature which he has established" (EAP I, vii [530b]). This realization "ought to banish pride and arrogance from the most mighty of the sons of men" (ibid.). And active gratitude, because the power we have is in fact "one of the noblest gifts of God to man" (ibid.). For this "bounty of heaven" we should both be grateful, and stir ourselves to use it properly. For it is in fact "perfectly suited to the state of man, as a state of improvement and discipline. It is sufficient to animate us to the noblest exertions. By the proper exercise of this gift of God, human nature, in individuals and in societies, may be exalted to a high degree of dignity and felicity, and the earth become a paradise" (ibid.).

What Reid happens not to mention in this passage is the most fundamental component of Reidian epistemological piety: trust. Not only is the transition that occurs in perception, from sensation to conception and belief of the external object, not a transition effected by reason. We can also neither establish the reliability of this transition without falling into practical circularity nor can we offer an explanation of it. In all those ways it is ungrounded: *rationally ungrounded*. Yet we are so constituted – or so ruled – that we do in fact trust its reliability. Ungrounded trust, trust without reasons for trusting, that's what is deepest in Reidian piety. Though that's not putting it quite right. According to the Reidian, that's what's deep in the piety of all humanity. What's deepest in *Reidian* piety, is acknowledging that fact, and acknowledging the darkness which that fact implies, and not railing against the mystery but accepting it humbly and gratefully.

Index